The Discourse of Text Messaging

CONTINUUM DISCOURSE SERIES

Series Editor: Professor Ken Hyland, University of Hong Kong

Discourse is one of the most significant concepts of contemporary thinking in the humanities and social sciences as it concerns the ways language mediates and shapes our interactions with each other and with the social, political and cultural formations of our society. The *Continuum Discourse* Series aims to capture the fast-developing interest in discourse to provide students, new and experienced teachers and researchers in applied linguistics, ELT and English language with an essential bookshelf. Each book deals with a core topic in discourse studies to give an in-depth, structured and readable introduction to an aspect of the way language in used in real life.

Other titles in the series:

Discourse of Twitter and Social Media, Michele Zappavigna
Workplace Discourse, Almut Koester
Discourse of Blogs and Wikis, Greg Myers
Professional Discourse, Britt-Louise Gunnarsson
Academic Discourse, Ken Hyland
School Discourse, Frances Christie
Historical Discourse, Caroline Coffin
Discourse Analysis, Brian Paltridge
Using Corpora in Discourse Analysis, Paul Baker
Metadiscourse, Ken Hyland

Continuum Discourse

The Discourse of Text Messaging

Analysis of SMS Communication

CAROLINE TAGG

continuum

Continuum International Publishing Group

The Tower Building   80 Maiden Lane
11 York Road   Suite 704
London   New York
SE1 7NX   NY 10038

www.continuumbooks.com

British Library Cataloguing-in-Publication Data

A catalogue record for this book is available from the British Library.

ISBN: HB: 978-1-4411-7409-3
PB: 978-1-4411-7376-8

Library of Congress Cataloging-in-Publication Data
Tagg, Caroline.
The discourse of text messaging : analysis of text message communication / Caroline Tagg.
p. cm. – (Continuum discourse)
Includes bibliographical references and index.
ISBN 978-1-4411-7409-3 (hardcover : alk. paper) – ISBN 978-1-4411-7376-8 (pbk. : alk. paper) – ISBN 978-1-4411-3268-0 (ebook (pdf)) – ISBN 978-1-4411-6153-6 (ebook (epub))
1. Discourse analysis–Data processssing. 2. Text messages (Telephone systems) 3. Instant messaging. I. Title.

P302.3.T34 2011
401'.410285–dc23
2011035033

Typeset by Deanta Global Publishing Services, Chennai, India
Printed and bound in India

CONTENTS

CHAPTER ONE

Situating text messaging: what, who, how and why

1.1 Introduction

'It started as a message service, allowing operators to inform all their own customers about things such as problems with the network. When we created SMS (Short Messaging Service) it was not really meant to communicate from consumer to consumer and certainly not meant to become the main channel which the younger generation would use to communicate with each other'

Cor Stutterheim, inventor of texting (Wray R., 2002)

Why should linguists be interested in studying the discourse of SMS text messaging? There are many reasons, but the one that first attracted me, back at the turn of the millennium, was the initial *unlikeliness* of it all. People are now so used to text messaging that it's difficult to step back and appreciate how unlikely it would once have seemed that millions of people might one day be interacting through tiny messages typed into tiny mobile phones by relatively large thumbs. And what interaction! Text messages are not always simply electronic notes to remind someone to pick up the milk or that they are meeting you in half an hour (although this kind of 'micro-coordination' is one important aspect of texting), but they can also be heartfelt, expressive, chatty messages that sustain friendships and convey complex emotions. The following text message, one of the many I collected and studied, offers an example of this. (All names throughout the book have been anonymized.)

1.1   Thankyou for ditchin me i had been invited out but said no coz u were cumin and u said we would do something on the sat now i have nothing to do all weekend i am a billy no mates i really hate being single

Susie, in her late teens, writing to her sister

Of course, the exploitation of an initially unlikely technology is not unusual. People have always pushed creatively at the constraints of a technology for expressive or communicative purposes: think of the cave wall, telegram, or postcard. Seen in the light of a progression of technological and social developments, texting is simply one more means of communication. I explore and challenge the apparent 'uniqueness' of texting, and where it fits in a tradition of informal written interaction, later in this chapter.

As the quote above from its inventor shows, the text message was initially designed as a way for phone companies to get in touch with consumers rather than for inter-consumer communication. This is the second aspect of text messaging that I liked, and still like – the way it has been embraced by people, especially young people; the way it symbolizes that sometimes large corporations trying to sell things cannot determine what people want to do or say and how they want to do or say it. And, despite the advent of smartphones and of video messaging, people still seem to prefer these tiny, abbreviated typed messages and they keep on sending them. In 2010, for example, it was estimated that 200,000 text messages were being sent every second, a threefold increase from 2007 (ITU World Telecommunications Database, 2010). This is motivated, purposeful writing – intimate and often highly personal. Of course, the private nature of texting has practical implications for the linguist, which I also explore in this book (Chapter 2) and which explains the relative dearth of data-based studies: how do you get hold of such personal data and is it ethical to try to do so?

Fortunately, another reason for my interest was that I and the people I know text. On the one hand, this made it easier to get hold of data. Unlike other forms of communication often favoured by linguists, such as hip hop, online chatrooms and gaming, here was a form of communication which I could easily relate to and which my friends (and, alarmingly, my parents) were using. What struck me about text messaging is that so many people do it; those who don't certainly see it going on around them. My interest was aroused by texts which people around me were sending and receiving, such as this.

1.2   Hey i know ur at work but i just wanted to let u know that i found my
       pen lid . . . it was in the bin:)x

(From exchange between two students at art college)

What interested me about this text message was, firstly, the friendly, informal tone it manages to convey. It does this partly through speech-like constructions: *hey I know ur at work but* and *I just wanted to let u know that* . . . . The text message is primarily **phatic** in that it is concerned with fulfilling a social or interpersonal function rather than conveying information. It is humorous with its delayed punchline: *. . . it was in the bin:)*; it speaks to an intimate, shared background. It is also – given the fact that it has little real content to convey – relatively long; there is scant indication that this is a texter concerned primarily with **brevity**, that is, with saving time and space. Throughout this book, I shall argue that the discourse of text messaging – including abbreviations and phonetic spelling (Chapter 3) and speech-like interjections (Chapters 4 and 5) – is shaped as much by people's awareness of who they are texting and how they want to come across as it is by any attempt to abbreviate.

A final thing that drew me towards texting was the way in which text messaging is integrated into people's lives. Texting does not require you to be sat at a computer; rather than being an interruption or a distraction, it is part of people's everyday lives. It is used alongside other means of communication, in the sense that you may use it to arrange a face-to-face meeting or to let someone know you have arrived home after the meeting; you may have it beside your computer as you work. Of course, any distinction between computer-mediated communication (CMC) and mobile communication is already blurring, and has been for some time, with the advent of smartphones that allow email to be checked on the move or posts to be sent to Twitter in the middle of everything from concerts to travel delays; while, of course, the use of Wi-fi means that the internet can be accessed in cafes and hotel lobbies. Yet, there is still a sense that when you send a text message, it goes straight to the people you are texting – straight to their pocket, their bedside cabinet, their hand. This intimacy has an effect on the language used. It encourages the emergence of particular practices between people who text each other frequently, that is, the use of expressions, abbreviations or spellings that others may not understand.

This book is about the communicative practices evident among a diffuse network of texters, based across the UK, who range in age from late teens to late sixties. The network starts from people I know and then spreads out to people *they* know. Based on discourse analyses of a corpus of over 11,000 text messages that I call CorTxt, I discuss the variation in spelling, the typical phraseology, grammar, discourse markers, everyday creativity and the construction of identity that emerged from close analysis of the data. I outline these topics in greater depth at the end of this chapter, and they form the respective bases of the following chapters.

However, while reading through these chapters, it is important to bear in mind that this is just one, highly **localized** group of users. That is, their communicative practices are likely to have emerged from a particular set of circumstances – particular individuals and relationships – and may not be typical of other 'texting communities' or networks. Many of the practices I describe may be ones that you recognize in your own texting practices, but there will be others that won't resonate. One of the purposes of this book, then, is to serve as an example against which you can consider your own communicative practices, and those of people around you. For example, given the average age of my texters (most are in their late twenties or thirties) and their location in the UK, you can begin to speculate on the extent to which the practices of the people you know may differ from the ones to be described here.

As well as inviting you to compare your findings with mine, I also wish for our localized practices to be set in the context of the millions of other people who are, even as you read this, sending text messages around the globe. Text messaging is a global phenomenon, although it is realized in a myriad of distinct localized practices. In other words, texting is a **glocalized** practice. This is a widely and variously used portmanteau term that combines *global* with *local* in an attempt to capture the way in which local groups make up or drive a global phenomenon. To give one example of what I mean by this: text messaging is characterized by its restricted character length, and this has resulted in surprisingly similar word abbreviations and play in English-speaking communities across the world, but different **respellings** (a term used to describe the use of unconventional spellings to convey meaning) will emerge within different networks, perhaps due to particular regional pronunciations. As you saw in the first text message above, Susie regularly omits <g> from the end of words, as in *ditchin* and *cumin*, suggesting a spoken pronunciation. In the following text message, you can see how replacing the letters <th> with <d> allows the South African texter to suggest a local pronunciation through respelling. (See Chapter 9 for more analysis of this message.)[1]

> Brur its 2bed one matras my darling is going 2 put me in shid in church. My money i have save have been decrease due 2 *da* Aunt Mayoly's funeral, & miner problst. So *da* case is coming very soon 3 months preg. I'll c then. Sharp.
>
> (Sent by Matsuka, in Deumert and Masinyana, 2008, p. 126)

Before going on to look at the localized practices of the texting community that I researched, I look in this chapter at three aspects of the wider world of texting. Firstly, I want to explore what people (or the media) say about texting and the attitude this suggests. The description of texting that circulates as part of media discourse has tended to be somewhat pessimistic over the impact of texting, and below I ask why and what impact this wider discourse may have on how people text. Secondly, I balance media myths by describing texting as an 'unremarkable' practice, that is, as one more advance in a long line of communicative technologies that have shaped how people use language. Texting does not represent a break from past communicative practices, but a continuation, in the sense that people have always exploited new technologies for their own communicative ends, while worrying over their impact. Finally, I discuss the social impact of texting in emerging 'mobile societies' and the way it has shaped how people communicate, that is, the intimate and interpersonal functions that explain some of the language practices denounced by the media. I will consider the extent to which texting has encouraged new practices or mediates existing ones. These discussions serve to contextualize the following study. The discourse of texting is shaped not only by the constraints of the mobile phone but also by the social functions of the technology, by existing social practices and by the attitudes people have towards it.

Terms used

Discourse in this book is understood broadly as language in use – that is, as naturally occurring, purposeful and coherent stretches of language that emerge through social interaction. Discourse is also socially situated, in the sense that communicative practices emerge from particular social and cultural contexts. My investigation of a corpus of text messages cannot therefore be assumed to be a description of all texted discourse.

Text messages are often shortened to 'texts', a practice that I shall avoid here. This is because the word 'text' throughout this book is used in a wider sense, to refer to any coherent stretch of speaking or writing, through any medium: this book is a text, as is an email and as is a spoken conversation. 'SMS' is also used by many researchers of text messaging; again, I prefer 'text message', 'text messaging' and (most frequently) 'texting' on the basis that they are the more recognized term among people in Britain, from where I write.

1.2 Meta matters

Cell phones are evil. Well, grammatically speaking. . . .

I knew this was coming. From the first time one of my friends sent me the message "I've got 2 go, talk to U later," I knew the end was near. The

English language as we once knew it is out the window, and replacing it is this hip and cool slang-induced language, obsessed with taking the vowels out of words and spelling fonetikally.

(Uthus, 2007)

It is hardly an exaggeration to say that texting has had a bad press. Despite the jocular, teasing tone of the journalist cited above, his sentiments reflect those found across the printed media. My evidence for saying this comes not only from my own experience but also from a survey carried out in 2006 by the linguist Crispin Thurlow. Thurlow analyzed newspaper coverage of 'issues related to young people, language and new technology' (p.671), which included 101 articles mainly from English-speaking countries. Many of these reflect the view in the above newspaper extract that texting is doing 'evil' things to language. Thurlow found texting described across the articles as:

reprehensible, frightening, depraved, infamous, criminal, jarring and abrasive, apocalyptic, execrable, pointless, and aberrant . . . inflicted on the innocent public . . . creating a whole new culture in the country . . . , dumbing down the English language . . . , and lowering standards all round.

(Thurlow, 2006, p. 677)

These are harsh words, and strong claims. As Thurlow acknowledges, the media's negative portrayal of texting is far from absolute, and it should be pointed out that newspapers have since picked up on and reported academic work that suggests more positive implications for literacy. Take, for example, an article entitled 'Texting boosts children's literacy ;-)' in *The Sunday Times* (May, 2008). Nonetheless, it seems not unfair to suggest that, to the casual reader, the print media remains to some extent sceptical of such reports.

One of the recurring assertions across the articles is that 'textese' represents, in Thurlow's (2006, p. 672) words, a 'decisive and dramatic break with conventional practice'. In the newspaper extract cited at the start of this section, the journalist suggests that the end is near and that 'The English language as we once knew it is out the window' (Uthus, 2007). According to this popular conceptualization, texting is unprecedented, new and unknown and is radically transforming how people communicate. The view is perhaps more prevalent in earlier articles, as journalists puzzled over what was then an emerging technology.

Not since man uttered his first word and clumsily held a primitive pencil nearly 10,000 years ago has there been such a revolution in language. From tapping abbreviated words into a mobile phone to emailing people on the other side of the Atlantic, today's technology is changing the way in which we communicate at an alarming rate.

('Net spawns a new teen lingo: Noticed some odd spelling when looking over your kids' shoulders they're on line? Here's why' in *The Vancouver Sun*, December 17, 1999)

The brief history of communications technology captured in the above extract is obviously over-simplistic, ignoring as it does the invention of printing, the telegram, the telephone and the postal service, to name but a few of the technological developments that have changed how people communicate. In the following section, I explore the argument that texting is simply one stage in a long line of developments in technology: it represents evolution in communication, as Thurlow puts it, not revolution.

What is interesting is that texting is by no means the first technology to face such an extreme and concerned reaction, as Gillen and Hall (2010, p. 173) point out in relation to the postcard in Edwardian Britain:

> for some the postcard transgressed social standards . . . For others, just as it is for some with today's texting and email, the new medium was going to ruin the English language.

The irony is that in their defamation of texting, media reports tend to *affirm* the association between the medium and a particular kind of discourse. One way in which this happens is that newspapers tend to select extreme cases which confirm the public's fears but which do not have a basis in widespread practices. For example, in 2002, a 13-year-old teenager handed in a school essay that began:

> My smmr hols wr CWOT. B4, we used 2 go 2 NY 2C my bro, his GF & thr 3:-@ kds FTF. ILNY, its gr8. Bt my Ps wr so {:-/ BC o 9/11 tht thay dcdd 2 stay in SCO²

The story hit the headlines (from *The London Times* to the *Montreal Gazette*). Putting aside for the moment the question as to whether the teenager knew exactly what she was doing, how representative is this of teenage behaviour? And how representative is it of texting practices? A text message such as the following from an 18-year-old texter to her aunt is probably more normal and hardly likely to make the news or inspire condemnation. (All names within text messages have been replaced with a code, such as NAME30 here – see Chapter 2 for details of the anonymization process.)

1.3   Hi C, jst 2 let u know I passed my driving test an hour ago! I am delighted. Sorting insurance this wkend then will get peugeot! Hooray! Pls let NAME30 know too x

The second way in which media coverage tends to reaffirm the nature of textese lies in what Thurlow calls their 'fictionalised accounts' of the language which texters use. It seems unlikely that anyone would actually use the unintelligible kind of heavy abbreviations invented by journalists in the following two articles.

> Mst f d tym dey usd ds knd f lng'ge 2 tlk 2 1 anthr nt 1ly n txt bt evn n wrtng ltrs 2
>
> > ('Text messaging cr8ts a hul nu cltur: Is that gud or bad?' 18 December, 2000, *BusinessWorld*, p. 1)

> lfYaMthWozNEBiGrUWdntHavNEFAcLft2Wsh
>
> > ('Text messaging breeds new dialect — the Queen's English meets the cellphone'. 4 May 2001, *Asian Wall Street Journal*)

Playing with language in this way seems to be as irresistible to those commenting on texting as it is to those using it. In 2008, the linguist David Crystal weighed in on the textese debate, challenging the notion that such extreme abbreviations are actually used by most people who text, at least in the quantity suggested by the media. However, even Crystal cannot resist perpetuating popular conceptions of textese in the title of his book, *Txt Msg: the Gr8 Db8*. He also provides lists of reported spelling variants which include abbreviated phrases strongly associated with texting, but which are not always attested or at least found to be infrequent in empirical studies (*AFAIK, ASLMH, BION, ICWUM, PTMM, TTYL8R...*).

What journalists are doing when they use unconventional spelling such as the number homophones <2> and <4> in 'Children's love 4 e-mail is threat 2 English' (*The Times*, 2000) is very similar to what texters do when they manipulate spellings: they are engaging with their reader and they are making a point. Compare the respelling <fonetikally>, used by the journalist cited at the start of this section to emphasize the point that texters are changing the way words are spelt, with the respellings in the text message from Susie which you saw earlier. Susie's respellings emphasize her immediate, heedless irritation and so, as with the journalist's respelling, they add to the meaning of the message: *Thankyou for ditchin me i had been invited out but said no coz u were cumin.*

Crystal's argument (which would be shared by most linguists) is that, where it occurs, the type of language play noted in texting suggests a degree of linguistic awareness and ability and is thus more likely to have beneficial effects on literacy than to harm it. We could speculate that the teenage writer of *My smmr hols wr CWOT* was not making a series of ignorant spelling mistakes; she was deliberately and defiantly flouting the rules of English spelling. However, in order to break the rules, she first had to know them. This argument is elaborated on in Chapter 3, where I explore the principles and patterns that underlie spellings in **Txt**.

Txt

The discourse of texting has been popularly referred to as 'textese', a term which I've used here in my discussion of its portrayal in the media. Tim Shortis, a researcher into orthography and texting, prefers the term **Txt** in order to distance academic treatments of the discourse from the media representation. In Chapter 3, I adopt Shortis's (2007b) term, which has been widely used in linguistic discussion of texting. I go on to use it slightly differently from Shortis, to refer not only to practices of respelling but also to the discourse that emerges through a configuration of texting strategies.

So you can see in the media a somewhat extreme and overly pessimistic portrayal of texting, in which certain assumptions are made: firstly, that the language of texting is somehow new and signals a break with conventional language use; secondly, that the language of texting is synonymous with abbreviation; and thirdly, that it heralds the decline of language and literacy as we know it.

To what extent does newspaper coverage impact on how people text? It is hard to tell. It probably has very little direct effect, if at all. I can't imagine somebody reading *The London Times*, and on that basis deciding to fundamentally change the way they communicate with friends; neither can I imagine someone reading David Crystal's book and deciding, hmm, I might try *PTMM* in my next text message. But, in a general sense, the media both reflects and feeds into a wider discourse that shapes how people feel about texting. The decisions that people make as to how to spell and which words to use are highly complex, and their choices depend on who they are texting, how they want to put themselves across and the expectations that their interlocutors have. The **value** that people place on the features associated with textese, as it is popularly framed – that is, what they think unconventional spellings mean and will mean to the people they text – will determine how they spell and the kind of grammar they use. It is worth bearing this in mind as you read through this book, as it feeds into the argument that the discourse of Txt cannot be understood as emerging from a straightforward attempt to keep messages short, but that texters' linguistic strategies play a role in self-expression and the conveying of particular identities.

1.3 Interactive written communication

Having a lovely time here in Wales. Came Sat last. Scenery delightful. such a wealth of trees. Weather glorious. Been out all the time.

> (Postcard, 1909. Collected and distributed on Twitter by the Edwardian Postcard Project (http://www.lancs.ac.uk /fass/projects/EVIIpc/))

My dearest Eliza, i just received your welcome letter and was very pleased to Receive it i was rather Disappointed as i hurried home for you but i know it cant be helped at all times . . .

> (Opening of letter to a 'fallen woman' at the London Foundling Hospital, 19th century; Kesseler and Bergs, 2003, p. 79)

LEAVING TONITE STOPPING OVER KC ARRIVE HOME SUNDAY MORNING SEVEN THIRTY DON'T WORRY EVERYTHING OK WILL GIVE DETAILS WHEN ARRIVE WALT.

> (Telegram from Walt Disney to his brother and business partner, Roy, on the night that Mickey Mouse was born, 13 March, 1928)

As the above extracts illustrate, people have been sending each other informal written notes of varying lengths for a long time. What do the above have in common, and to what extent can texting be compared to them? Like most text messages, the above appear to have been sent between people who know each other well, presumably people with whom the writers also share face-to-face relationships. (In contrast, certain kinds of correspondents, such as penfriends or contributors to online chat forums, may never meet.) Furthermore, they were not written by elite literary figures but by people who would not necessarily expect their writings to be preserved or that anyone else would read them – at least at the time, for the young Walt Disney.

The nineteenth-century love letter, for example, is one of many found among the possessions of working-class women admitted to the London Hospital as 'fallen women'. Eliza's lover is unconventional in his use of capitals (in terms of fairly long-established grammatical conventions in English), capitalizing the start of *Receive* and *Disappointed* but using a lower-case *i* for the first person pronoun, as well as omitting the apostrophe in *cant*. The letter is very speech-like in the way it runs sentences together without punctuation, relying instead on conjunctions *and* and *but*. We can compare this to many of the text messages in my corpus.

1.4   Dude, if you see NAME10 then dont mention that you've spoke to me, she wants me to go to the pub and i cant be bothered and my mom goes on holiday tomorrow.

In comparison, the other two texts have short, abbreviated sentences such as, in the postcard: *Came Sat last. Scenery delightful. such a wealth of trees.* The telegram has no full stops, but otherwise feels very similar: *LEAVING TONITE STOPPPING OVER KC.* Note also the spelling of *tonight* (<tonite>) and the initialism <KC> (*Kansas City*), both practices evident in texting. Again, I have in my collection text messages that reflect the short, curt style of the earlier postcard and telegram.

1.5   Hi. Do u want to join me with sts later? Meeting them at five. Call u after
       class.

Chloe, teacher in her early 30s

Motivations behind these linguistic choices include space and financial constraints. Telegrams are widely believed to have inspired a new style of writing, based on compressing a message into the smallest possible number of words to keep costs down – while, however, maintaining intelligibility, so that a longer, clearer word may be chosen over a shorter, more ambiguous one (Baron, 2002, p. 36). Since the development of the postcard as we know it today – whereby the written message shares space with the address, leaving room for a picture on the other side – the writer similarly needs to fit the holiday greetings into the small space beside the address. Despite these constraints, however, note how the writers of each are not simply concerned with getting a particular piece of information across, but also show signs of being concerned with *how* they come across: *DON'T WORRY EVERYTHING OK* and with expressing opinions or sentiments: *SCENERY DELIGHTFUL.* As I shall explore in greater depth in the next section, texters also combine a fairly functional purpose (as in *Missed the bus! Be there in 35mins*) with an awareness of interlocutors and displays of self-expression.

In discussions around texting, there is a tendency to assume an earlier 'golden age' when standards were much higher and when people maintained a careful and polished control of grammar. In comparison, writing now is seen as being sloppy, uninformed and less expressive or literary. This is the notion of language decline, if you like – the feeling that standards are worsening and that what we need to do is reverse changes; to turn back the clock. Arguably, however, this can be described as the *myth* of language decline, based more on how people now feel about language than on any evidence as to how people actually used to write.

What we know about people's writing in earlier times can in fact only ever be partial, dependent as it is on what survives. The documents that reach us from the past are generally those written by elite and often literary figures. This is often not made explicit, so it is easy to assume that Samuel Pepys' diaries represent the average seventeenth-century Londoner's life and literary style; or that Byron's poems reflect how people generally expressed their love in the 1700s and 1800s. Of course, throughout these centuries, most people were illiterate. By the late nineteenth century, those who could write were writing letters that diverged wildly from those penned by English novelist Jane Austen to her sister, for example, as the above letter to Eliza shows. Its writer wrote much as people do today: hurriedly, informally, with mistakes and reflecting how one would speak. Literacy standards, at least in the UK, have never been *higher* than they are now – if anything, they were always lower in the past, and certainly less inclusive: fewer people were literate at all.

Is texting, then, nothing more than today's version of a miniature nineteenth-century letter or a postcard sent by phone? Developments in transport and communication technology have moved written correspondence on from the letter, through the postcard and the telegram, to the email and the text message. With each step, the world shrinks while time (how long it takes to send and receive written correspondence, as well as to compose it) speeds up. Accompanying these technological advances are certain shifts in how people communicate. It would appear inevitable that expectations of speedy responses grow as time and space shrink. Letter writers could wait days or even weeks to receive a reply. By the early 1900s, Britain had for a time three postal deliveries a day, and so postcards sent in the morning could receive a response that afternoon. The space allocated to the written message also seems to have shrunk if the text message is compared with the letter, although the history of constraint should not be underestimated in this respect – the cost of sending a letter in the eighteenth century depended on its size, so people went to extraordinary lengths to reduce it: one technique was 'cross-writing' whereby people would finish the page and then write across what they had just written.

However, the particular configuration of features that make up texting may be encouraging new conventions and alleviating existing ones: the fact that they are so particularly constrained in terms of character allowance (as the telegram was so constrained in terms of word count), that they are so intimate and can so be quickly exchanged that interactions begin to resemble spoken conversation perhaps explain why greetings and sign-offs are generally dispensed with, for example, and it may become permissible to more hastily put together your message with the acceptance of 'mistakes' or inconsistencies. As a consequence of all this, there may be somewhat less value placed on the increasingly transient message: although some people do store and treasure text messages (see the next section), people do not tend to keep them to the extent that they might have treasured letters or picture postcards.

The argument here is not that texting is nothing more than an electronic postcard. But it is misleading to assume that texting has come from nowhere, and that it interrupts a golden age when everyone could write 'perfectly'. Instead, texting is one stage in a long line of developments which people have exploited in their desire and need to communicate.

1.4 Text messaging in mobile cultures

What is texting exploited for, and how and to what extent has it changed the way people live? Many people have integrated texting (and the mobile phone in general) into their lives so effectively that they can no longer imagine how they coped without it. However, this does not mean that texting has transformed lives; rather, it has added to existing practices. What people choose to use it for and who they communicate with shapes the language used.

In their study of Norwegian teenagers and their families, Ling and Yttri (2002) charted the development of the mobile phone from its role in heightening security to what they call 'hypercoordination'. Initially, as an unfamiliar device with which people were yet to become comfortable, the mobile phone was reserved for extraordinary situations, namely, in case of personal accident or emergency. I remember, back in the mid-1990s, when only two of my university friends had mobile phones. For one of them, the phone was a security device given to her by mother to carry when walking back from campus in the dark from student union meetings. As I remember, she did not use it to make everyday calls; we had a landline in our shared accommodation for that. As more and more people bought mobile phones and their use became more routine, mobiles began to play a role in what Ling and Yttri call 'micro-coordination'. Micro-coordination refers to the everyday organization of meetings and other social events and activities on the hoof, as it were. The text messages I collected exhibited a great deal of micro-coordination, including most of the interaction between a mother, Charlotte (in her late 50s), and her daughter, Laura (aged around 30). In the following exchange, Laura is arriving home from holiday.

1.6	Laura:	Hello we are back waiting for luggage, not sure if will make the bus! Will let you know
	Laura:	We made it! Eta at taunton is 12.30 as planned, hope thats still okay?! Good to see you! :- xx
	Charlotte:	Yes i will be there. Glad you made it

To what extent are mobile phones changing how people interact? With respect to its instrumental role of micro-coordination, you could point out that texting is not replacing or challenging face-to-face meetings. Instead, it is used to facilitate social events which could of course take place, perhaps with more careful organization beforehand, without the intervention of the mobile phone. However, as Ling and Yttri point out, how people organize these social activities may be changing. The traditional notion that transit and interaction must be controlled from geographically fixed nodes is being challenged: previously, you would arrange your trip from home and then set out on it. The mobile phone, however, allows people to set out with a vague idea as to where they are going, who they are meeting and when, and to reach a 'progressively exact arrangement' (in Ling and Yttri's words) as they go. So, although texting mediates existing practices and rituals, it also reshapes them.

Linguistically, how might this function of the mobile phone be expected to affect the language used in text messages? We might posit that people are likely to be in a rush; they may be in a place where texting is difficult (on a bus; driving; in a shop); and they may be focused on the message rather than the niceties of social interaction. The impact of some of these are perhaps evident in the above exchange: there are shortened, somewhat brusque phrases such as *Will let you know* and a lack of punctuation (no full stops or apostrophe) and capitalization (*i* in the last message), which suggests speed or carelessness. I have seen a similar curtness in other text messages:

1.7   Missed the bus! Be there in 35mins, where are you now? NAME94 x

1.8   U still in the joint place? I'll b there in 20ish – am on bus

At the same time, a lot of interpersonal or relationship work is being carried out in the initial exchange above and this is evident in the linguistic features that occur. In the second message, the daughter is careful to check *hope thats still okay?!* and adds that it will be *Good to see you! :- xx* to which her mother responds *Glad you made it*. In this respect, decisions made regarding punctuation are not signals of haste, but appear to play a role in reaching out to an interlocutor. The emoticon (:- xx) functions in this instance as a kiss, and the exclamation marks add emphasis to the sentiments expressed (*hope that's still okay?!* and *Good to see you!*). What this exchange shows, then, is that while the instrumental functions of texting may encourage brevity and lack of attention to punctuation or capitalization, coordinating events together requires that consideration is given to the interlocutors and this is carried out through linguistic and paralinguistic features.

I mentioned above that I had two friends with mobile phones back in the mid-1990s and that for one it was still mainly a security device. However, for my other friend, it was definitely a symbol of status; a piece of cutting-edge technology to flash around. In this respect, he was anticipating the way in which phones would become both an 'accessory' and an important part of people's sense of identity. The third function of the mobile phone described by Ling and Yttri is that of 'hypercoordination': as, alongside the coordination of activities, people start to use the technology for social and emotional purposes. It becomes expressive as well as instrumental. As you saw above, even the most instrumental text message involves at least a nod towards social niceties, but in other cases this purpose can be foregrounded. We saw this above with Susie's message, whose purpose was to express disappointment and anger. The following exchange is between Laura, recently back from her stay in the forest of the Congo, with a friend of a similar age.

1.9   Alison: I've set that picture of the big spider i took in watermarque as the wallpaper on my phone, but i'm gonna have to change it reckon, cos everytime i see it, it makes me shudder! Ugh!

    Laura: You will develop an irrational fear of mobile phones! I gave myself a nightmare by watching primeval with giant spiders, then sleeping in my sleeping bag first time since the jungle!

    Alison: I watched that too! I'd be more scared of centipedes in your sleeping bag! Why did you have to sleep in your sleeping bag?

    Laura: Didnt seem worth fighting with duvet covers for just a couple of nights-anything to avoid a little housework!

    Alison: Absolutely. I cleaned my carpet today and now i can't go in my bedroom!

    Laura: For fear of fainting with the realisation of all that housework you just did? Quick have a cuppa!

    Alison: No, my carpets are all wet!

There is little instrumental function evident here; the purpose is solely phatic, that of keeping in touch, passing on everyday anecdotes and amusing each other. What do you notice about the language used in this, and by Susie (in the 'billy no mates' example)? I've already commented on the way in which 'billy no mates' reflects a spoken pronunciation in her text messages; as well as the <g> dropping, she also uses <coz> for *because*. Perhaps most interesting is the effect of <u> (for *you*) in the message. It does not in fact alter the standard pronunciation in the way that *ditchin* does, and yet it adds to the speech-like feel of the message: *coz u were cumin and u said we would do something on the sat*. I return to this use of what is known as **eye dialect** in Chapter 3. For the moment, I'd like to note that emotion is not conveyed solely through spelling. The use of one long sentence by billy no mates, in which clauses are strung together rather than being punctuated by full stops, heightens the sense of a breathless indignation. In the exchange above, other features that heighten the expressiveness of the messages includes the use of speech-like interjections: *Ugh!*, *Absolutely*.

In many respects, then, texted communication resembles spoken conversation – in its purposes as well as the linguistic form it takes; and this is something that I will explore in this book. Many studies have approached the study of texting or internet language on the basis that the situation and the language used sits 'somewhere' between speech and writing: it is a bit like speech, but also shares some features with other written texts.

However, this view downplays the role that people play in determining what a discourse looks like. Because people want to fulfil expressive, speech-like purposes, they adopt practices associated with informal spoken chat: speech-like sentence structures; discourse markers such as 'oh and'; and they use spelling to suggest spoken forms. In other words, texters draw on spoken practices in order to heighten the sense of speech-like informality and intimacy.

At the same time, text messages are of course written. One impact of this is that texters have the time to craft messages: even messages that appear to have been hastily put together may be stylized to seem that way. In their study of teenagers in Finland, Kasesniemi and Rautianen (2002) note that texters would often engage the help of friends in compressing what they wanted to say into a text message, and as a group spend a significantly long time crafting what they want to say. Nonetheless, through this collective process of stylization, text messages may still *appear* private and intimate to the recipient, who remains unaware of the group effort. The other impact of the written medium is that the sweet intimate nothings of the kind whispered in the ear or treasured in conversation can actually, in text messages, be kept.

Taylor and Harper (2003), in their study of British teens, build on the idea that text messages can have emotional value. They suggest that the success of mobile phones can be explained by their role in young people's existing exchange ceremonies, or gift-giving, in which phones, credit and text messages act as currency. Sending a message, or not sending one, signals the status of the friendship between interlocutors and their place in the social group. Through these gift-giving rituals, phones and texting can confirm and strengthen alliances and friendship. Keeping text messages similarly signals the importance of a particular text message, as well as the significance being placed on the original gift and what this means in terms of friendship. Kasesniemi and Rautianen note how significant text messages may even be written down to overcome the limited phone memory – chiefly by girls but also by boys, as this conversation with a 17-year-old male Finn shows:

Researcher: Have you ever written them down, if you've had to delete them for some reason:

Boy: Well at some point Emma sent me these poems. If I've had to delete them, I think I've had to delete one or two of them, I've written them down on paper then, the poems.

Researchers: What kind of poems were they?

Boy: What were they now . . . there was one that went 'When you look at me you seem distant, when you look at the clouds you seem close'. Stuff like that.

Researcher: Why were they so important you felt you had to write them down?

Boy: They just sounded so good somehow, so I thought I'd keep them.

Researcher: Where do you have them now?

Boy: They're on a piece of paper in a drawer.

(Kasesniemi and Rautianen, 2002, p. 179)

Grinter and Eldridge (2003) note a similar practice with teenagers' lists of contacts, which contain more phone numbers than they actually use – the numbers act instead as a show of status and belonging. (This practice has since been reflected in the collecting of Friends on social network sites such as Facebook.)

Taylor and Harper (2003) point out that the value placed on phones can depend on the form of the language, and *not* sticking to punctuation rules or abbreviating the language so as to avoid sending more than one message can lower the value assigned to the message. In these cases, the fact that abbreviating is perceived as an attempt to save money or time is seen as reflecting an interlocutor's attitude towards the recipient of their text message. Given the fact that people have the choice to respell in various ways, then spelling words conventionally carries value in the same way as respelling them in unconventional ways does. In my conversations with teenagers, I have been surprised at how often they express a dislike of abbreviations and what they see as 'sloppy' language. In looking at how spelling varies in the messages I have collected, I have come across texters whose consistent use of particular respellings is a sign of identity; and those to whom 'standard' spelling is important. Text messages from the first texter below are consistently characterized by, in particular, her use of alphanumeric sequences (where numbers, symbols and letters are run together – see the underlined parts of the first message below). The second texter below is careful in his use of conventional spelling, but is less concerned with question marks and capitalization, both of which he described to me as 'unnecessary' in getting his message across.

1.10   Hiya! I finished uni on thurs + am home now. In lyme regis wiv mum + sum others2day, start my3wk placement on mon, wiv kids, arrggh! Then working@barnados! Xxx

Alison, aged around 30

1.11   I've just discovered a new found love for driving in london. its awesome. hows the walk. Proper beautiful isn't it. make sure you explore

Darcy, in his early twenties

To what extent does the mobile phone's involvement in existing social rituals change behaviour or relationships? It has been noted that texting, like online communication, removes inhibitions and allows for freer expression. Kasesniemi and Rautianen (2002) describe its use in initiating and even maintaining relationships to the extent that shy teenagers may enact two distinct lives: the daily face-to-face meetings at school and the deeper relationships played out through text messages. I would imagine that many people have had some experience of dual online and offline relationships: perhaps with a colleague who is achingly funny by email and dull when you bump into them at work; or a friend who is willing to discuss things over an online instant messaging chat which they would never do face-to-face.

An English friend and I converse in Spanish, which we are both learning, using Windows Live Messenger (an instant messaging tool) – but we would always choose to speak to each other in English. Why is this? In this case, there is safety in distance, both in terms of time and space. As well as having the time to think about and craft exactly what they want to say, people do not feel threatened by the physical proximity of their interlocutor. There is also a sense in which one can hide behind the written words; in my case, it alleviates the need to worry about how I sound in Spanish; in other cases, it can allow people to create new identities through text. Secondly, such forms of CMC are, like texting, centred chiefly on a limited amount of written text, and what this tends to do is encourage language play and inventiveness. I explore this idea further in Chapter 4. Finally, in the case of texting, at least, the medium encourages intimacy and thus trust: as Kasesniemi and Rautianen (2002, p. 171) put it, 'a text message finds its way to times and places where a call would be impossible'.

Text messaging has not transformed life or language as we know them; instead, like other communicative technologies, it has facilitated and added to existing social practices. In the particular case of texting, the technology has increased the extent to which people are able to correspond with each other from a distance on a daily basis, through personal, private and intimate written messages. It is this which encourages the kind of discourse which has been reported on and treated so warily by the media; and to an extent this is no surprise: personal communication of this kind encourages group codes, realized as respellings or in-group phrases. At the same time, the creativity involved in respelling and adopting speech-like practices into a written medium suggests linguistic awareness and an ability to use language for expressive and interactional purposes. The discourse that emerges, at least among one extended texting community, is explored in the rest of this book.

1.5 Investigating text messaging: an outline of chapters

The background to **Chapter 2: A Corpus of Text Messaging** lies in corpus linguistics – an approach to language study which involves the use of large language databases – and, in particular, the principles and practicalities of corpus construction. I start by describing the corpus used in this study, CorTxt, and highlight how the nature of text messages (the privacy and intimacy of the medium and the unconventional language used) complicates the process of collecting data. In particular, I look at the anonymization of CorTxt, exploring whether and why it is necessary, to what extent it is possible, how it can be carried out. As such, the chapter not only is a groundbreaking look at how this new data set can be managed but also picks up on the description in Chapter 1 by probing in greater depths aspects of the medium of texting and how the data shapes the methods used.

Chapter 3: Respellings in Text Messaging outlines the sociocultural model of spelling that, by situating spelling within the wider literacy practices of a particular society, enables us to see the choices people make as to how they spell, and respell, as both principled and meaningful. Respellings in texting can carry social meaning: they create a sense of spoken informality and intimacy, they signal deviance from the norm and they create an illusion at least of brevity: that is, texters are performing spoken informality, deviance and brevity. Here I suggest that these work together in the performance of social identity (a theme returned to in later chapters).

A great advantage of this chapter over other studies is the wealth of data it brings, enabling respellings across 11,000 text messages to be categorized according to both form and function, and for patterns to emerge from across the corpus.

Chapter 4: The Grammar of Text Messaging addresses assumptions among the public that that the grammar of text messaging is in any way deficit or incorrect, and argues instead that it is appropriate and motivated. The chapter uses corpus-based descriptions of spoken grammar – which have themselves challenged perceptions of speech as fragmented or lacking complexity – to highlight the 'speech-like' nature of grammatical features of Txt. These features include clause combination, headers and tails, situational ellipsis and deixis, and they combine to create a speech-like sense of intimacy, immediacy and informality. However, texters are free to make other choices and produce constructions that you would not expect to hear being spoken. Thus, the chapter also reveals the active role that texters play in constructing this grammar which in turn contributes to their creation of texted identities.

Chapter 5: Discourse Markers in Texting builds on the previous, by looking at the occurrence of spoken discourse markers in texting. Against a background of research into various (written) texts which similarly draw on discourse markers because of their association with speech, the chapter shows again how texters draw on features of spoken grammar in self-presentation and to fulfil intimate and interpersonal functions through texting.

Chapter 6: Frequent Words and Phrases in Text Messaging highlights how texting differs from other written and spoken varieties though investigation of the frequent phrases which characterize CorTxt and which can be said to comprise a linguistic 'fingerprint' of texting. It does this by adopting a 'corpus-driven' inductive approach to corpus study, whereby word and phrase frequency is used as a 'way in' to the data. The corpus driven approach reveals that the distribution of words in CorTxt is startlingly different from other corpora. Most noticeable is that *the*, usually by far the most frequent item in any corpus, is less frequent than *a*, which is generally three times less frequent. This cannot be accounted for wholly by the omission of *the*, nor by the speech-like nature of texting, but must also be explained by the frequent phrases in which the two items occur. The chapter also reviews approaches to the study of phraseology, drawing on a range of sources including those in both corpus linguistics and psycholinguistics.

Chapter 7: Everyday Creativity in Text Messaging shows that creativity in texting is not limited to abbreviations and phonetic spelling, but also includes the repetition, manipulation of idioms and morphological inventiveness found not only in written literary texts but also in spoken conversation and in informal written and online correspondence (postcards, letters, online chat). This chapter highlights how the need for brevity and other constraints of text messaging encourage creative wordplay, and how some instances of creativity are very speech-like while others emerge from the particular affordances of the medium.

Chapter 8: Performing Identity through Text Messaging draws on research into the discursive construction of identity to show how the linguistic choices made by texters, and the resources on which they draw, contribute to their performance of identity through texting. In particular I draw on the concept of performativity, used by Judith Butler to describe how gender identities are created and reaffirmed through being repeatedly performed, in distinct ways in differing contexts, in interactions with others. My argument here is not to highlight the usefulness of the term *perform* to describe how texters actively respond to varied circumstances, expectations and discourses and to argue that it is the effects of this performance that creates and reaffirms the nature of Txt. In doing so, the chapter draws on examples from throughout the book to show how brevity, a speech-like informality and deviance are performed through linguistic resources in texting.

Drawing on strands running through the book, **Chapter 9: Text Messaging in the World: the State of the Art and its Future** looks at texting in the wider world. English is used in text messages by communities across the world, and in this chapter I look at how similar practices emerge in places as diverse as Europe, South Africa and the Middle East. At the same time, English in many of these communities is just one language used alongside home vernaculars, and I explore what motivates the choice to use one language or another, and the kind of discourse that this multilingualism produces. The second aspect that this final chapter asks is what the future for the language used in texting is likely to be, as globalization takes hold, as the technology develops, as smartphones enable both texting and CMC and as social networking sites expand. The chapter explores the place of texting alongside these other media in a globalizing world and the impact this will have on the discourse that emerges.

1.6 Further reading

For further discussion of texting in society, see collected papers in Katz and Aakhus (2002). For a linguistic overview, see Thurlow and Poff (2012).

Notes

1   The brackets < > denotes how a word is spelt: so, we may say that the sound /k/ can be spelt <k> or <c>. The forwards slashes // denote how a word sounds: so, the plural <s> in dogs or cats may be pronounced /z/ or /s/.

2   My summer holidays were a complete waste of time. Before, we used to go to New York to see my brother, his girlfriend and their three screaming kids face to face. I love New York, it's great. But my parents were so worried because of 9/11 [the attack on the twin towers in New York] that they decided to stay in Scotland.

CHAPTER TWO

A corpus of text messages

2.1 Introduction

For a long time after Facebook claimed the best part of most of my friends' days, we still had one friend who carried on sending us updates of her life by text message or email. I must admit that we railed at them a little. No greeting, no enquiry as to how we were; the assumption that we were interested in hearing about the minutiae of her day; and no suggestion that reciprocation was welcome. It was ironic, then, that that was essentially what we were doing everyday on Facebook through the status update facility: posting short, fairly self-centred announcements. Somehow, though, what was acceptable on the social network site felt wrong through email and texting. You can argue that this is because Facebook lends itself better to such communication, and I wouldn't necessarily disagree: it allows people to post messages rather than directing them at any one person, for example (although it also allows for private, directed interactions).

However, there is nothing inherent to the technology that says people *have* to use it like that. Take the social network and microblogging site, Twitter, as an example. When the site launched in 2006, it asked users to post short messages in response to the question 'What are you doing?' But, increasingly, that's not what people wanted to use the site for. When, in 2009, Twitter changed its question to 'What's happening?' the new wording was a direct reflection of the fact that people were using the site to pass on and evaluate information, and not simply to update people on what they were doing. In fact, Twitter has constantly incorporated user-generated devices into the site (such as the use of the hashtag [#] to indicate topics; @ to address someone; or RT to retweet or resend a message).

How we use technology depends as much, if not more, on how we perceive and value that technology as it does on the nature of the technology itself. In other words, how a technology is used in any particular place at any one time depends not on some homogenizing effect of the technology but on the people using it (at that time and in that place). It is true that some technologies may lend themselves to certain uses. However, rather than seeing technology as determining how people will respond, we can see technology as offering possibilities (or **affordances**) that people are free to exploit in a number of ways. We saw this particularly vividly with the unpredicted popularity of texting itself, as people exploited what had been designed as a tool for engineers (see Chapter 1); and we saw it again with Twitter. You may be able to think of other illustrative examples.

What this means, for present purposes, is that this book on the discourse of text messaging is in fact not a book about the discourse of text messaging at all – it is in fact a book about the communicative practices of a particular group, or groups, of people through text messaging. What they are doing is likely to find some resonance with what other texters are doing, but generalizations can at best be cautiously put forward. In practical terms, what this means is that it's important to know something about who the texters being researched are, and to bear in mind that their personal characteristics are likely to influence their texting practices.

The purpose of this chapter is twofold. Most importantly, I want to describe my corpus, CorTxt, and how I perceive the people who have contributed to it, as well as the methods followed in its compilation and preparation. This is necessary in light of the book as a whole, because what I say about text messaging in later chapters needs to be evaluated in the knowledge of who we are talking about. However, in the process, I will explore some of the challenges to corpus compilation that text messaging throws up. In particular, I look at two of the aforementioned challenges: how social and technological features of texting complicate data collection and how its linguistic nature problematizes the process of anonymization.

2.2 Describing CorTxt

This book is based on CorTxt, a corpus of just over 11,000 text messages (190,516 words) collected between March 2004 and May 2007. Many of the observations made will still be relevant by the time you read this, but changing practices and technologies will also mean that the studies in this book are ripe for comparison with what texters are now going on to do (this is a theme returned to in Chapter 9). They may, for example, be increasingly accessing the internet through their phones while on the move and making nuanced choices between text messaging, on the one hand, and

Facebook, Twitter or email, on the other. Throughout the book, I will ask you to compare my findings with your own experiences (and even where I don't, this is something you could do at most junctures).

Have a quick look through Table 2.1. As you do, consider the strengths and limitations of the recruitment procedures, and what the reasons might

Table 2.1 Corpus Specifications

	CorTxt
No of messages	11,067
No of words	190,516
Average no of words per message	17.2 words
Collection period	March 2004–May 2007 (3 years 2 months)
Collection methods and procedures	From friends and family (10,626 messages) Contributors were recruited informally through email and requested to submit all received and sent messages with dates, times, and senders' names or initials. Number submitted was up to contributors. It was made clear messages would be anonymized, and all senders required to complete consent forms and personal profiles. Finally, my interest in exploring how people text on a day-to-day basis was highlighted and participants were asked not to select interesting or amusing texts (although it was made clear that they could omit private text messages they did not feel comfortable submitting). 'Templates' were attached as Excel files into which participants could enter messages. AOL anonymous online public forum (441) A further 441 messages came from an anonymous public forum provided by AOL for forwarding text messages. After it was discontinued, people kept using it: that is, messages used in this study were those which were sent to the service but not forwarded.
Composition of texters	Mainly British English speakers, aged 19–68, professionals and students
Language of communication	English (mainly British English)
Type of communication	Mainly personal communication, although some business text messages evident, including: Hi, Are you interested in working taster day at Cornwall College, Camborne 27.4.06 4hrs@£6 per hour? Ring if interested. NAME173

be behind the method of data collection. Given the participants in the study, how cautious do my conclusions regarding the discourse of text messaging have to be?

Choices over various recruitment procedures are discussed in section 2.3 below. However, one outcome of the friends and family approach has been that participants in my study tend to share similar characteristics: contributors were almost all British, spoke English as a mother tongue, were aged over 18, and tended to be well-educated students or professionals. What this means is that conclusions I draw regarding, for example, the creative use of language in texting may not be applicable to groups of texting individuals who differ in this respect.

Table 2.2 provides further details regarding the contributors to the corpus. Before you look at it, let me flag up two points. Firstly, it should be noted that contributions to the corpus were uneven, that is, people submitted very different numbers of text messages. The largest contribution came from a texter who supplied 14.1% of the total number, while many participants contributed only one message. Secondly, it should also be noted that contributors submitted text messages that they had received as well as those which they had sent. The ethical concerns raised by this are explored later in this chapter.

As you go through the characteristics mentioned in Table 2.2, think about how each might affect the way people text. Which, if any, do you think are the most important factors? And how does the breakdown compare to the people you text? Are the people you text younger? More varied? Are they more prolific texters? Are they from a greater variety of national backgrounds? Although not thorough or systematic, such observations can underlie the comparisons you make between your own experiences and the findings reported in this book.

This table shows a somewhat greater variety in backgrounds than the initial table suggested. The fact that my contributors submitted text messages they had received as well as those they had sent resulted in the incorporation of various networks into CorTxt, that is, the corpus does not simply comprise my immediate network. Prominent in the corpus (in terms of numbers of messages) are the messages sent to and from a female speech therapist (aged around 30) in Cardiff; a male design student (in his mid-twenties) in south-west England; a female secondary school teacher (in her mid-thirties) in north-west England; and a female postgraduate student (in her early thirties) in the West Midlands. Contributors work in a variety of occupations, although nearly half are employed in some capacity in the education sector: students, teachers and support staff. One important variable is age, given that we can assume younger texters' practices diverge from those of older adults: the most represented groups in CorTxt are people in their early thirties and their twenties. Most had at the time been texting for between 5 and 7 years – that is, texting was not something new but neither was it something most people had grown up with; and

Table 2.2 Contributors to CorTxt

CorTxt			
Total number of contributors (those directly recruited who submitted messages)	16		
Total number of named senders (including contributors plus those whose messages were sent to and submitted by contributors)	248 (sending 10,022 messages – the rest are either from the AOL site or senders who could not be identified by their recipients)		
Age range	−21	3%	
	22–25	25%	
	26–29	23%	
	30–35	30%	
	36–39	5%	
	40–45	3%	
	46–49	4%	
	50–55	3%	
	55–59	6%	
	60+	3%	
Gender	M	41%	
	F	59%	
Occupation	Education	48%	Students, teachers, student support and information management
	Health and community care	9%	Social services management, medicine, nursery officer, counselling, speech and language therapy
	Engineering and construction	7%	Construction management, architectural technology, technology

(Continued)

Table 2.2 (Continued)

	CorTxt		
	Office and administrative	6%	Office assistance and administration
	Arts, craft and entertainment	4%	Publishing, photography, design
	Other (no one category over 3%)	26%	
	Hospitality IT Legal and Financial Management and Executive Manual work Public Service Retired Unemployed		
Native language	English	96%	
Use of 'predictive texting' (a device found in most phones which uses a dictionary to predict the word being typed, and which may influence whether people abbreviate, and the kinds of abbreviations that they make)	Yes	83%	
	No	17%	
Average length of time texters have used text messaging	Under 5 years	28%	
	5–7 years	58%	
	Over 7 years	14%	
Frequency of texting	Infrequent user (one or fewer messages a day)		
	35%		
	Daily user (around one or two messages a day)		
	20%		
	Frequent user (more than one or two a day)		
	45%		

the overwhelming majority used predictive texting. The gender balance is biased towards females.

Exactly what impact these factors can be said to have on the discourse produced is hard to say. Much of the concern that centres around texting in society is directed at children and teenagers: people still at some stage or other of learning to be literate. In general, the make-up of contributors to CorTxt suggests a population of literate, educated adults and we can expect a more sophisticated linguistic awareness. Indeed, in later chapters we will see evidence that some of these texters take great delight in language play and amusing each other (e.g. Chapter 7) – this may or may not be something that other texters engage in. How does your texting network compare to the characteristics described here?

In the next section, I look at some of the assumptions made in the collection of the corpus, and the challenges faced.

2.3 Challenges and decisions behind CorTxt

2.1   Dude, if you see joanna then dont mention that you've spoke to me, she wants me to go to the pub and i cant be bothered and my mom goes on holiday tomorrow.

In the last chapter, I touched on reasons why you might want to study the language of text messaging. In this section, I look at *how* you might go about doing so. My assumption here is that the best way to study the language used is to collect and look at real data: that is, to gain access to actual text messages sent between individuals. I spent three years collecting the 11,000 text messages that make up CorTxt. Given that you may well have better things to do or a shorter period of time in which to do it, I hasten to add that the *amount* of data is not necessarily important. However, what is important for our purposes is that the messages are representative of everyday practices, rather than being cherry-picked (or should that be Orange-picked) because they are particularly interesting or controversial. There are two related issues here.

Firstly, you are likely to find that the people who contribute text messages struggle to believe that you are interested in what they may see as normal, fairly mundane texts and dismiss them as boring or even as unrepresentative of 'real' texting practices that they see documented in the press: in Chapter 1, I gave the example of a13-year-old schoolgirl whose school essay resembled code: *B4, we used 2 go 2 NY 2C my bro, his GF & thr 3:-@ kds FTF.* What people tend to want to do is contribute the more outlandish or playful of their text messages.

Secondly, as a researcher, it is easy to make your own assumptions based on popular accounts of texting and to let these assumptions guide analysis. Most scholarly accounts of texting start from the premise that texting is heavily abbreviated – and often find that it is not. As well as having representative text messages, then, what is also important is *how* you decide *what* to look at, that is, how you find your way into the data. This question is central to a branch of linguistics known as **corpus linguistics**.

Corpus linguists adhere to an approach which requires the collection of a substantial amount of data and which takes frequency of use as a starting point for analysis. A **corpus** in this sense is a collection of texts which are stored electronically, and which are accessed using computer software. A corpus is not read like a book (from start to finish), but instead it is searched like a library; an online library in which you can search not only for book titles but for each word (Ramesh Krishnamurthy, pers. comm). Thus, you might search for *thing* in CorTxt and generate the following examples, in what are known as **concordances**. The concordances below in Figure 2.1 are sorted alphabetically on the word to the left of the central **node**, *thing*. (And they begin to show an evaluative use of *thing* as a marker of vagueness – see Chapter 5.)

Chapter 6 looks at the language patterns that emerge from this kind of analysis. In this chapter, I am more concerned with challenges regarding the collection of data, and how they manifest themselves (and are sometimes amplified) when the corpus is one of text messages. The text message at the start of the chapter, and reproduced below, illustrates many of the challenges involved in text message collection.

> Dude, if you see Joanna then dont mention that you've spoke to me, she wants me to go to the pub and i cant be bothered and my mom goes on holiday tomorrow.

The first challenge is the effect of message length on corpus **size**, which is traditionally measured in words (the limitations of trying to identify and demarcate words in Txt given the shifting word boundaries is discussed in Chapter 7). The above text message can be said to comprise 33 words. However many I collected, at an average of 17.2 words (as calculated by the corpus exploitation tools) I was never going to compile a large corpus in terms of its word count. Although comprising over 11,000 text messages, CorTxt contains less than 200,000 words, which is tiny compared to an equivalent corpus of, say, 11,000 newspaper articles. The British National Corpus (BNC), built in the 1990s, comprises 1 million words. The Bank of English, a growing corpus largely comprising newspaper texts and held by the University of Birmingham and Collins publishers, was nearing 500 million words in 2010. At this time, The Oxford English corpus (Oxford University Press) contained 2 billion words. The rapid growth in corpus size is partly because of technology: the more sophisticated both the hardware and the software, the greater the number of texts that can be stored and analyzed. But size also reflects the starting assumption within corpus linguistics that the more examples you have, the more sure you can be of

48 quite a few ppl hav had the same kinda **thing**.she's better now stil a bit dazed i th

49 party, how could I resist. That kinda **thing**. Texting you is always interesting but

50 ME67. I'm sure a phone call is the last **thing** she wants, but would appreciate no whe

51 ng – am getting the whole hugh laurie **thing** – even with the stick – indeed, especial

52 ds me i still need 2go.did u c d little **thing** i left in the lounge?it was free but i

53 And crap mirage thing. One more little **thing** maybe? X" "Is the cd somewhere i can s

54 was lovely. See ya on tues. You lucky **thing** with your big hols to go!" "hi. Am com

55 ly bad – totally rejected that kinda me **thing**. Think I might work till we im to the

56 lies for dad, and mats. And crap mirage **thing**. One more little thing maybe? X" "Is t

57 think i have decided to keep this mp3 **thing** that doesnt work. May sound odd, but i

Figure 2.1 Concordance lines for **thing**

your conclusions. It is difficult to fault this assumption, especially when determining the significance of various statistical calculations.

However, at the same time, there has been a parallel move towards smaller, more specialized corpora. The principle that emerges here is not size but **representativeness**. A corpus can be said to be representative when its composition reflects that of the variety it pertains to represent (Hunston, 2002). To what extent can statements based even on vast corpora such as the Oxford English corpus be made about language *in general*? Can or should generalizations be made?

Recognition of the need to study language as it occurs in different contexts has led to the construction of corpora of academic articles and of particular sections from articles or theses, fiction or particular fictional genres, electronic communication in general or certain online domains, with the argument that these can perhaps claim to be representative of the object of study (academic introductions, vampire fiction, emails and so on). Or can they? Groom (2006) based his research on a corpus of US stem-cell patents, a corpus which included all the US stem-cell patents that existed. His findings, therefore, can be said to be entirely pertinent to this particular subset. In other cases, statements about a corpus can only be statements about that corpus, and all generalizations are extrapolations (Hunston, 2002, pp. 22–3).

Ultimately, representativeness is probably an unobtainable, even fictional, goal. What is important is that the data you use is carefully documented and that care should be taken not to over-generalize in your interpretations of it. As I said in Chapter 1, my aim was to document the practices of a localized group of texters – but even here it is difficult to generalize findings across all individuals or to assume that the practices evident in the corpus are anything more than what these people were doing in a particular context and at a certain time.

The second issue is the private nature of text messages: what would happen if 'Joanna', the woman mentioned in the text message above, happened upon this book? The fact that text messages are often private and personal raises two issues. Firstly, it means that it can be hard to convince individuals to part with them and this, along with the practical difficulties of getting messages off a phone and into computer-readable format, can further reduce the amount of data easily collected. It also raises the question as to *how* messages can best be obtained, and from *whom*: questions I explore further below. The second issue raised by the private nature of the data is the question of participant protection and the need for **anonymization**. Joanna, above, is not of course her real name. For the sake of this example and its readability, I replaced her real name with a pseudonym; throughout the corpus itself and in this book I have replaced names with a code. Whether to use codes or names is a complex but engaging issue which I shall explore below; and whether a text message can ever be anonymized so that somebody's identity is completely concealed is an interesting question. I discuss anonymization as an example of the ethical issues involved in data collection later in this chapter.

A final three concerns are specific to this kind of data: transcription error, message selection and spelling normalization. The problem of **transcription error** is either that typos can be made in transcribing messages from phones into computer-readable formats or that spellings such as <dont> and <cant>, or the lack of capitalization of *i*, for example, may be corrected in the process of transcribing, by the computer spellchecker if not the transcriber. The problem is that there is little alternative to transcription, unless messages are forwarded to the researcher's phone, which incurs cost. Software does exist to transfer data directly from phone to computer, but at the time of data collection, it was neither widely used or very reliable nor able to keep up with developments in mobile technology.

The second concern is **message selection**, as I discussed above: that participants may select shocking or special text messages to submit and withhold ones they perceive to be uninteresting. It is also hard to ensure that participants have not simply made up messages. Of course, some selection will always be necessary, so that participants need not contribute highly personal messages or others they are not comfortable sending, and it is difficult to get round this issue when dealing with a private medium. In fact, message selection can form a central part of the ethical procedures by which data is collected, in that it allows participants to control which data should or should not be used in the analysis. As with the issue of transcription error, the approach to the problem of message selection must be a pragmatic one and, to the extent that both are to some extent unavoidable, the potential for bias and possible errors in transcription must be acknowledged.

The final issue is **spelling normalization**, that is, whether unconventional spellings should be 'corrected' into a more conventional English. If, as I argued in Chapter 1, spelling is an important resource for making meaning, then the argument is that respellings should be retained. However, if you intend to search for words (such as *thing* above), the fact that the computer cannot recognize respelt forms of the same word needs to be addressed.

In the rest of this chapter, I look more closely at two of these issues. Firstly, I discuss how the nature of text messaging complicates data collection; secondly, I explore how the nature of its language problematizes both the process of anonymization and the processing of the data.

2.4 How to get hold of text messages

As we saw in Chapter 1, text messages are generally sent from one individual's mobile phone to another's; and the individuals in question tend to be intimately related: friends, family members, colleagues or classmates. There are, then, two main obstacles to the collection of text message data: firstly, this potentially private nature, which may mean that individuals are reluctant to part with text messages; and secondly, the fact that text messages are stored on an individual's mobile phone so that even if someone grants a researcher access, they still have to get messages off and into a computer-readable format. These factors may go some way to explain the relative dearth of studies of text messaging (especially ones exploiting large databanks) compared to open-access public internet chat rooms. Given the challenges in accessing personal online correspondence, how is text message data best collected?

There are two main approaches to collecting text messages. Which do you think would be more effective and why?

- in-depth approaches which probe the texting practices of a few individuals

- large-scale approaches often using anonymous and web-based methods

In-depth approach

The research started by the Information Society Research Center (INSOC) in 1997 into the mobile phone use of Finnish teenagers is interesting because in 1998 they were able to document the sudden and unforeseen take-up of text messaging. All at once 'instead of talking about calling and changing colour covers on their mobiles, all teenagers wanted to give their views on text messaging' (Kasesniemi and Rautiainen, 2002, p. 171). These teenagers had been recruited through a variety of ways, including advertising and directly through teachers and families. Once recruited, however, close relationships were established with the researchers, and their interpretations and observations were seen as shaping the development of the research as much as those of the researchers. As well as amassing an 8000-word corpus of text messages over five years, the researchers carried out participant observation and interviews and collected observation journals, notes that accompanied the text messages, and email and text correspondence between the 'informants' and the researchers. Apart from the richness of the data, the immediate advantage of this approach in terms of collecting text messages is that the teenagers appeared to have a sense of responsibility over their involvement and to have sustained their practice of transcribing messages over time.

> Collecting messages has become part of my daily rhythm. It's been an interesting experience! I've written down every single message, I'm pretty conscientious!
>
> (Girl, 17)

> First I wrote the messages down right after I had got them and read them, but later I started to write them down the same night. In the end I would write them down when there was no more space for them [in the memory]
>
> (Girl, 17)
> (Kasesniemi and Rautianen, 2002, p. 174)

Given their involvement, and the fact that teenagers were discussing their text messages with the researchers, there was a greater likelihood of ensuring authenticity, that is, that the teenager was not making up messages for the researchers' attention. Aside from these practical advantages, what should be noted is the fit between the approach adopted and the research aims of the project. The qualitative approach allowed for greater familiarity with participants' backgrounds, heightened the ability to acquire personal information and so achieved depth (a greater understanding of individuals' behaviour) rather than prioritizing breadth (a larger and more varied sample).

Large-scale approach

Text messages, perhaps surprisingly, can comprise valuable evidence in court. Tim Grant of the Centre for Forensic Linguistics, Aston University, has been collecting text messages since 2006 when he began his project at the University of Leicester. His aim is to build what is known in corpus linguistics as a **reference corpus**, that is, a large and very general corpus against which more specific corpora or individual texts can be compared (the aforementioned Bank of English, BNC and Oxford English Corpus may be used as reference corpora). In this case, Grant's reference corpus specifically comprised text messages, against which particular text messages can be compared. Participants in the study are asked to submit 10 messages to a website, along with details pertaining to each individual message and to themselves.

What Grant is interested in is exploring the extent to which he can establish the authorship of any one text, based on the individual's idiosyncrasies in spelling, that is, whether we have recognizable texting idiolects and whether, as the case may be, they can be used against us. In 2001, for example, when a young girl Danielle Jones went missing and was subsequently found to have been murdered, Grant's evidence played a vital role in identifying her uncle, Stuart Campbell, as the killer. Having killed his niece, Stuart then sent messages from her phone, pertaining to be from Danielle, and thus providing himself with an alibi. What he didn't realize, however, was Danielle's spelling practices: for example, he spelt *what* as <wot> whereas Danielle preferred <wat>.

The advantages of the online collection procedure are self-evident: it is easy to administer and easy to reach a large number of people, and it avoids the time and cost which need to be invested in a more qualitative approach. The disadvantage is the lack of background detail and sense of context; with web-based questionnaires, the disadvantage is that they favour texters with internet access and know-how. If you advertise online, you are only going to reach people who are also online. Again, however, the research focus is important. Studies such as Grant's which aim to describe the orthographic features typical of texting require breadth and variety of textual data rather than prioritizing in-depth knowledge of participants' backgrounds.

Both of the above projects took advantage of a **snowballing** approach to recruitment. The snowballing technique involves initial participants being urged to invite friends to join the study, who then invite their friends and so on. For Kasesniemi and Rautiainen (2002), it was simply an effective way to reach new recruits. For Grant, the advantage of the snowballing technique for his purposes was that it enables researchers to explore not only how individuals vary in linguistic practices but how *networks* of texters differ, that is, how the people you text influence your texting practices. Participants were asked to devise ID codes for themselves and the recipients of the submitted texts, to allow the researchers to identify whether their own recipients later joined the study as participants in their own right.

Making use of what you have: family and friends

A third method for obtaining data, and the one I took in compiling CorTxt, is to recruit family and friends. Again, the advantages of this are self-evident: these were people I had access to and upon whom I could rely to undergo the tedious process of saving and writing out text messages. I was also familiar with their backgrounds and, in some ways, many participants shared similar text message practices to myself. At the same time, because I requested messages that people had both sent and received, my initial network expanded to include people I did not have direct contact with and so using friends and family was a starting point, rather than the entirety of the network.

What may be lost with this method, however, are claims to representativeness. To what extent is a network emanating from friends and family representative of the wider texting population? As discussed above, the question is somewhat moot, because representativeness is anyway a questionable notion. In the present case, obtaining representative samples of the 'texting population' would require accurate knowledge of who texts (and how much?) and this, as with other types of language interaction, is not possible to know. For example, figures cited in text message studies suggest that the texting population is predominantly young, but older age groups, however, cannot be ignored. According to the Mobile Data Association, the average age of mobile users in 2003 was already rising above 30 (Jellinek 2003). Faulkner and Culwin (2005) note that phone ownership in Finland is even across all age groups except those aged over 60 who live alone, who are less likely to own a mobile. Gender and other sociological variables such as education and employment are equally difficult to ascertain. The book remains a discussion of the particular network(s) under investigation, and generalizations must be cautious.

In this section, I have compared a qualitative and quantitative approach to text message collection; and mentioned a couple of methods of recruitment, including web-based questionnaires, the snowballing technique and the use of family and friends. What emerges is the importance of practical considerations and the need to be pragmatic; while taking care to document your data.

2.5 How to anonymize the data

2.2   Bloody hell, cant believe you forgot my surname Mr Jones. Ill give u a clue, its spanish and begins with m . . . X

For a smaller-scale study, anonymization will be more straightforward than it proved for my relatively large text message corpus; nonetheless, it highlights important principles and raises interesting questions.

To what extent is it possible to anonymize a text message – that is, to remove any information that might potentially lead to anyone being identified? If you look at the text message above, you'll notice how personal information about the texter and the textee is intricately embedded into the text message. Does anonymizing the text message significantly alter it, and risk making it potentially unusable as authentic data? Which is the best way to anonymize it – by substituting other names or with codes? The answers to these questions lie in a balance between the practicalities of what can feasibly be anonymized (while maintaining data as much as possible in its original form); and the principle of protecting participants.

The principle of protecting participants requires the replacement of all information pertaining to specific individuals who could subsequently be identified or contacted by people who do not otherwise closely know them. Note here that it is impossible to ensure that *nobody* will ever recognize the participants. The data anonymized in CorTxt is tabulated below. You can also see in these examples how name codes are numbered to enable different name-forms to be tracked. All occurrences of Aaron, for example, would be NAME1 (although they may refer to more than one Aaron).

What to anonymize, what to leave unanonymized and where to draw the line between the two are harder questions than you might think. One distinction is that between private and public information – a distinction that, as we shall see, is not always clear-cut. Let me illustrate this with reference to place. How would you anonymize the addresses in the following two text messages?

2.3   NAME238 what number High Street do u live at? Is it 11?

2.4   Ok thats cool. Its 16 Church Road, just off either raglan rd or edward rd. Behind the cricket ground. Gimme ring when ur closeby see you tuesday.

The embedded personal information in the first text message relates to a specific individual and so the name of the street was replaced (in this instance) with the code STREET.

2.5   NAME238 what number STREET do u live at? Is it 11?

In contrast to the anonymization of the street above, only the specific house number was changed in the second text messages. The mention of the other road names was not sufficiently associated with the individual concerned to warrant removing them.

> 2.6   Ok thats cool. Its POSTALADDRESS, just off either raglan rd or edward rd. Behind the cricket ground. Gimme ring when ur closeby see you tuesday.

But the decision as to whether mention of a place could lead to the identification of an individual is ultimately arbitrary. *The UK*, presumably, would not be a risk; nor *London* or even *Bristol*, the city where this research was conducted; but what about *Moseley* (a district of Birmingham), or the *Selly Soak* and *The Country Girl* (pubs around Selly Oak, Birmingham)? Imagine you had sent these text messages. Which, if any, would you want anonymized?

> 2.7   Hiya! How was christmas? I'm back in birmingham and anxious for the next excuse to party . . . How are birthday plans progressing?
>
> 2.8   Ooh, 4got, i'm gonna start belly dancing in moseley weds 6.30 if u want 2 join me, they have a cafe too. G
>
> 2.9   Hi NAME502. I'm thinking of heading 2 the country girl if u or NAME321 will be there. I need more stickers :-)
>
> 2.10   In selly soak pub in selly oak

At which point should the line be drawn? Decisions must be based on the context. While *Selly Soak* and *The Country Girl* were left in, the following mention of a pub, which relates specifically to the new landlord (the texter), was anonymized.

> 2.11   Hithere.Wehavenowmovedin2ourpub,PUBNAME,POSTALADDRESS. PHONENUMBER. Would be great 2 c u if u cud come up.

See Table 3.2 for a list of anonmyised items. Missing from the markers of identity are terms of endearment. Terms such as *honey* were retained, but nicknames directed at particular people changed. Again, however, where does the line fall between generic terms (*honey*, *darling*) and terms that resemble nicknames? Incidentally, this does not address the problem arising in the contrasting situation, where one person uses a particular name to address a range of interlocutors and the nickname becomes part of their idiolect which could be used to identify the sender. This was the case with *bird*, used by one sender to address a number of interlocutors. The first message below is to a friend, and the second to his mother.

Table 2.3 Contact details and replacement codes

Detail	Code	Freq.	Examples
First names	NAME + number	3180	Oh, great NAME46, you're a star! Yes, pop round tomorrow eve. I'm home about six.
Surnames	SURNAME + number	88	Was it you that said something to me recently about someone we used to go to school with, NAME344 SURNAME1?
Phone numbers	PHONENUMBER	69	Hey gorgeous man. My work mobile number is PHONENUMBER. Have a good one babe. Squishy Mwahs. Xx
Extension numbers	EXTNUMBER	1	Message from NAME214 SURNAME32. I am at Truro Hospital on PHONENUMBER ext EXTENSION. You can phone me here. as I have a phone by my side
Postal addresses	POSTALADDRESS	38	Come round, it's POSTALADDRESS. Xxx
Postcodes	POSTCODE	5	Oops: 4 got that bit. POSTCODE
Email addresses	EMAILADDRESS	13	Hi my email address has changed now it is EMAILADDRESS
Car registration numbers	REGNUMBER	3	Yes, my reg is REGNUMBER. Ciao!
Sort codes and account numbers	SORTCODE ACCOUNTNUMBER	33	My sort code is SORTCODE and acc no is ACCOUNTNUMBER. The bank is natwest. Can you reply to confirm i've sent this to the right person!
Dates and times of birth	DATEOFBIRTH TIMEOFBIRTH	11	Hi NAME256 here. NAME11 have birth at *TIMEOFBIRTH* on the *DATEOFBIRTH* to NAME485 at 8lb 7oz. Mother and baby doing brilliantly.

2.12   Hey bird. I'm really sorry but i don't think i'll be able to drive on saturday
       cos the car is being used by NAME40. Can you still dive. If you don't want
       to drive all that way then i could drive some of it for you. What d'ya say?

2.13   Hello bird. Sorry i didn't ring. I'll give you a shout tomo at some point x

The possibility that texters can be identified through individual texting styles raises the question as to whether the formal replacement strategy outlined above is ever sufficient in concealing identity. Can authorship be attributed on the basis of texting idiolects, as forensic linguistic analysis such as that carried out by Grant would suggest? Or is it more likely that only those in regular texting contact could recognize each other's orthographic preferences? Think about the people you text – could you tell who was texting you if their number didn't appear on your phone?

What to replace markers of identity with is also no straightforward process. The obvious possibility involves systematic replacement of names with other, randomly selected names, but this can be problematic. One issue with the random selection of names, such that *Maud* may be replaced by *Britney*, or *Eric* by *Jennifer*, is the loss of social information such as age and gender retained in, or inferred from, original names. The desire to retain social information can be addressed through the concept of equivalence: that is, in making connections between the social implications of original names and those of pseudonyms. Gender is the one variable regularly recognized during anonymization, that is, that male and female names and speakers are matched. However, if gender is so naturally assumed to be important, why not other social factors: age, social background and ethnicity?

Another practical problem is that replacement names cannot already occur within the corpus, unless you are careful; real names (such as, say, *Paul*) cannot be changed to fictitious ones (say, *David*) if there is (to take our example) a real *David* who is then accidentally anonymized (say, to *John*), with the result that the real name *Paul*, first changed to *David*, may inadvertently be changed again to *John*. If there are also real *John*s, to take this to an extreme, then all *David*s, *Paul*s and *John*s may end up merging together as *Tom*s. Furthermore, even if pseudonyms do not occur as real names, it is difficult to spot names missed during anonymization. This means names must be successfully anonymized in one go, so to speak. In contrast, the replacement of names with codes (or with fictional names) means missed names are easily spotted.

In the light of complications involved in randomly selecting replacement fictitious names, the more effective option is to replace names and other personal information with codes. Drawbacks to the basic codes used in this book include the fact that many texters use number homophones (such as <2> and <4>) throughout CorTxt. Confusing sequences were therefore created, of which the worst is perhaps the following, where *2* (*to*) runs into NAME115 which itself runs on into the homophone *4*.

2.14   say thanks2NAME1154me. Xx

Another disadvantage of codes is that the depersonalization can distort readers' sense of the data. How have you felt reading messages punctuated by NAME codes and numbers?

Methods for anonymizing data can be manual, automatic or a combination of both. Small sets of data can of course be manually processed, although even these can become time-consuming and troublesome. Given the labour intensity involved in manual anonymization, some degree of automatization is often required. By automatization, I mean that a computer is programmed to automatically identify and replace certain indicators (such as common names) throughout the corpus. Fully automated methods bring their own problems, not least because of the problem of over-anonymization. Can you identify the problems in the over-anonymized text messages below?

2.15   All sounds good. Fingers cNAME513ed. Makes it difficult to type.

2.16   Hey mate. Spoke to the mag people. We're on. NeNAME211 the isNAME349 deliverNAME211 by the end of the month. DeliverNAME211 on the 24th sept. Talk later. NAME182

2.17   We're up wk beg 18th NAME301

2.18   Hello! I've just accepted an invite to a restaurant in st NAME348's square – leaving now – we are a random bunch and should be in the actress and the bishop by nine thirty. Would you like to join us there?

2.19   I've got2ring NAME82 on monday to let NAME82 know if its beta or not

2.20   NAME348's mine hands off. Even old he's got something about him. Mmm NAME348 SURNAME21...

2.21   Double eviction this week – NAME438 and NAME299 and good riddance to them!

In the first two, parts of a word (<ross>, <ed> and <sue>) have been identified as names and automatically changed; in the third, the month of June has been mistaken for the name June and anonymized; in the fourth, the name of a public square has unnecessarily been anonymized (it is St Paul's Square in Birmingham). The fifth is impossible to retrieve solely from its context, but the anonymized word is 'em', an abbreviation of *them* rather than of the name Emma. Finally, in the last two examples, the people being referred to are public figures: Paul Newman in the first and two contestants on a reality TV show in the second. Because of problems such as these, the process I followed can best be described as semi-automatic, in that names were initially identified and anonymized automatically, but this was then followed by a substantial amount of manual checking.

These were just a few of the decisions and challenges that emerge in an attempt to anonymize text message data. Other decisions were raised in the selection and presentation of examples for this book. At times, in order to provide some background information, I have selected text messages that were written either by participants from whom I was able to gain specific consent or by those who were sufficiently removed from myself that connections between us would be difficult to reconstruct and identification thus unlikely. (The downside of this is that examples are sometimes limited to a smaller pool of participants than I would otherwise have drawn on, and that I cannot be consistent in providing background information.) The names given to the senders of text messages are, like those people mentioned in the text messages, also anonymized throughout.

What the process of anonymization reveals is not only some of the methods and associated pitfalls, but also a lot about the intimate, personal nature of text messaging. Finally, the above is also useful in that it highlights the principles of anonymization and questions the extent to which anonymization is possible. While efforts must be made to ensure that participants are adequately protected from risk, the caveat remains (as in any research) that true and complete concealment of identity can never be wholly ensured.

2.6 Chapter summary

In this chapter, having described the data and the people on which this book is based, I outlined some of the issues to consider when collecting text message data for linguistic analysis. Some of these are general concerns, while others emerge from the particular nature of text messaging. To recap, these issues include:

- Size: how much data you can accrue is always a concern for corpus linguists. In this respect, text messaging raises particular challenges; partly because of the shortness of text messages and partly because the challenges in collecting data will tend to limit how many messages you can reasonably acquire.

- Representativeness: In this chapter, I used the word 'representative' in two respects. I questioned whether a corpus can ever be truly representative of a population (particularly where it pertains to represent intimate practices such as text messaging) and warned against generalizing. However, I also pressed the importance of obtaining texts representative of how people actually text – rather than Orange-picking the more 'outrageous' (to use the language of the press) text messages.

- Message selection: Balanced against the above, is the possibility that people will self-select text messages – and the fact that this is necessary in ensuring ethical concerns are met. This can be addressed to some extent through informed consent (so that people are aware of what you require) but must be acknowledged as a potential limitation.

- Transcription error: The other challenge to text message data collection is transcription error. As messages must be transcribed from phones, there is always the possibility that mistakes may be made or, indeed, that they may be 'corrected'. Again, to the extent that this is unavoidable, it should be acknowledged.

- Spelling normalization: as we shall see in later chapters, unconventional spelling can be a problem if you intend to conduct word frequency counts or statistical measures; but at the same time, as we shall also go on to see, variation in spelling is an important meaning-making resource that should not be ironed out.

- Ethical issues: I touched on one aspect of this issue, anonymization. Anonymization is complicated by the very personal nature of the text messages: people and places are frequently mentioned and, even where they are not, idiosyncrasies and topic choices often facilitate identification; in practical terms, it is complicated by the irregular spelling and capitalization of names in text messaging.

In the process of exploring these issues, much is revealed about the language used in text messaging. Data collection is complicated firstly by the fact that texting is such an intimate and private practice. It is also complicated by the technology. However, all is not bleak. Despite the private nature of text messaging, there may be a sense in which people are either fond of or proud of their texts and willing to show them off. (Despite the facility to erase messages, and the often limited memory space, people save special texts, sometimes in computers.) Studies such as Kasesniemi and Rautianen's (2002) document how people share messages, and show other people favourite texts. (I have a friend who regularly picks up my phone and reads through my messages; simply, I assume, to find out what I have been up to.) In my experience, most people are also quite fascinated by text messaging, and interested in how they and their interlocutors text. As I mentioned earlier in the chapter, when approaching friends and family, I was initially surprised at how willing people were to part with text messages – perhaps in part because, contrary to what I've just written, many texts are impersonal or harmless: *i'm in solihull, do you want anything?* Some form of relationship with the people you approach no doubt helps, be that pre-existing personal relationships or strong researcher-researched bonds. These links can also help to overcome issues of message selection and error transcription.

Ethical issues are also interesting in the light of the nature of text messaging. Ethical guidelines must always be carefully considered in relation to a particular research project. However, as a relatively new and under-researched data set, text messages have generally not been considered in the writing up of general ethical guidelines; and so these existing guidelines must be drawn from selectively. Text messaging is highly private, suggesting the need for greater sensitivity; yet often fairly mundane in comparison with, say, medical data comprising doctor–patient consultations. Finally, as suggested above, the process of anonymization highlights features of the very personal, somewhat idiosyncratic and unconventional language of text messages.

Before moving on to my analyses of CorTxt, I'd like to reiterate some of the limitations of the corpus which are alluded to throughout this chapter. The collection comprises only 11,067 text messages – remembering that, by 2010, an estimated 200,000 text messages were being sent every second – and they were sent within a three-year period between a loose network of people who are, in the main, highly literate adults with professional and academic occupations. Generalizations cannot be made; instead, this book must be seen as detailing the linguistic practices of a particular group of texters at a particular time. There are other limitations – for example, my study is data based and as such does not involve interviews that could attempt to gauge how participants themselves described their practices; furthermore, I have tended to make statements about the corpus as a whole, rather than attributing certain practices to particular individuals. These limitations must be borne in mind in considering the significance of my results.

2.7 Further reading

On corpus linguistics and corpus compilation in general, see Hunston (2002), McEnery et al. (2006), O'Keeffe et al. (2007), and McEnery and Hardie (2011). For an overview of texting corpora, see Tagg (forthcoming).

For the anonymization of linguistic data, see Rock (2001).

For information on ethical guidelines, see those drawn up by the British Association for Applied Linguistics (BAAL), which can be retrieved from their website (www.baal.org.uk); and, for electronic data, the Association of Internet Researchers (AoIR) at http://aoir.org/. Most universities will also have their own guidelines and procedures, and these must also be consulted.

CHAPTER THREE

Respellings in text messaging

3.1 Introduction

3.1 Hi NAME219 hope unis ok&u'r feelin gud Hows it bin wiv NAME227
since u got bac? Gud news bout the playscheme Lookin4ward 2seein u soon
hav missd u lotsa love NAME330

Alison, in her early thirties

Text messaging is often defined, at least in the media and in much public
debate, by its spelling. The text message above encapsulates popularly held
conceptions as to what Txt looks like. Words are shortened in various ways
(*feelin*, *bout*, *hav*, *missd*) and some are spelt phonetically (*gud*), while other
spellings reflect how we might say the words in fast, informal speech (*bin*,
wiv, *lotsa*). Words may often be run together without spaces between them.
As you'll notice above, words may instead be separated by punctuation (*u got
bac?Gud news*) or by number homophones such as 2 and 4 in *Lookin4ward*
and *2seein*.

The paradox with Txt, however, is that the popular conception doesn't
always match how many people actually text. Since I started studying text
messaging, I've had several conversations which go along the lines of:

Me: Actually at the moment I'm looking at the language of
text messaging.
Interested person: Oh, I never use text language. I write everything out
normally.

The assumption made by the 'interested person' (who is in some cases simply being polite) is that by 'language of text messaging' I mean the kind of abbreviated and unconventionally spelt language discussed above. And their response tends to be that they do not text in this way. One caveat here is the unreliability of self-reports – the possible discrepancy between what people do and what they say. Nevertheless, what these people tell me is reflected in my data. In fact, what struck me first when looking through CorTxt was the *absence* or infrequency of unconventional spellings in many text messages. Here are some examples.

3.2   Everybody had fun this evening. Miss you.

3.3   Men like shorter ladies. Gaze up into his eyes.

3.4   No, but you told me you were going, before you got drunk!

3.5   Sorry NAME352. I will be able to get to you. See you in the morning.

Admittedly, neither my data nor my conversations involve many teenagers, and it may be this age group (or younger) that tends to abbreviate. (Although, interestingly, so far the people I've encountered who are most voraciously critical of 'textese' were a group of English Literature undergraduates.) Indeed, my informants will sometimes extend the above conversation by describing what they see as the more idiosyncratic and indecipherable spelling practices of offspring, nieces and nephews. So it is useful in this context to note the similar infrequency of unconventional spellings found across studies. Thurlow and Brown (2003), for example, report that although 82% of the 19-year-old university students participating in their study claimed to use 'textisms', they found only an average of 3 per text message (which they describe as 20% of message content). According to Taylor and Harper (2003), the value placed on text messages by young people can depend on the language used, and abbreviating to avoid sending more than one message can in fact *lower* their value. It might be worth reflecting on your own practice – and your own inbox. To what extent do you, and the people you text, play with spelling conventions? (And do your practices shift to accommodate those of your interlocutors?) How do you judge messages with unconventional – and those with conventional – spellings?

Another question worth considering is how intelligible you find your friends' and family's spelling practices. One of the fears expressed in the media is that Txt is indecipherable. And it may well be – to those looking over their children's shoulders. We may all have received the odd text message (in both senses of the word) which we puzzled over. In general, however, it is fair to say that when we text we are aware of what our interlocutor will understand. Textisms are difficult for outsiders to understand precisely because they draw on intimate contextualized practices and shared knowledge between those involved. As Thurlow and Brown (2003, p. 15) point out, most textisms are 'semantically recoverable', that is, they can be understood in (or 'recovered' from) context. When people shorten a word by omitting the vowels, for example, they recognize the fact that consonants carry the greater information load: *please* can be recovered from <pls> but you would hardly recognize it if you removed the consonants and were left with <eae>; while phonetic spellings can often be interpreted simply by reading them aloud. Spaces are often only omitted where words are broken up by numbers or punctuation: hence the alphanumeric sequences *Lookin4ward* and *2seein* described above. Ultimately, these forms emerge from interaction and are likely to be understood by the people involved: in this respect, as Thurlow and Brown put it, textisms are fairly 'unremarkable'.

Why do people sometimes choose to spell certain words unconventionally? The obvious answer is that they are abbreviating words to save time, effort and space (and hence money), and that this is encouraged by the constraining physical features of the mobile phone – the tiny keypad, the limited character allowance. As Crystal (2008, p. 20) points out, abbreviated messages in full form would tend to be longer than unabbreviated ones (as illustrated in the text messages above), suggesting that people are trying to compress longer messages, or hasten their delivery. Two points emerge here.

Firstly, if we look at the data, it becomes apparent that the need for brevity is not only motivated by technological factors. It is also dictated by communicative demands, such as the expectation that responses will be quick (Thurlow and Brown, 2003). So, abbreviations may be a response to **interpersonal** as well as technological factors. That is, when people decide how to spell, they are concerned with how their spelling will be received by their interlocutor as well as how much space, time or money they can save. The question then becomes: if people abbreviate with an eye to their audience (rather than to save space), will they not also lengthen words or play with spellings in a way that does not result in truncation? Is brevity the only result when people play with spellings? Once we accept that spelling practices may be shaped by interpersonal considerations, we can assume that spelling plays a greater role in communication than simply speeding it up. Is the need for brevity enough to explain the differences in spelling and the effect they have in these two messages, for example?

3.6   Thankyou for ditchin me i had been invited out but said no coz u were cumin and u said we would do something on the sat now i have nothing to do all weekend i am a billy no mates i really hate being single

3.7   Hi, how u? R u getting ther? I'm in bank quein up-payin in stuf4alice-who I Wrk4. We'l av2go out4drink soon-let me no if u wan2 ova nxt few days-not thur. Sux

In their study of text messaging in the UK, Thurlow and Brown posit three motivations for respelling. These are as follows:

1 'brevity and speed' (seen in lexical abbreviation including letter-number homophones; and the minimal use of capitalization, punctuation and spacing);

2 'paralinguistic restitution' (such as the use of capitals to indicate emphasis or loudness, or multiple punctuation, which compensate for the lack of such features as stress and intonation)

3 'phonological approximation' (i.e. often playful attempts to capture informal speech such as <ya> or <nope>).

Often, more than one of these motivations can be fulfilled within one spelling: <ya> for *you*, for example, serves both to abbreviate *and* recreate a spoken utterance. In other cases, however, the desire to approximate an informal spoken form may result in additional characters, as in <nope> or <okie dokie>.

In this chapter, I work within the assumption that how we spell (and 'respell') can be meaningful. It is meaningful because the way we choose to spell words contributes to the effect that a text message has and what the text message says about the person who sent it. In other words, how we spell contributes to our portrayal of social identities, as we choose to express them through text messaging. In taking this approach, I adopt a sociocultural model of orthography, one which posits spelling choices as a socially meaningful practice.

Below, I first explain what is meant by a sociocultural model of orthography and by the term respelling. I then describe the respellings which occur across CorTxt and, working within the model, try to explain their significance in terms of making meaning. They may be unremarkable – but they are not meaningless.

Conventions Used

Throughout this book, I italicize linguistic items under discussion. When I focus on a word as a respelt form, or when presenting an orthographic letter, it is framed by angled brackets, so that I can talk about alternative spellings of *what* being <wat> or <wot> . This practice draws on Sebba (2007). In contrast, representations of sounds are captured within slashes, so that I can say that the letter <c> is pronounced /s/ in *ceiling* and /k/ in *cat*.

3.2 A sociocultural model of spelling

Any guesses as to what these words have in common?

cerise, interning, semaphore, condominium, ratoon, narcolepsy, odontalgia, vivisepulture

The answer is that they are all words with which young American children bagged first place in annual spelling competitions (taken from every decade from 1926 to 2006) (see *http://www.spellingbee.com/champions-and-their-winning-words*). 'Spelling Bees' have been hugely popular for years in the United States, and have recently caught on in other countries, including Britain.

What do spelling bees tell us? Firstly, they remind us of what every schoolchild knows – spellings are either right or (more often, it would seem) wrong. These contests wouldn't work otherwise. Quite why spellings are viewed through the rigid perspective of right and wrong is not entirely clear. It certainly wasn't always the case. In the Middle Ages and up to the time of Shakespeare (also known as Shakespere and Shakspeare), people's spellings would reflect their local pronunciation; but more than that, there simply wasn't the belief that each word should have one spelling. The notion of correct spelling emerged as a result of the invention of printing and the establishment of mass schooling, both of which encouraged the perception that one word needed one stable form. In comparison to, say, punctuation, it is also fairly easy to standardize spelling – it is tricky to generate rules that account for the placing of commas in whatever people choose to write, but fairly easy to dictate which letters should make up each word. And dictionaries have proved an effective, popular and trusted way to codify and disseminate spellings.

Secondly, spelling bees tell us that how good someone is at spelling matters. Not being able to spell well tends to carry a stigma in literate societies – it suggests you are uneducated or even unintelligent; the flip side of this coin is that being able to spell well is a great achievement. So, correct spelling is not neutral; it is a highly evaluative activity around which cultural practices are built up. Spelling bees award good spellers, while bad spellers are met with some social opprobrium. In other words, adhering to the correct model or diverging from it, both carry social meaning – it says something about who you are and how society sees you.

Is the social meaning carried by 'incorrect' spelling always the same? Or does it depend on who is involved, where they are writing, and with what intention? Advertisers, for example, often use respellings to sell products. A prominent and enduring advertising slogan in the UK is *Beanz Meanz Heinz*, for Heinz Baked Beans (where <z> replaces <s>). If an advertiser uses unconventional spelling such as the above, can it be described as a mistake or the result of ignorance – or as an attempt to catch the eye of consumers in a memorable way? What about graffiti sprayed onto a wall or scratched into a desk, which include respellings such as in *I woz ere*. Is this so widely used because successive generations of graffiti artists are unable to spell, or because it signals through its unconventional spelling the casual and transgressive intentions of its author?

The significance and status of orthography and spelling can only be appreciated when its context is taken into account. A vivid example of this is the clash in literary practices between Spanish missionaries and local Mexican linguists as they devised orthographies for previously unwritten Mexican languages (Barros, 1995). The missionaries brought with them their assumption that reading and writing were solitary and silent practices (as they largely continue to be in many places) and so favoured alphabetic Spanish orthography. The local linguists, however, came from a society with a focus on collectivity and orality, and so they argued for 'mural texts' or 'wall-newspapers' and for a phonetic script resembling a phonemic transcription (Barros, 1995, p. 282). As Sebba (2007, p. 24) puts it, different orthographies support different literacy practices, emerging from different ways of seeing and doing things. To take another example, in the 1700s, spelling played a significant role in signalling the unity and identity of the United States and its independence from Britain. I grew up thinking that American spelling was a more 'logical' system; it turns out to be much more to do with forging an American identity.

What's the difference between: spelling and orthography?

The difference is crucial in understanding how unconventional spellings work. **Orthography** refers to the conventions of a particular written language, which determines possible letter-sequences and the sounds that written letters represent. For example, English orthography allows the lengthy consonant clusters <sch> or <ght> , but does not allow <ng> at the beginning of a word (which is possible in, e.g. Vietnamese); while the sound /u:/ can be represented by <oo> but not by <uu> . **Spelling** is the application of these orthographic principles to particular words. So, for example, although English orthographic principles would allow the spelling <gudz> , the correct spelling is <goods> .

As the above examples show, decisions by individuals or groups to spell according to prescribed usage or to depart from prescription by varying spellings can have various social meanings. The fact that unconventional or non-standard spellings can be deliberate and meaningful is captured in the term **respelling** (e.g. Sebba, 2007), which avoids the evaluative perception of incorrectness that colours the alternative term 'non-standard'.

There is, however, only a restricted set of options from which people can pick in respelling. Any variation from conventional norms must follow language-specific orthographic principles to remain recognizable to readers and thus be effective (Sebba, 2007, p. 32). That is, when people respell words, they alter spellings in line with existing orthographic principles. What this means is that respellings draw on the same orthographic conventions as conventional ones. <woz>, for example, works as a respelling of *was* because it follows the principles of English orthography. The particular principles involved here state that the vowel sound of *was* (/ɒ/) can be represented by the letter <o> (consider *cos* and *hot*); and that the sound /z/ can be written with the letter <z>. In fact, we could argue that <woz> adheres more strongly than *was* to the sound-symbol correspondences we expect to see (so that <cos> arguably works better as an abbreviation of *because* than <cause>). The spelling of *was*, in contrast, is phonetically more irregular. This is how phonetic spelling works, and how it derives the social meaning it does.

Look at two respellings of *school* scratched on a school desk. Which one is more effective, and can you explain why the other does not work?

Down with skool

Down with zguul

The second option <skool> is often used as a respelling of *school* (Ministry of Sound released the dance album *Back to the Old Skool* in 2011, *Skool Daze* was a 1980s computer game and the online site *skool UK* provides creative teaching solutions, to pluck a few examples). The phrase *Down with skool* is itself taken from the title of Geoffrey Willans' (1953) book about a boy's experiences at school (cited by Sebba, 2007, p. 31). The respelling is chosen to make a rebellious yet humorous point against schooling: yet, to do so, the choice of <skool> conforms to English sound-spelling conventions. In contrast, <zguul>, while recognizable, is not a meaningful deviation from the spelling of *school* because it does not follow English orthographic principles: <zg> is not a permitted sequence in English orthography, while <uu> is very rare (occurring in a few words like *vacuum* and *continuum*). <Zguul> has no meaning at all. This shows that respellings are neither freely nor randomly chosen but that the choice is restricted according to orthographic principles.

These ideas constitute what is known as the **sociocultural model of orthography** according to which, respellings can be both principled and meaningful. Can you think of other contexts in which people – either individuals or societies – engage in respelling? Can these examples be described as both principled and meaningful?

The context we are interested in now is that of texting. If respelling in texting adheres to the same orthographic principles as in other contexts, as indeed it must, it follows that textisms will reflect or extend existing patterns of respelling. That is, respellings that occur in texting are not unique but resemble those that occur elsewhere. Kesseler and Bergs (2003), for example, compare their corpus of valentine text messages with love letters written by lower-class 'fallen' girls at the London Foundling Hospital in the 1800s. (We saw one example in Chapter 1.) The two are similar in that both tend to be written on the spur of the moment and combine emotion with everyday purposes. Kesseler and Bergs (2003) found that, like texting, Victorian letters contained phonetic spellings such as <bcoz> (*because*) and <luv> (*love*), graphic symbolizations of kisses (*xx*) and roses, shared metaphors and figures and grammar and spelling mistakes. They conclude that popular perceptions of an earlier, literate age are based unfairly on letters composed by highly literate, public individuals who knew their writings would be retained (see Chapter 1). The letters of lower-class writers, however, was much more an everyday practice comparable to present-day texting; and spelling variation in texting is a continuation, or development, of these earlier practices. Their findings are reflected by Shortis (2007a,b), who describes texting as extending, popularizing and legitimizing an existing yet devalued 'orthographic palette' of spelling options. The 'palette' extends the traditional binary of 'correct' and 'incorrect', and provides texters with a range of meaningful options.

So, what respellings occur in text messaging, and what do they mean? In the following section, I address these questions, using examples from CorTxt. After exploring the most frequently occurring respellings in the corpus, I look at how these can be categorized, based on both form and function. I then explore three functional categories in greater depth: colloquial contractions (which reflect spoken forms), phonetic spelling and abbreviations (the last two rely for effect solely on their visual form). In each case, I argue that the respellings say something about how the texter who used them wishes to come across.

3.3 Respellings in CorTxt: a study

Table 3.1 lists the 50 most frequently occurring words in CorTxt which also appear in a respelt form. (That is, frequent words that were not respelt, such as *I*, *a* and *me*, are not included.) The numbers to the left indicate the position of the word in the overall frequency list. *The*, for example, is the 6th most frequent word once *I* and *a* are included. What, if anything, do you notice about the list in terms of the respellings?

One observation is the proportion of frequently occurring words that are respelt – of the 79 most frequent words in CorTxt, 50 occur also in a respelt form. In fact, frequently occurring words such as the above are more likely to be respelt than those further down the frequency list. One reason for this

Table 3.1 The top 50 most frequent groups including respelt forms

	Headword	Respelt forms	Freq of group
1	you	u (3043), ya (256), yer (14), ye (9), uu (2)	7,884
2	to	2 (690), ot (3)	4,976
3	x	xx (833), xxx (635), xxxx (11), xxxxxx (3), xxxxxxx (2), xoxox (1), xxxxx (42)	3,689
6	the	d (21), da (6), th (8), hte (3), te (2), ze (2)	3,553
7	and	n (182), an (19), adn (10), amd (2), annd (2)	3,171
8	in	iin (2)	2,387
9	for	4 (357), fer (2)	2,057
11	have	av (8), hve (6), ave (5), hav (106)	1,993
13	be	b (375)	1,567
16	are	r (422), ar (2)	1,478
20	good	gud (40), gd (25), goodo (3)	1,265
22	see	c (248)	1,255
23	just	jus (18), jst (6), jurt (2)	1,240
24	i'm	im (280)	1,216
25	so	soo (1), sooo (5), soooo (1)	1,159
27	will	wil (12)	1,124
28	that	tht (1), dat (4), tha (2)	1,118
29	your	ur (286), yor (2), yer (9), yr (13), u'r (2), ure (1)	1,111
30	not	nt (4)	1,106
31	do	d' (12), du (5)	1,061
32	ok	okay (75), okey (27), k (33), okej (1), okie (12)	1,040
34	with	wiv (82), wid (4), wiht (3)	1,002
35	was	woz (4), ws (3)	952
36	yes	yep (69), yeh (22), yea (15), yeah (382), yup (13)	952
39	can	cn (1)	894
40	tomorrow	tomoz (9), tomorro (6), tomorow (4), tomora (3), tomo (361), morrow (6), mora (1), tom (24), 2mora (14), tomoro (10), 2morrow (9), tmw (9), 2morow (4), 2morro (4), 2mrrw (4), 2moz (3), 2mrw (2), amoro (2), tomorrrow (2), 2moro (42)	888
41	what	wot (148), wat (37)	839
43	know	no (57), knw (1), kno (2)	776

(Continued)

Table 3.1 (Continued)

	Headword	Respelt forms	Freq of group
44	about	bout (123), abt (4)	768
45	hope	hpe (2)	746
47	back	bak (38), bac (7), bck (3), bk (11), bek (2)	733
49	no	nope (19), nah (18)	714
50	now	nw (9)	713
51	going	goin (60)	710
52	its	It's (240), tis (21)	696
53	how	hw (2)	692
54	don't	dont (198), dnt (4)	671
57	i'll	ill (46), il (21), i'l (30)	628
58	this	dis (6)	598
59	when	wen (75)	589
60	there	ther (2)	588
61	night	nite (105)	586
65	from	frm (9), fm (3)	568
67	had	hd (1), ad (2)	562
68	too	2 (61)	554
71	come	cum (8), com (2)	537
73	well	wel (5)	520
74	one	1 (88)	514
78	sorry	sori (3), sos (12)	502
79	soon	sn (6)	499

may be that common words tend to be more irregularly spelt and are thus open to being respelt phonetically (Weber, 1986, p. 418). Examples from the above list include *was* (as discussed earlier) as well as *what* and *come*. Another reason may be that respelling frequently used words also ensures recognition (between texters) of variants used. Grinter and Eldridge (2003) similarly observe that the teenage texters in their study shortened everyday words such as *tomorrow* and *school*. Here we see that texters also regularly respell common functional words such as *you* (<u>, <ya>, <ye>, <yer>), *to* (<2>) and *the* (<d>, <da>, <te>, <th> and <ze>). This is in contrast to the complex list of abbreviated phrases often found in online text dictionaries (and in Crystal 2008).

Also evident in this list is the tendency for more frequent words to be respelt in more varied ways. Of those words that have more than two respellings, most tend to be higher in the frequency list. *You*, for example, has 5 respelt forms, and *the* 6; whereas at the other end of the list words like *had*, *come* and *sorry* just have 2. (The fact that *tomorrow* stands out in the list below with 20 variant forms is perhaps due to the fact that its length renders it amenable to different forms of respelling.) In many cases, it is interesting that texters appear to have choices as to how they spell any one particular word. This is illustrated by <ya> and <u> as respellings of *you*, which are very different approaches to respelling the same word. In other words, texters have choices not only in *whether* they respell but *how* they do so. This point is returned to throughout the chapter.

Forms of spelling variation practice

The above respellings can be grouped into four categories: letter substitution, letter omission, letter appellation and letter transposition, with each subdivided into vowels, consonants and numbers. For example, <thanx> can be described as the 'substitution' of <ks> with <x>, <jst> as the 'omission' of <u>, <soooo> as the 'appellation' of <o>'s and <adn> as a transposition of <n> and <d>. (Unlike other categories, transpositions appear to be mistakes or typos.) In several cases, one respelling exhibits two or more patterns. In <plz>, for example, <s> is replaced by <z> (substitution) and the vowels <ea> are omitted (omission) (see Figure 3.1).

Letter Substitution

- Vowels
  - <o> for <a> (/ɒ/) in *wot* and *woz*;
  - <u> for <o> du (/uː/); *cum*, *luv* and *gunna* (/ʌ/);
  - <a> for <er> (/ə/) in *betta, numba, lata*; <a> for <ou> (/ə/) in *ya*; <a> for <ow> (/ə/) in *tomora*);
  - <e> for <ou> (/ə/) in *ye*;
  - <i> for <ee> (/ɪ/) in *bin*;
  - <o> for <au> (/ɒ/) in *cos* and *coz*; <o> for <ow> (/əʊ/) in forms of *tomorrow* (*tomoro*);
  - <u> for <oo> ((/ʊ/) in *gud*; <u> for <oul> ((/ʊ/) in *wud, cud*;
  - <er> for <our> (/ɔː/ /ə/) in *yer*; *ur* for *your* (/jɔː/)

Figure 3.1 Categories of respelt forms

- ○ <u> for *you*
- ○ <ite> for <ight> (/aɪt/) in *nite, 2nite, mite*
- consonants
  - ○ <z> for <s> (/z/) in *coz*(24), *cuz*(3), *cz*(2), *plz*(4), *plez*(3), *howz*(8), *woz*(4)
  - ○ <d> for <th> (/ð/) in *wid* and *dis*; <f> for <ph> (/f/) in *fone*; <v> for <th> (/ð/) in *wiv*; <x> for <ks> (/ks/) in *thanx*
  - ○ <b> for *be*; <c> for *see*; <r> for *are*; <n> for *and*; <ne> for *any*
  - ○ <v> for *very*
- numbers
  - ○ <2> for <to> (tu:) in *2morrow, 2nite, in2*
  - ○ <4> for <for> (/fɔː/) in *b4*
  - ○ <8> for <ate>, <eat> (/ ɛɪt/) in *m8* and *gr8*

Letter Omission
- vowels
  - ○ vowel omission   (gd, hve, thx, frm, lv, plz, cld, wld)
- consonants
  - ○ double letter reduction   (beta, tomoro, i'l, stil, wel, gona)
  - ○ final letter omission   (an, com, goin, bac, wil, jus)
  - ○ first letter omission (<h>, <th>)   (av, ello, em)
  - ○ mid-position omission of h   (wat, wen, wot, te)
  - ○ other mid-position omissions   (gona, thx)
- syllables
  - ○ final syllable omission   (tomo, prob, num, mess)
  - ○ first syllable omission   (k, bout, cause)

Letter Appellation
- o appellation (so → soooo)
- p appellation (yeah → yep; no → nope)

Figure 3.1 (Continued)

- y appellation (please → pleasey)

- doubled letter (summort, summing, untill, till)

Letter Transposition
- *adn* for *and*

- *hte* for *the*

- *ot* for *to*

- *thrus* for *thurs* (*Thursday*)

Figure 3.1 (Continued)

What sense can we make of these patterns? Transpositions, as mentioned above, may be the only category to involve non-deliberate mistakes or typos. Omissions and substitutions involve systematic replacements of less frequent spellings with what Carney (1994) describes as the 'default' or most frequent spelling for the sound. To elaborate on my previous example, <o> replaces <a> to form <wot>, <woz> and <coz> because <o> is the more frequent representation of the sound /ɒ/ (as in *pot, toggle, forgot*). Other examples are <u> which is used to represent /ʊ/ in <gud>, <wud>, and <cud>, as well as the sound /ʌ/ in <cum>, <luv> and <gunna>; <a> to represent /ə/ in <betta>, <numba>, <lata> and <tomora>. In the case of consonants, it is not frequency which governs the choice of respelling but the more marked or prototypical association of certain letters with certain sounds. The letter <z>, for example, is associated with the sound /z/ (you may think this self-evident, but in fact /z/ is often represented by the letter <s> in *realise, dogs* and *has*, for example); and /f/ with <f>, rather than <ph>, which is historically restricted to words of Greek origin (Carney, 1994, pp. 228–30).

Economy of expression is an obvious motivation for substitutions and omissions. This is inevitable in the case of omissions, but most substitutions also involve reductions in the number of letters used. In many cases, one letter replaces two (or three): <d> for <th> (<wid>), for example, <u> for <oo> (<gud>), or <ite> for *ight*. The only example which does not involve some reduction in letters is the replacement of <a> with <o> in <woz> (for *was*). However, the patterns do not suggest that abbreviation and the need for brevity are the only, or even the predominant, motivations. Certain substitutions, for example, show alteration in pronunciation. Replacing <th> with <d> in <with> suggests a change of pronunciation which, as we shall see, reflects a Caribbean pronunciation. The final letter omission in <goin> also reflects a regional informal spoken pronunciation; while <er> in <yer> reflects the pronunciation of /r/ in some English dialects. Nor, clearly, do appellations such as <soooo> or <pleasey > serve to abbreviate. As suggested previously, these respelt forms also function to reflect spoken forms.

The functions behind spelling variation

The functions of variation that emerge from categorizing these formal patterns can be described as in Figure 3.2 below.

- **Colloquial contractions** (Weber, 1986) in *CorTxt* include: *n, av, yer, wiv, goin, bin, allo* and *fink*.

- Other **colloquial respellings** include *goodo, pleasey, nope* and the informal variants of *yes: yep; yeah, yup*.

- **Regiolectal respellings** (Androutsopoulos, 2000) include <summat>, <summort>, <sumfing> and <summing> for *something*; and <wid> and <dis> for *with* and *this*;

- Examples of **phonetic spelling** include: 2, 4 *u, 'b, c, gud, woz, coz, thanx, wot, nite, cum, luv, fone, cud,* and *wud*.

- **Abbreviations:** clippings include *tomo, cause* and *bout*; while the final letter is omitted from a number of words including: *are, have, will, just, all, back*;

- **Consonant writing,** in which the vowels are omitted, is evident in *gd* (*good*), *jst* (*just*), *thks, thnx* or *thx* (*thanks*), *bk* (*back*), *frm* (*from*), *wk* (*week*), *lv* (*love*), *pls* or *plz* (*please*), *cld* (*could*), *wld* (*would*), *nxt* (*next*), *txt* (*text*), and *wknd* (*weekend*).

- The **omission of apostrophes** is evident in the otherwise standard contractions: *im* (*i'm*) and *ure* (*you're*) (categorized as a type of abbreviation).

- **Visual morphemes** (Bolinger, 1946) are present in the symbol *x*, or a series of *x*'s, which occur frequently, apparently to represent kisses in order to sign messages off, sometimes alongside *o*'s, representing hugs.

- **Mistakes or mistypings** such as *thrus, iin, adn* and *jurt*.

Figure 3.2 Functions of spelling variation in CorTxt

In the rest of this chapter, I shall look at three of these categories: colloquial contractions, phonetic spelling and abbreviations. The forms that fulfil these functions in CorTxt are listed in Figure 3.3 below.

1 abbreviations

    a)   apostrophe omission (im, its, dont ill)

    b)   double letter reduction (2morow, wil, beta, gona, hapy)

    c)   mid-letter(s) omission

        i.   h (nigt, wat, wich, wen, tnx)

        ii.   c from ck (bak)

        iii.   n (thx, thks)

        iv.   e (havnt), <a> (hve, yeh), ou (abt), <i> (finshed)

        v.   ee (wkend), eek (w'end),

        vi.   lea (pse)

        vii.   shd

        viii.   bday, b'day

    d)   final letter(s) omission

        i.   e (sum, luv, ar)

        ii.   h (o), k (bac), s (thur), w (kno)

        iii.   rs (thu), gh (thou)

    e)   final syllable(s) omission (fri, num, mess, eve, tomo, tom)

    f)   initialisms (v, sth)

    g)   substitutions

        i.   sos for sorry

        ii.   z for rrow (tomoz)

    h)   standard abbreviations (pm, xmas, 1ˢᵗ)

2. phonetic spelling

    a)   number homophones

        i.   1 for one (/wʌn/)

        ii.   2 for to (/tuː/)

        iii.   4 for fore (/fɔː/)

        iv.   8 for ate /ɛɪt/

Figure 3.3 Functions and the forms that realize them

b) letter homophones

    i.   b for be (/biː/)

    ii.   c for see (/siː/)

    iii. r for are (/ɑː/)

    iv. u for you

    v.   f for ph (/f/)

    vi. ne for any (ɛnɪ)

c) ur for you're and your (/jɔː/) – not phonetic

d) other homophones

    i.   ite for ight (2nite, rite, mite)

    ii.   y for why (/waɪ /)

    iii. yt for ight (/aɪt/) (myt)

    iv. no for know (/nəʊ/)

e) schwa (/ə/) represented (see section 3.4 on the sound 'schwa')

    i.   a for er (/ə/) (lata, afta, ova, betta, numba)

f) letter o

    i.   o for <a> (/ɒ /) (wot, wots, wot's, woz, coz, cos)

    ii.   o for ow (/əʊ/)

g) letter u

    i.   u for au (/ɒ/)

    ii.   u for <o> (/ɒ/)

    iii. u for <o> (/uː/) (du)

    iv. u for <o> (/ʌ/) (cumin, cum, luv, dun)

    v.   u for oo or oul (/ʊ/) (gud, cud, wud, shud)

h) other vowel sounds

    i.   ar for <a> (/ɑː/) (arvo)

    ii.   or for ough (/ɔː/) (thort)

    iii. or for our (/ɔː/ /ə/) (yor)

Figure 3.3 (Continued)

    i)   consonants

        i.   x for <ks> (/ks/) (thx)

        ii.   z for <s> (/z/) (coz, cuz, plz)

        iii.   doubled letter (m) (summat, which shortens the previous vowel sound)

    j)   eye dialect or clipping (tho, although)

3. colloquial contractions

    a)   first letter omitted

        i.   h (ad, ell, ere, avin)

        ii.   th (em)

        iii.   a (n)

    b)   first syllable omitted (though, cos, till, bout, k, morrow, mora)

    c)   mid-syllables omitted (satdy)

    d)   mid-letters omitted (probaly)

    e)   weak sounds represented

        i.   schwa (/ə/)

            1.   a for <e> (/ə/) (da)

            2.   a for ou (/ə/) (ya)

            3.   a for ow (/ə/) (tomora)

            4.   a for to (amora)

            5.   d for th (/ð/) (d, dat, wid)

            6.   e for ou (/ə/) (ye)

            7.   er for our (/ɔ:/ /ə/)

        ii.   /ɪ /

            1.   i for ee (/ɪ /) (fil, bin)

    f)   f for ph (sumfing)

    g)   t for th (/θ/ /t/) (tank)

    h)   z for th (ð) (ze)

Figure 3.3 (Continued)

i)   v for f (/f/) (arvo)

j)   final letter omitted

    i.   d (an, n)

    ii.   e (th, d)

    iii.   g (avin, goin, mornin, somethin)

    iv.   t (jus, tha, tex)

k)   final syllable omitted (prob, morn, mo, avo, arvo)

l)   tis

m)   something (summort, summat, summing)

Figure 3.3 (Continued)

In the following sections, I explore the three functional categories in greater depth. I look at their use in historical and other written texts, and consider how and why they are used; and then I begin to speculate on their use in CorTxt.

3.4 Colloquial contractions

In this section, before turning to CorTxt, I outline what colloquial contractions have been seen to 'mean' in other written texts. *Colloquial contractions* such as <ya> or <gonna> are reduced or contracted written forms which reflect informal pronunciation as well as suggesting various emotions (Weber, 1986, p. 420; Androutsopoulos, 2000, p. 521). These contractions can involve word shortenings (<you> to <ya>) or combine two words (<going to> to <gonna>). Although, as Crystal (2003, p. 275) points out, many now have established written forms, they differ from standard contractions (such as *I'm* or *can't*) in not being formally recognized in dictionaries or schools, not using apostrophes and involving at times just one word. Colloquial contractions are largely limited to written discourse representing direct speech: comic strips and jokes, dialogue in prose fiction, advertisements, and pop and rock songs such as 'I wanna hold your hand' (The Beatles) and 'Never gonna happen' (Lily Allen).

Colloquial contractions 'mean' by evoking aspects of identity and register through writing. Their function is **indexical**. Indexical reference describes the way in which features of language relate directly to personal or social characteristics of the language user. For example, if I say *'im* instead of *him*, it is likely that this says something to a particular community about my social background or level of education. In other words, reflecting a certain pronunciation is not the ultimate purpose of respelling; what is important is what this means for readers regarding the level of formality and/or speaker identity (Jaffe and Walton, 2000).

This is evidenced by the use of **eye dialect**, such as *wot* for *what* and *sez* for *says*. Eye dialect is the respelling of a word in a more straightforward yet unconventional way; in Sebba's (2007, p. 34) words, '[u]sing sound-symbol correspondences which are conventional for the language, but are the wrong ones for the particular word': eg, <thort> for <thought>'. Unlike colloquial contractions, eye dialect does not alter the pronunciation of a word. For example, <thort> and <thought> are both pronounced the same, unlike <you> and the colloquial contraction <ya>. So, eye dialect forms like <thort> or <wot> represent a standard pronunciation in a non-standard way – rather than representing an informal or non-standard way of speaking. However, through their unconventional form, they can tap directly into a particular social identity. They often indicate an act of transgression or difference (discussed in the next section), or they suggest a lack of education, in that the phonetic spellings can be interpreted as mistakes made by people who write what they hear. *Down with skool*, for example, can be interpreted as signalling a schoolboy's rebellion against the school, as well as the school's failure to teach him to spell.

Eye dialect and colloquial contractions are thereby often used to characterize or ridicule people of low educational, economic or social status and/or those with strong regional accents. For example, the coarse language used by the porter in Macbeth is accompanied by respellings suggesting colloquial contractions which contrast with that of the **unmarked** voices of other characters – unmarked in the sense that they embody common, expected, default features. In contrast, the features in the example below are **marked** – unusual, unexpected, informative.

> Knock, knock, knock! Who's there, i'th'name of Belzebub? Here's a farmer that hang'd himseld on th'expectation of plenty: come in time; have napkins enowa about you; here you'll sweat for't.
>
> (The porter, Act II, Scene III)

Colloquial contractions can also be used in self-representation (rather than the portrayal of others), and in these cases are used overwhelmingly in positively affirming community values and identities (Jaffe, 2000, p. 508). We can see this in Irvin Welsh's (1993) *Trainspotting*, in which spellings reflect the characters' Scottish pronunciation, as well as in Roddy Doyle's Dublin-based novels. The extract below illustrates Doyle's portrayal through respelling of the speech of an Irish working class family in *The Snapper* (first published 1990).

Jimmy Jnr walked back in.
   —What's *tha'*? A rat?
   —It is not a rat, Jimmy Rabbitte, said Tracy. —It's a dog.
   —It's a dog, *righ'*, said Linda.
It was warm and quivering. Jimmy Snr could feel its bones.
   —*Wha'* sort of a dog is it but? he asked.
   —Black, said Tracy.
   —Go *'way*! said Jimmy Jnr.
   —I'm your new da, Jimmy Sr told it.
They all laughed.
   —*An*, look it. There's your mammy *makin'* the tea.

Doyle (1998, p. 165)

Caribbean poets often use respelling reflecting pronunciation of their creoles.

wi feel bad
wi look sad
wi smoke weed
an if yu eye sharp,
read de vialence inna wi eye;
wi goin smash de sky wid wi bad bad blood

   Dread Beat an Blood (Johnson, 1975, cited in Crystal, 2003, p. 348)

Androutsopoulos (2000, p. 528), to take a final example, describes colloquial spelling variation in German underground music magazines as establishing informal, intimate arenas between writers and readers. The difference between these fanzines and the derogatory descriptions of 'others' is that, with the former, the respellings do not contrast with conventional surrounding text (often the language of educated or higher-standing persons) but occur throughout the fanzines in an unmarked manner. Fanzines and Caribbean poetry show that, while colloquial and regional respellings used to represent others are contrasted unfavourably with the conventional language of educated persons, colloquial respellings can also affirm group boundaries, evoking shared identity and intimate, personal and informal relationships. This performance of intimacy and informality also occurs in texting.

   As we saw above, colloquial contractions are widely used throughout CorTxt. They include the omission of final letter <g> from progressive verbs such as in *goin*; and of <d> after <n> in <an> and <n>. The drop-ping of <h> can be seen in <ad> and <avin> and other shortenings seen in *ok* (<k>), *because* (<cause>, <cos>, <coz>) and *about* (<bout>). The letter <a> is used to represent **schwa**, in <ya>, <da>, <tomora> and <amora>, as well as <gonna>, <gunna>, <gona>. Schwa is a vowel sound that occurs only on unstressed syllables in a word and unstressed words in a sentence: *tomorrow*, *about*, *computer*, *I'm going to pick up the kids*. As you can see, it can be represented by various letters and letter combinations (<o>, <a>, <er>), but in respelling it tends to be represented by <a>. (Although in the Middle and Early Modern English periods, schwa was often represented by <e>.) Like other colloquial contractions, the respelling of schwa serves to create an informal and speech-like feel, which is exploited to good commercial effect in the 1950s advertising slogan: *Drinka Pinta Milka Day* (Carney, 1994, p. 447). Other examples of colloquial contractions in CorTxt are the deletion of <t> in <jus>, <tha> and <tex>, for example, which we saw in the novel dialogue above, 'What's tha'? A rat?' (Doyle, 1998). In general, although Txt may seem to comprise 'new' spellings, they in fact repeat or extend existing functional patterns.

The implications are that colloquial contractions used in texting not only reflect those seen in other texts, but that texters also fulfil functions which are historically and widely fulfilled by these contractions: namely, they are striving to set the tone of the message, indicate emotions or construct identities through their texting practices, and they adopt and exploit well-established linguistic devices for doing so. As in other texts, therefore, the effect created is of intimacy, informality and, at times, a certain nonchalance.

Text messages which include colloquial contractions, and other attempts to capture spoken forms, include the following. Other kinds of respellings such as letter homophones <r> and <u> also occur – these are explored below.

3.8   Hello beautiful r u ok? I've *kinda ad* a row *wiv* NAME99 and he walked out the pub?? I wanted a night *wiv* u Miss u xx

3.9   Thought *praps* you meant another one. *Goodo*! I'll look tomorrow xx

3.10 NAME79 says that he's quitting at least5times a day so i wudn't take much notice of that. *Nah*, she didn't mind. Are you *gonna* see him again? Do you want to come to taunton tonight? U can tell me all about NAME79!

3.5 Phonetic respellings

Phonetic respelling involves substituting letters in irregular conventional spellings for those which more regularly correspond to the particular sound. They are thus found with common words more likely to be irregularly spelt. As mentioned above, one use of phonetic respelling is eye dialect: where the respelling serves (often derogatorily) to indicate an individual's social identity and speech.

In other contexts, phonetic respelling creates modern, dynamic, eye-catching effects, through the visual effect of its deviance from expected spellings. Many brand names involve what Androutsopoulos (2000) calls 'grapheme substitutions': the substitution of one letter for another such as in *Beanz Meanz Heinz*. Back in the early 1900s, Pound (1925) identified a 'Kraze for K', which has not disappeared: *KitKat, Kwik Save, Kleenex*. Many phonetic respellings are shorter than corresponding conventional variants, due to a tendency to reduce vowel pairs and consonant clusters: studies of trademark respellings by Jacobson (1996) and Praninskas (1968) include *Protex* (where <x> replaces <ks>), *Tru-Blu, Fre-Flo, Mildu* and double-consonant reduction – *Hot-Stuf, Chil-Gard, Fly-Kil*. Use of letter and number homophones is noted by Carney (1994, p.448), who cites *Spud-U-Like, U2, INXS* and *IOU*. Another well-established example in advertising is the reduction of *ight* to *ite* (Moon, 2008) as in *Miller Lite*.

What impact are advertisers after? (Think back to your earlier musings on *Beanz Meanz Heinz*.) The aim of phonetic respelling in advertising is ultimately to attract consumers. It achieves this through respelling because distinct, unexpected spellings contrast with the surrounding text, disrupt readers' scanning and so catch their eye (Jaffe, 2000, p. 510). In other words, the impact of these respellings lies in their divergence from expected norms.

Another example of the impact of phonetic respelling is the fanzines explored by Androutsopoulos (2000). Use of <x> to represent <ks>, <cks> and <gs> in English and German words produces <punx>, <thanx>, <sonx> (*songs*), <lyrix> and <demnaxt> (*demnachst = soon*) positions the fanzines in the subculture and marks them as radical, tough and original (Androutsopoulos, 2000, pp. 527–8). However, their phonetic respelling not only affirms group identity but also creates deviance by marking the subculture as distinct or opposed to mainstream ideology: the two functions of convergence and opposition operate simultaneously. Similar observations have been made of the texting practices of teenage groups, in that parents and other adults are often unable to penetrate what they describe as a secret code known only to members of the texting circle (e.g. Ling and Yttri, 2002). Despite not being teenagers, the texters in this study can be seen as similarly adopting respellings to affirm close relationships and cement shared practices in a way that inevitably excludes those who do not share the code.

As with colloquialisms, phonetic respelling in CorTxt reflects existing patterns of variation. Texters use number and letter homophones, as in other domains, often combining the two: <b4>, <m8>, <cu> and <ur> (*you are*). Other grapheme substitutions include <ite> for <ight> (in <mite>, <2nite>, <rite> and <lite>); the more unusual <yt> in <myt> (*might*), which appears to extend the spelling of /aɪ/ with <y> in *my* and *dry*; and consonant substitutions <x> for <ks> in <thx> and <z> for <s> in <coz>, <cuz> and <plz>. As mentioned above, these consonant forms are the most salient spellings of particular phonemes, rather than the most frequent spellings. Vowels used in phonetic spelling include <o> for <a> in <wot>, <woz> and <coz>; <u> for <o>

in <cum>, <cumin>, <luv>, <dun>; and <thort> for *thought*. Most are familiar from other domains: ite from advertising; <woz> and <wot> from graffiti; <gud> and <luv> from informal personal writing; <x> from Androutsopoulos's fanzines. Other forms in CorTxt which seem less familiar extend existing patterns or practices: representations of schwa in respellings like <betta>; <u> for <oo> or <oul> in <cud>, <wud>, and <shud>; <cumin> (*coming*) and <myt> (*might*).

There are respelt forms in CorTxt which are less well-documented elsewhere. These include <ne> (*any*) with 8 occurrences and <y> (*why*) with 7 occurrences. Below are some examples.

3.11 Ive only ever been 2 1 that 1 lol. Don't think there r *ne* others. U goin 2 cardiff 2morow?

3.12 Mam said dont make *ne* plans for nxt wknd coz she wants us to come down then ok (ps u still havnt got the hang of txtin ppl back have u!) x

3.13 Love u loads! *Y* didn't u take new phone and charger with u? Aah, we need 2 check they fit! My day is slow but ok, voda sorted, running out of time now ;-(c ya

3.14 Had some letters bout stuff i need to take and confirming my start dat, not really. Tried2ring woman2day2see if she cud recommend some reading, but think they're al on holiday at mo, which is *y* my start date was to far off.

Use of <ur> in respelling *your* is interesting in that it is not strictly phonetic – yet it occurs more often in place of *your* (286 occurrences) than it does of *you are* (177 occurrences). Below are randomly selected occurrences of <ur> as the possessive *your*.

3.15 Hi will be thinking about u tomorrow and hope u can sit down in *ur* dress!! Have a good day xxx

3.16 Hello. Gd joke, by the way! So wots *ur* plan4the rugby tomo, apart from winnin . . . I will mostly be watchin bonobos shaggin . . . One of them stole my watch 2day, ripped it right off my arm, damn animal. I get back at 3 on wed, u around for coffee? If im not too travel smelly . . .! hav gd weekend X

3.17 I admire *ur* commitment. Save me some x

In personal correspondence with one contributor to my corpus, she suggested that she 'probably substituted the *u* for *you* and then added the *r* to make it *your*' – a complex practice which starts with a phonetic respelling.

Text messages in CorTxt using phonetic respelling (and other respellings) include the following.

3.18   *Thnx* dude. *u* guys out *2nite*?

3.19   Ok that would *b* lovely, if *u r* sure. Think about *wot u* want to do, drinkin, dancin, eatin, cinema, in, out, about . . . Up to *u*! *Wot* about NAME408? X

3.20   Hey! Congrats *2u2*. id *luv* 2 but ive had 2 go home!xxx

3.6 Abbreviations

It is perhaps abbreviation with which texting is most often associated. It may surprise you to consider the long history of abbreviation, and the variety of formal and informal contexts in which it occurs. Handwritten medieval manuscripts from across Europe were heavily abbreviated (Bradley, 1919, p. 4) for two main reasons: because at that time spelling had not been standardized and to fit words on the page. Elizabethan scribes were paid by the inch and thus invented lengthier versions of words (*pauvre* for *povre*, for example) (Scragg, 1974, p. 52 in Baron, 2000, p. 98). These practices continued with the development of technology. Although early printing, for instance, played a leading role in standardizing spelling and punctuation, Elizabethan printers also varied spellings due to space constraints and cost. The need to justify the right-hand margin of printed pages and to ensure text fit the page, for example, prompted the use of an elaborate system of abbreviation and variable spelling: *busy* could be spelt <busie>; *here* as <heere> (Baron, 2000); *on* as <onn>, <hon> and <ho> and *say* as <sai>, <say>, <saie> and <sei> (Bennett and Smithers, 1968 in Baron, 2000, p. 104). Other strategies employed by printers included increasing or decreasing gaps between words, and substituting words for phrases, or vice versa.

The pragmatic flexibility of these practices is not dissimilar to those used in texting. A more recent example than pre-standardization printing is the nineteenth-century telegram, the cost of which was calculated according to the number of words it contained, encouraging highly abbreviated styles (Crystal, 2003: 425, and see Chapter 1). However, abbreviated forms occur in greater number across a wider range of current texts than might be thought. In 2001, the *Acronyms, Initialisms & Abbreviations Dictionary* listed over 586,000 entries (Crystal, 2003, p.121), and the extent to which abbreviations such as laser, DVD-ROM, scuba and NATO have entered our lexicon is often illustrated by ignorance as to what the full terms of some are.

Abbreviation fulfils functions other than that of shortening. Other reasons include the value often placed on linguistic economy or attempts to achieve concise styles, the desire to convey social identity or be part of the social group to which the abbreviation belongs. EFL, ESOL, IATEFL,

CELTA and TOEFL, for example, belong to the British English language teaching community, while abbreviations abound in science, technology and specialist fields such as cricket, computing and the armed forces. As argued in this book (see Chapter 8), abbreviation in texting is not chiefly motivated by any need to be brief but instead contributes to texting identity through performances of brevity and informality and through acts of divergence or separation from mainstream norms.

Abbreviations tend to follow certain formal patterns and can be categorized into the following types (see Figure 3.4).

- **Initialisms**—Phrases which are shortened to the first letter of each word (or syllable): BBC, BA, EEC, TV, PhD.

- **Acronyms**—Initialisms which are pronounced as single words, such as NATO, laser and UNESCO.

- **Clipping**—Words formed through either the beginning, end or middle of a longer word being clipped: *demo*, *exam*, *bus*, *plane*, *fridge*, *flu*, *maths*, *specs*.

- **Blends**—Words made by blending other words together, such as *brunch*, *heliport*, *smog*, *Eurovision*.

Figure 3.4 Types of abbreviation

While colloquial contractions mirror contracted spoken forms, abbreviations are largely driven by attempts to alter the written form. In cases where written abbreviations correspond to spoken phrases, the spoken shortenings arise from the written abbreviation rather than the other way around. Interestingly, in saying web addresses, people tend to use the written abbreviation *www*, which in spoken form is longer than *World Wide Web*. Abbreviating tends to reduce the written form, not the spoken. (Although the spoken form is relevant in distinguishing between initialisms and acronyms.)

Examples of familiar patterns of abbreviation in CorTxt include consonant writing, with the omission of <a>(<tht>, <bck>, <lst>), <e> (<txt>, <nxt>, <snd>), <ea> (<pls>, <spk>), <o> (<2mrw>, <nt>, <hpe>) and <ou> (<cld>, <wld>, <shld>). Other abbreviated forms in the text messages depart in marked ways from respellings elsewhere. However, as with other functional categories we have looked at, in most cases unusual forms emerge from extending or combining existing patterns. For example, double-letter reduction, producing <stil> (*still*), <gona> (*gonna*) and <beta> (*betta = better*), although appearing unusual, has been seen to occur not only as a medieval printers' trick but in advertising slogans such as *Hot-Stuf* (Carney, 1994:447), and the omission of other final letters such as <e> in *hav* and *sum* can be explained as part of phonetic spellings: *sum* represents the phoneme /ʌ/ better than *sume* where, by English orthographic conventions, the <e> lengthens the vowel.

To take another example, although the following forms are unconventional in that they are not widely used elsewhere: <kno> (*know*), <bac> (*back*), <thou> (*though*), <mess> (*message*), <thu> (*Thursday*), <tomo> and <tom> (*tomorrow*), they can be described as extensions of the practice of clipping. It may be the case that clippings are favoured by the predictive text devices particular to mobile phones, whereby the phone predicts the most likely letter sequence as you type. Pressing the 8 key (tuv) and then the 6 key (mno) produces *to*, the third press suggests *too* as the most likely sequence, but by the fourth, *tomo*. Another example may be the final letter reductions in <i'l>, <stil>, <wel>, <com>, <hav> and <jus>, where the phone has apparently recognized the word before the last letter has been typed and thus affords a convenient abbreviation.

Other unfamiliar forms include <sos> for *sorry* and <tomoz> for *tomorrow*. <Sos> is a variant of <soz>, with both <soz> and <tomoz> recent, largely online abbreviations of, respectively, *sorry* and *tomorrow*. Omission of certain mid-letters is similarly unusual: <h> from *nigt*, *wat*, *wich*, *wen*, *tnx*; <c> from *bak*; <leas> from *pse*; and <n> from *thx* and *thks*. In these examples users seem to rely on the *shape* of the word, rather than the sound, to convey meaning. The use of <x>'s to represent kisses, a common feature of personal correspondence (Kesseler and Bergs, 2003), is similarly a visual device. This is important, because it reminds us that texting is not simply about sounding speech-like, but that texters are also aware of and play with the visual appearance of words.

Text messages with abbreviated forms include the following. Again, abbreviations tend to combine with other kinds of respellings.

3.21   V skint too but fancied few bevies.waz *gona* go meet NAME211&*othrs* in spoon but *jst* bin *watchng* planet earth&sofa is *v* comfey; If i *dont* make it *hav gd* night

3.22   Ok. Can be later showing around 8–8:30 if you want + *cld* have drink before. *Wld* prefer not to spend money on nosh if you don't mind, as doing that *nxt wk.*

3.23   That's a shame! Maybe *cld* meet for few *hrs tomo*?

3.7 One implication: choice in texting

As mentioned towards the start of this chapter, it is evident that many words can be respelt in varied ways. *You*, for example, can be spelt conventionally as <you> (4560 times in CorTxt); or with the letter homophone <u> (3043 times), or <ya> (256), <ye> (9) and <yer> (14), used to reflect regional or informal spoken forms. Other examples include those listed in Figure 3.5. What, if anything, strikes you about the choices that texters seem to make?

av (8), hve (6), ave (5), hav (106)
gud (40), gd (25), goodo (3)
jus (18), jst (6),
tomoz (9), tomorro (6), tomorow (4), tomora (3), tomo (361), morrow (6), mora (1), tom (24), 2mora (14), tomoro (10), 2morrow (9), tmw (9), 2morow (4), 2morro (4), 2mrrw (4), 2moz (3), 2mrw (2), amoro (2), 2moro (42)
wot (148), wat (37)
2nite (45), tonite (10), 2night (12), 2nigt (3),
thanx (32), thx (5), tank (2), sanks (2), thnx (2), thks (1), thanxs (1), tnx (2),
cud (48), cld (19),
luv (46), lv (4), lov (4)
wud (38), wld (22)
cos (226), coz (24), cause (4), cuz (3), cs (2), cus (2), cz (2)
pleasey (4), plez (3), pls (35), plse (3), plz (4), pse (2)
gunna (11), gona (6)
sth (9), somethin (8), summort (3), sumfing (2), summat (2), summing (2)
msg (7), mess (8)

d (21), da (6), th (8), te (2), ze (2)
n (182), an (19)
havin (24), avin (6)
mornin (23), morn (18)
l8r (20), lata (5), l8er (2)
mite (9), myt (6)

Figure 3.5 'Competing' respellings

Some competing respellings illustrate how one function (say, abbreviation) can be achieved in different ways. The various ways in which words can be colloquially contracted is illustrated in <ya>, <ye> or <yer>; and in <havin> (where the <g> is dropped) or <avin> (where the <h> is also dropped), as well as in *and*, contractions of which are captured by <an> or <n>. Respellings of *something* show several regional pronunciations: <summort>, <sumfing>, <summat> and <summing>. Contrasting forms of eye dialect of *later* are <l8r> and <lata>; and of *might*, <mite> and <myt>. Others seem to indicate choices open to texters in reducing the number of characters used, depending perhaps on how much they wish to abbreviate: <thurs> or <thu>, for example, and <pls>, <plse> or <pse>. The choice between clipping or consonant writing in some examples may depend on texters' use of predictive texting. *back*, for example, is abbreviated either as <bac> or <bk>; *give* as <giv> or <gv>; *have*, as <hav> but also as <hve> and as <av> (8); *tomorrow* as <tomo> or <tmw>.

Other examples suggest choices between two functions of respelling, that is, forms of abbreviation or attempts to reflect speech: the aforementioned variants of *you* (<ya> and <u>) are echoed in the spoken chatty form of *please* as <pleasey> versus the brief abbreviated <plz>. Elsewhere, eye dialect forms contrast with consonant writing in, for example, *would*, which occurs both as eye dialect, <wud>, and as consonant writing, <wld>. Similarly *could* is spelt either <cud> or <cld>; and similar examples include *good* (<gud> or <gd>); and *love* (<luv> or <lv>).

The choice of <wot> or <wat> as variants of *what* is interesting as an example of conventional versus apparently new spelling forms. <wot> is a phonetic respelling used in graffiti, as in 'Wot, no butter?' (Crystal, 2003, p. 275). 'Wot no . . . ?' was a popular post-war graffiti in Britain, accompanied by the picture of a figure peering over a wall which commented on the lack of various items in the aftermath of the World War II. According to Crystal, it occurred in similar forms in other countries.

Whether the less conventional form, <wat>, is a competing form of phonetic respelling or simply an attempt to cut down on characters is difficult to determine. The form is reflected also in <wen>, for *when*. A similar process may be in evidence with *come*, which occurs both as the conventional eye dialect form *cum* but also as the less conventional clipping *com*.

3.8 What do 'textisms' mean?

In this chapter, I have given some indication of the meaning-making potential of respellings in texting. Two initial observations were made: that most spelling variation in CorTxt follows or extends English orthographic principles; and that it thus reflects historical and current spelling practices. By choosing to spell in principled ways which deviate from expected conventions, texters use respellings in meaningful ways. The fact that texters make choices, vividly illustrated through 'competing' respellings such as <u>, <ye> or <ya> for *you* implies texters actively and creatively choose how to present themselves, albeit constrained by situational factors and orthographic principles.

It is naturally not possible from the text messages alone to determine what texters intend to mean through respellings, nor how the respelt forms are interpreted by interlocutors, but research into other writing domains (such as fanzines or graffiti) allows us to speculate on what spelling in texting may mean. As in other attempts to reflect spoken or regional pronunciations, colloquial contractions and respellings are likely to fulfil an indexical function and to create and sustain an arena for participant relationships which, as in spoken interaction, are informal and intimate. A sense of informality is thus constructed by texters drawing on their awareness of features of everyday, face-to-face conversation. However, texters also draw on existing patterns of abbreviation which contrast with the speech-like language described above and so add what could be described as illusions of brevity to otherwise lengthy, expressive messages. The purely visual device of phonetic spelling also disrupts the relaxed intimacy with unconventional and eye-catching forms which evoke the originality and radicality of advertising, graffiti and underground subcultures. Through signalling deviance or divergence from expected, mainstream norms, these respellings affirm both group identity and distinguish the group from other social groups. Putting all this together, we can see that texters can express attitudes and emotions, define relationships and construct texting identities simply through the choices they make when spelling. Identity construction is discussed further in Chapter 9.

3.9 Some notes on methods

To conduct this investigation of respelling, I generated a word frequency list, and used it as the basis for the grouping of respellings around headwords, using the corpus analysis tool *WordSmith Wordlist*. *Wordlist* must be purchased as part of the *Wordsmith* set of tools; AntConc is free, accessible online and can similarly be used to generate a word list. Of course, an analysis of respelling in text messaging does not have to be as wide or as thorough as mine: it can work just as well on a small number of text messages which you can process manually.

The categorization of respellings into groups requires several decisions to be made. One problem is ambiguous respellings with more than one referent, such as <2> (which can refer to *to*, *too* or the numerical value) and <prob> (*problem* or *probably*). These cannot be handled simply by looking at a frequency list but must be checked through sorting concordance lines, and adjusted manually. Other ambiguous respellings constituted the standard form of another word (<ill>, for example, as a respelling of *I'll* and a word meaning to be sick; <no> as a shared respelling of *know* and *number*, and as a negative marker). Elsewhere, respellings proved difficult to identify and label. For example, it was difficult to know whether *wk* in the following referred to *work* or *week*.

5.11 Hi, wkend ok but journey terrible. *Wk* not good as have huge back log of marking to do

3.10 Further reading

Urban Dictionary (www.urbandictionary.com) is a great resource for looking up the meaning and origin of slang and newly coined words. The dictionary is compiled by its users, who contribute definitions and examples – an understanding of word's complex usage and meaning builds up through these sometimes contradictory entries.

CHAPTER FOUR

The grammar of text messaging

4.1 Introduction

4.1   Sorry im getting up now, feel really bad- totally rejected that kinda me thing.

Student, in his early twenties

To what extent does the above text message read like something someone would say? Is there much you would change to make it sound more speech-like? If not, can you explain how the texter has managed so effectively to capture a spoken form of expression – using only a mobile phone keyboard?

You might point to some of the spelling – *kinda*, for example, is a colloquial contraction suggesting a spoken form. However, what really makes this text message look speech-like (if that's not a contradiction in terms) is its grammar.

What can we say about the above text message, in terms of its grammar? We could start by noting that the text message contains just one sentence; and by counting the **clauses** it divides into. *I'm getting up now* and *feel really bad* can be considered clauses because each has a main verb, *get up* and *feel*. *Sorry*, on the other hand, is not a clause (it has no verb) and instead functions as a type of **discourse marker** which sits outside the clausal structure of a sentence. Similarly, *totally rejected* and *that kinda me thing* would normally be considered to lie outside the main clausal structure. They are described in grammars of speech as **tails** – words or phrases that refer back to the preceding clause to strengthen or clarify what has just been said. In this case, *totally rejected* expands on what the texter means by feeling *really bad*, and *that kinda me thing* further explains how he feels. (The tails can also be analyzed – in *that kinda me thing*, for example, we find the **deictic** use of *that* to indicate a shared understanding.) Notice that the clauses are separated not by conjunctions (such as *and* or *if* – or *or*), but simply by commas, while there is no punctuation at all linking the discourse marker to the clause (*Sorry im ..*). This stringing together of clauses and other elements creates a very speech-like feel. In other words, it would seem from this text message that the grammar of texting is very much like spoken grammar, at least in the way that clauses and other elements combine.

However, text messages do not always read like snippets of speech. Look at the message below.

4.2   Evening v good if somewhat event laden. Will fill you in, don't you worry . . .
       Head ok but throat wrecked. See you at six then!

What really distinguishes the grammar of this text message from that of 4.1 is its **situational ellipsis**. Situational ellipsis refers to the omission of certain words or phrases, generally in spoken or informal language, which we might expect to see in full sentences or in formal written text. So, for example, *totally rejected* above (which feels a natural thing to say in conversation) can be expanded to the more explicit 'I feel totally rejected'. This omission of subject and verb at the beginning of a clause is typical of informal spoken language because, it is argued, you do not need to spell everything out to the friends or colleagues with whom you are speaking – they can fill in the gaps. However, in this second text message, the ellipted elements are not those which would normally be omitted in spoken conversation. Omitted from 4.2 are not initial but medial elements – *Evening [was?] v good*; *Head [is?] ok but throat [is/was?] wrecked* – utterances that you might expect to see in a scribbled written note but would be surprised to hear someone say. Here is a post-it note I produced using the online site www.SignGenerator.org – although not genuinely produced for communicative purposes, it serves to illustrate how the utterances described above would not be out of place in a written note.

Why might we want to explore the question as to how speech-like the grammar of texting is? One reason is that it might tell us something about how people perceive text messaging and what kind of communication they think they are having. Is texting a kind of written conversation, in which texters write as if they were talking; or is it the equivalent of a written note, with information condensed into something which functions rather like an electronic post-it note? This choice (somewhat starkly put) suggests firstly that texters are free to exploit the medium in different ways – they are not just compelled by the constraints of the mobile phone to focus narrowly on abbreviating but can make their own decisions about what texting is for and how they will use it. Take the following text message (which you saw in Chapter 1), and consider how its grammar differs from that of the *Evening v good* text message. What differences would you posit between the two text messages in terms of how they were meant and received?

4.3   Thankyou for ditchin me i had been invited out but said no coz u were cumin and u said we would do something on the sat now i have nothing to do all weekend i am a billy no mates i really hate being single

The freedom to make grammatical choices in order to come across in different ways flags up people's awareness of the features that comprise informal spoken conversation and their ability to exploit those features to conduct similar kinds of interactions through texting. For example, we saw above how texters seem to indicate through commas the stringing together of clauses that is typical of spoken language. So, texters play an active role in constructing the 'grammar of texting', drawing on written and spoken features which they use to construct a certain kind of interaction.

The grammatical analysis of texting is also useful in challenging the assumption that certain features typical of text messages and internet chat can best be described as 'incorrect'. Entering this debate involves us asking the question, what is grammar? On the one hand, prescriptive grammar can be seen as dictating how people *should* use language. On the other, grammar can be understood as a mechanism underlying all language, encompassing the selection and ordering of words, the combining of clauses, markers of time (*im getting up*), plurality, and so on. The ways in which grammar operates in informal, unregulated contexts such as texting and many spoken conversations are not incorrect; they are different realizations of the same underlying mechanisms. And not *very* different, at that – if you look back at the text messages above, you'll see that they generally follow recognizable grammatical principles of English, such as word order. Where they differ from conventions normally seen in formal writing is in response firstly to the increased informality of the situations in which the text messages were produced, and also because of the particular functions being fulfilled, the nature of the relationship between the texters, and the affordances of the mobile phone.

In this chapter, I look at the grammar of text messages in CorTxt, and what it tells us about how these texters perceive texting and what they use text messages for. Before going on to this, it is worth thinking further about the issues that arise from the above discussion. What is grammar, and how does a grammatical analysis of texting fit into the wider picture?

4.2 What is grammar?

Before reading on, how would you answer the above question? It may seem obvious at first, but in fact it is easy to assume we understand what grammar is without looking more closely at what it does and doesn't entail.

There is a tendency to assume that certain types of language don't have grammar or use less grammar than other types. So, for example, a language learner might think that when they're speaking rather than writing a foreign language, they don't have to worry so much about grammar; when you write a letter to your linguistics teacher, you take extra care with your grammar; when you text, all thought of grammar goes out the window. But is it possible to have language without grammar? Arguably, my niece at 18 months spoke such a language: she said 'water' if she wanted a drink; 'up' to be picked up or when she went upstairs; 'aunty' if someone pointed at me. But there is a limit to the complexity of the ideas she could express, or how unambiguous she could be with these words, and she soon started making connections between them. These connections may rely, as they often do in English, on word order ('Alice want water'); or with grammatical inflections ('Alice goed up'); or with the use of grammar or function words such as prepositions and determiners ('why aunty under the table?'). It is these connections between words that are known as grammar and all human language (eventually, in the case of child learners) has it. *Water* shows little evidence of grammar; *im getting up now, feel really bad- totally rejected that kinda me thing* has it aplenty (as my analysis suggested).

But can you have *bad* or incorrect grammar? When someone says, 'My grammar's awful', or of their children 'They forget their grammar when they speak', or 'Texting encourages bad grammar' (*Daily Observer*, Feb 2010), what they are referring to are certain rules that have been written about language. In English, these include the fact that you 'shouldn't' split infinitives or end a sentence with a preposition; you 'should' say 'my friends and I' rather than 'me and my friends' and 'I've spoken' rather than 'I've spoke'. These are part of what is known as **prescriptive grammar**. These are conventions laid down to govern English usage, most of which date back to the 1700s and 1800s, and some of which draw on an understanding of how Latin, not English, works. If you like, they are not grammar itself, but external observations regarding how language works. Nonetheless, grammars of this kind tend to be meant, or are at least taken, as guides to how one *should* speak. One can go as far as to say they are attempts to control variety and change in language. You'll notice that with all the rules above, it is in fact possible to break them and still make sense. Star Trek famously decided 'to boldly go'; people say 'me and my friends' all the time; it's very easy to write a sentence and then stick a preposition on. On the other hand, nobody prescribes against, say, *cat the mouse ate the* because nobody would ever say it. That is, prescriptive rules are only lain down because it is perfectly possible *not* to follow them and this must (so the prescriptivist argument goes) be controlled.

What variety do people try to suppress through prescriptive grammars? In some cases, any variety at all – there is no socially motivated reason why we can't decide to boldly split infinitives. In other cases, what is being proscribed is regional variety. There are dialects in which it is acceptable to say 'I've spoke' – it's part of the grammatical system. One famous example is the proscription of multiple negatives, now expressly forbidden in English on the basis that negatives cancel each other out. Does anyone really interpret 'I don't want nothing' to mean 'I want something', except to make a grammatical point? Interestingly, multiple negatives are not only used in languages other then English ('*no* quiero *nada*', in Spanish, for example – 'I don't want anything'), but also appear to have once been widely accepted in English. Chaucer in *The Canterbury Tales*, for example, said of his Knight that:

'He *nevere* yet *no* vileynye *ne* sayde / In al his lyf unto no maner wight'

(Merriam-Webster's Dictionary of English Usage, p. 365)*

The other kind of variety that has at best been ignored by prescriptivists is that of register. It may be best to write 'My colleagues and I feel . . .' in a complaint to your employer, but it might feel faintly incongruous to announce 'My friends and I are off to the pub' to your mum. The problem with much prescriptive grammar is that it is based on written language – understandably, given the lack of spoken data before the invention of recording equipment; and that it is based on formal, literary written work – again, understandably, given the fact that written works are generally more socially valued. The problem with this is that spoken language comes to be described and evaluated in relation to formal writing.

Instead of describing what could be called the grammar of speech, grammarians interested in spoken language have tended to describe what they hear in terms such as 'fragmented' (Chafe, 1982). The tail *that kinda me thing*, in a sentence like 'I feel really rejected, that kinda me thing', might with a traditional grammar have been labelled a 'right dislocation', not only suggesting an impairment, but using the written sentence as a basis for the description. That is, as written sentences run from left to right, the addition of a phrase at the end of an utterance can be seen as occurring to the right.

Even linguists such as Wallace Chafe, who documented differences between written and spoken grammar, tended to explain the latter with reference to the constraints that speakers face (rather than the affordances); the fact that they have to speak on the spot and that listeners cannot process dense complex sentences, for example. All perfectly true; but speech was still presented in terms of its deficiencies in comparison to writing.

The linguist MAK Halliday was one early exception. He used the term 'clause complex' to refer to the strings of clauses I described as being typical of speech: so that *Sorry im getting up now, feel really bad- totally rejected that kinda me thing* could be described as a (fairly simple) clause complex. Halliday (1989) suggested that speech in this respect was more complex than writing, and he also showed that its structure made speaking more flexible than written grammar and thus suitable for carrying out the interpersonal functions which speech typically fulfils.

More recently, **descriptive grammars** have moved away from prescribing rules towards offering a description of grammar which takes into account both spoken and written language varieties. In this study, I draw on Ronald Carter and Michael McCarthy's *Cambridge Grammar of English* (2006), which looks, as the subtitle suggests, at *Spoken and Written English Grammar and Usage* and is informed by investigation of naturally occurring language. Other such grammar books include the *Longman Grammar of Spoken and Written English* (1999) by Douglas Biber and colleagues. Their suggestion is not that speech and writing have their own grammar, but that people make different grammatical 'choices' in different contexts. To explore this, try taking this written sentence and imagine you wanted to convey its content in conversation (about breadmaking!) with a friend. How would you break down and present the information? What choices did you make, and why?

> By far the most important ingredient in the baking of bread, and the one most easily forgotten, is the addition of a teaspoon of salt at the very start of the process.

The grammatical choices that people make in different contexts are shaped by consideration of who they are addressing, how much time their addressee has to process the information (i.e. are they reading or listening to it), the function of the exchange, and the affordances of any technology at their disposal. If writing a book is a slow, prepared and largely solitary activity whereby an author addresses a largely unknown audience, then this explains why the written grammar of books is both complex and elaborated. Spoken conversation between friends is in comparison spontaneous and immediately interactive, as people think on the hoof and respond flexibly; as a result, conversational grammar includes features such as tails, whereby speakers go back to elaborate if necessary on what is said, as well as the ellipsis of words that people can assume their interlocutors will understand. Of course, writers can also choose to use features associated with spoken language in order to interact with audiences and draw them in. Compare the following paragraphs from two different discussions of palaeontology. Which is from an encyclopedia and which is a popular science book written by Bill Bryson?

> A fundamental premise of palaeoanthropology (the study of man in times past) rests on the contention that unequivocal evidence of human evolution would be found in fossils of known antiquity linking modern man to extinct ancestor. . . . However, the arbitrary nature of the fossilization process virtually eliminates all chance that such an ideal could ever be achieved or even approached.
>
> The shortage wouldn't be so bad if the bones were distributed evenly through time and space, but of course they are not. . . . Homo erectus walked the Earth for well over a million years and inhabited territory from the Atlantic edge of Europe to the Pacific side of China, yet if you brought back to life every Homo erectus individual whose existence we can vouch for, they wouldn't fill a school bus.

The vocabulary may be the more noticeable feature marking the second extract as a popular science book (*A Short History of Nearly Everything*), but one of the other features that Bryson exploits is the clausal structure. Does the information feel less tightly packed than in the encyclopedia extract (*Pearsons Cyclopedia*)?

In terms of the contexts in which online communication and text messages tend to be composed, the situations seem to sit somewhere between those associated with book writing and informal conversation. The channel of communication is written; interlocutors are unlikely to be face-to-face with each other; and they do not have access to resources such as tone of voice or gesture. However, the relationship between interlocutors is likely to be closer than that between book author and reading public, while the purposes of their conversations are likely to be informal and chatty, so it would be odd if texters decided to write in a way that resembled literary prose. The grammar they use is likely to reflect spoken grammar for two reasons – firstly, because they are doing similar things with language as speakers; and secondly, because they can consciously adopt spoken features in order to convey an impression of close, intimate informality.

In the following sections, I look more closely at the following features: clause combination, tails and headers, situational ellipsis and deictic language. In doing so, I use terms and categories suggested in Carter and McCarthy's grammar. The occurrence of speech-like grammatical features in CorTxt suggests that texters draw on spoken language to create speech-like informality and intimacy. Differences between spoken and texted grammar emerge, however, suggesting texters are also motivated by other purposes or affordances of the medium.

4.3 Clause combination in texting

For this study, I selected 100 text messages according to a random criterion (they were sent between 2pm and 2:35pm) to explore how clauses combined into sentences. Before going any further, it is worth revisiting 'clause' and 'sentence', as neither can unproblematically be applied to analysis of spoken interaction.

> Most sentences begin with full stops
>
> Chris Tribble

A **sentence** is one of those immediately understood words that are nonetheless notoriously difficult to define. Imagine you were defining 'sentence' to students who wanted to improve their writing. You could draw on two definitions: one orthographic and one grammatical. By orthographic, I refer to punctuation. Most people are probably aware that a sentence finishes with a full stop (question mark, exclamation mark), although there is also some truth in Chris Tribble's witticism above. However. Does that last word become a sentence because I've followed it with a full stop? A teacher would probably require a sentence to meet certain grammatical criteria: namely, that it contains at least one clause and, if more than one, that the clauses are combined in conventional ways.

A **clause** can be defined as a grammatical unit centring around a verb, which is the only compulsory element – so at its simplest the command *Stop!* is a clause. Other elements of the clause include the **subject**, indicating who has carried out the verb, such as the pronoun *I* in *I stopped*; and the **object** of the clause, who or what the verb is done to – as in *I stopped the microwave*, or *the child* (from running across the road). We could also add **adjuncts**, which explain how or when or why something occurred – *I might have accidentally stopped the microwave* or *stopped the child just in time*.

As the above definitions suggest, what is contentious about the 'sentence' is that it is a feature of *written* language. There are no full stops in speech, and as you shall see, clauses in speech are not neatly organized into something resembling a sentence. Instead, in speech, we can talk of clauses combining more loosely into **utterances**. In this study of texting, I refer to sentences, because text messages are written and units are demarcated through punctuation. However, note the contradiction inherent in the notion of 'speech-like sentences' in texting. A speech-like sentence is arguably not a sentence at all.

Nineteen of the sampled text messages (nearly a fifth of the total) comprised one sentence with one clause. The verb has been underlined in each. Note that all three are either questions or exclamations; this was the case with most one-clause text messages.

4.4   I <u>have lost</u> 10 kilos as of today!

4.5   Now that's <u>going to ruin</u> your thesis!

4.6   <u>Have</u> you <u>seen</u> who's back at Holby?!

These one-clause sentences do not, of course, involve any clause combining and so were excluded from the study. The remaining text messages were placed on a cline as more or less **speech-like**, depending on the number of clauses within each sentence, and how clauses and sentences are combined.

Speech-like clause combination

Let's start by looking more closely at 'speech-like clause combination'. There are **main clauses** and **subordinated clauses,** and they combine in one of two ways: two main clauses or two subordinated clauses can join in a relationship of **coordination** (using the coordinators *and, but, or* and *so*); and subordinated clauses can join to main clauses through **subordination** (using subordinators like *although, if, because* and *when*). Which of the two types of clause combination do you think is more typically associated with spoken language?

The answer is coordination; as I've already mentioned, people tend to string clauses together using *and* and *but* when they talk. Carter and McCarthy use the term **multiple coordination** to describe how spoken clauses often combine, and their description matches that of Halliday's clause complex: multiple clauses in speech strung together using coordinators. The following utterance may appear an impressive breathing feat if nothing else, but is probably quite typical of spoken language. Of course, punctuation is used to organize this transcription, but you can begin to see how the term 'sentence' does not satisfactorily describe the structure of the utterance.

> I'd gone to the bookshop with a friend **and** he went to collect me **and** I was just sitting in the bookshop chatting **and** my husband said, 'That coffee shop over the road,' **and** I thought, 'Oh this is good.' Then you came in **and** Sylvia was having a coffee with us **and** poor James was left running the bookship **and** nobody had made him a coffee **and** I said 'I know what I'm going to do. Can I buy him a coffee here?
>
> (Carter and McCarthy, 2006, p. 558)

Coordination can also occur between 'contact clauses': coordinated clauses that sit side-by-side without a connective. Try saying the above but omitting the connectives; do you find your voice rises between clauses? This is often indicated in linguistic transcripts by commas. The question mark also indicates a rising tone, and the full stop a slight fall, indicating that the speaker may have reached the end of the point they were making.

> Then you came in, Sylvia was having a coffee with us, poor James was left running the bookshop, nobody had made him a coffee, I said 'I know what I'm going to do'. Can I buy him a coffee here?

The text messages at the speech-like end of the spectrum are those in which clauses are combined in ways most typical of speech, including multiple coordination and contact clauses. Of my 100 text message sample, 22 were described as speech-like. How many clauses are there in the following example? Remember that each clause must have a verb (or verb group, like *cant be*).

> 4.7   Dude, if you see NAME10 then don't mention you've spoke to me, she wants me to go to the pub and i cant be bothered and my mom goes on holiday tomorrow.

The above text message contains seven clauses, including four main clauses and three subordinated. Which are which?

No	Clauses
	Dude,
1	*if you see NAME10*
2	*then dont mention*
3	*that you've spoke to me,*
4	*she wants me*
5	*to go to the pub*
	and
6	*i cant be bothered*
	and
7	*my mom goes on holiday tomorrow.*

It is easy to spot the three main clauses coordinated by *and* towards the end of the message: *she wants me to go to the pub and i cant be bothered and my mom goes on holiday tomorrow.* Of the remaining clauses, *then dont mention* is the fourth main clause, to which the others are joined by subordination, as is evident if we highlight the subordinators: *if* you see NAME10 | *then don't mention* | *(that) you've spoken to me* (where the subordinator *that* has been omitted).

Here are some other speech-like text messages. The first one has been analyzed into its component parts; try to analyze the second and third for yourself, before looking at the answers at the end of the chapter.

1.

No	Clauses
	Hiya –
1	*thinking about weekend*
	and
2	*realised*
3	*I was assuming*
4	*you would stay Saturday night too –*
5	*you will,*
6	*won't you?*
7	*(tho no prob*
8	*if you can't)*

2. Thankyou for ditchin me i had been invited out but said no coz u were cumin and u said we would do something on the sat now i have nothing to do all weekend i am a billy no mates i really hate being single

3. Hi- seems a small group will be going out on fri- i'll book at table for a meal at 7.30 – so try to get the earlier train and pack light if possible x

So, my argument here is that many text messages (a fifth of my sample) can be said to resemble spoken language in the way that texters choose to put the clauses together.

Note-like clause combination

Clauses in other text messages, however, depart significantly from this speech-like structure. Thirty-eight text messages are here described as *note-like* (i.e. more typical of written notes than spoken utterances). Look at the following, and try to divide them into clauses. What do you notice? (Sentences are divided by ||.)

4.8 No i'm not gonna be able to. || too late notice. || i'll be home in a few weeks anyway. || what are the plans

4.9 Not thought bout it. . . || Drink in tap & spile at seven. || Is that pub on gas st off broad st by canal. || Ok?

4.10 Hey, did you have a good time in porague? || I'm in ireland at the mo with the in laws! || Going ok. || \ yes love being on hol 2!

You may have noticed that the majority of the clauses are separated by full stops or question marks – that is, each clause represents a sentence. These text messages are categorized as note-like mainly on the basis that clauses are not strung together but are separated by full stops into sentences. Noticeable in places is a lack of clear relationships between utterances, with the result that texters appear to dart from one point to the next. See the example below: *I hate not knowing. What did Frankie say? How would she know? They'd be crazy not to take u. I'm worried.*

> God
> 1 *it's really getting me down just hanging around.*
> 2 *I hate not knowing.*
> 3 *What did NAME72 say?*
> 4 *How would she know?*
> 5 *They'd be crazy not to take u.*
> 6 *I'm worried*
>
> X

Where clauses are combined, the relationships tend to be of subordination rather than coordination – in contrast to the pattern we noticed with the speech-like text messages. In the following text message, clauses are divided by | and subordinating conjunctions underlined. Can you spot two coordinated clauses?

> 4.11 Hope | [that] you had a good time last night .\ || Bet | [that] NAME172 is ill. || Why didn't NAME262 go? || Just a text | to ask you | who did your bathroom | and | how much did it cost?

Who did your bathroom and *how much did it cost* are both subordinate to *to ask you* but coordinated to each other by *and*. (Well done if you spotted that!) Look at the following text messages, divided into 6 and 8 sentences, respectively. Can you identify the subordinated clauses in both?

> 1 *i'm not sure how to break this to you.*   MESSAGE
> 2 *there's no easy way to put it. . . .*
> 3 *i can't make the friday-night fun.*
>   *sorry.*
> 4 *however, feel free to text me during the evening if there are any lulls in conversation.*
> 5 *anyway, hope ur exotic trip goes well.*
> 6 *see u next term.*

1   *Good news indeed..*   MESSAGE
2   *But Prodi doesnt seem that good too.*
3   *In England,its pretty bad too.*
4   *Blair is a complete idiot.*
5   *Im gonna b more and more involved in political issues..*
6   *Im already a unionist but i think next year i'll b a member*
    in a political party.
7   *Its called Ligue Communiste Revolutionnaire.*
8   *I'll tell u more about it when we'll c each other.*

I started this section by saying that I was placing the text messages on a cline, and you may have noticed, even among those texts towards the far ends of the spectrum, that what I call note-like text messages include speech-like elements; and vice versa. Towards the middle of the cline, this mix of clause combinations was yet more evident with 21 text messages best described as mixed. In the text message below, for example, the first utterance is speech-like in that it comprises four clauses joined by *and* – but these are then followed by two note-like sentences each comprising one clause.

4.12   NAME78, NAME416, NAME366 and NAME417 | picking them up from various points | going 2 yeovil | and they will do the motor project 4 3 hours | and then u take them home. || 12 2 5.30 max. || Very easy x

4.4 Headers and tails

Look at the two spoken utterances below. What feature do they have in common, and how do they differ? Can you explain why the speakers might have chosen to construct their utterances in this way?

1.   He's amazingly clever, that dog of theirs
2.   Your sister, is she coming too?

(Carter and McCarthy, 2006, p. 194)

In both utterances, there is a noun phrase (*that dog of theirs* and *Your sister*) which sits outside the clause and is repeated *within* the clause with a pronoun (*he* and *she*). The first is a **tail**, an example of which we saw earlier, which occurs after the clause; the second is a **header**, and comes before the clause. Carter and McCarthy (2006, p. 196) argue that headers and tails are 'listener sensitive', helping, in the case of headers, to orient listeners and prepare them for new information and, in the case of tails, clarifying or reinforcing what has been said.

The problem with exploring tails and headers in texting (or indeed any large data set) is finding them. The only regular feature that can be searched for is the pronoun. By searching for pronouns (*she, it, they*, etc.) and looking line-by-line through the concordances for noun phrases occurring within a wide span to the left (headers) and the right (tails), I found a handful of occurrences in CorTxt.

Here are two examples taken from the text messages. The first is a header, and the second is a tail (noun phrases are in bold and pronouns underlined).

4.13   Well done, blimey, **exercise**, yeah, i kinda remember wot <u>that</u> is, hmm. Xx

4.14   Yep <u>then</u> is fine **7.30 or 8.30 for ice age.**

Here are some more examples. Can you identify the noun phrases and pronouns, and decide which are tails and which are headers?

4.15   Hasn't that been the pattern recently crap weekends?

4.16   it's really getting me down just hanging around.

4.17   My friend, she's studying at warwick, we've planned to go shopping and to concert tmw, but it may be canceled, havn't seen NAME54 for ages, yeah we should get together sometime!

4.18   NAME78, NAME416, NAME366 and NAME417 picking them up from various points

4.19   Hello! Just got here, st andrews-boy it's a long way! Its cold. I will keep you posted

There is no evidence that headers or tails are widely used in the corpus. However, it is interesting that they are used at all. Several reasons would mitigate against their use. Firstly, we might not expect to see many lengthy noun phrases (like *NAME78, NAME416, NAME366 and NAME417*) in texting. Secondly, tails and headers add words to text messages, which contradicts common assumptions about Txt. Thirdly, you could argue that texters don't need them. Text messages can be edited and scanned (rather than processed in real time), thus reducing the apparent need (as in speech) to orient listeners. Their occurrence thus suggests that texters' concern for creating a speech-like sense of involvement may override any tendency to abbreviate. Look through your mobile phone, and/or keep an eye out when new text messages come in. Can you find any examples of headers or tails, and explain why they were used?

4.5 Situational ellipsis

Have a quick read of the following spoken conversation, which illustrates situational ellipsis. Which words would you say were missing (ellipted)? What, if anything, do the omitted words have in common?

Martin: Think it might be time for a coffee! Fancy one?
Mary: Cup of coffee would be great.

The words I am thinking of are *I*, *Do you* and *a*. Are they the ones you decided on? The example highlights the observation that when people chat they generally do not need to use the elaborate and explicit sentences necessary if they wrote, say, a report to be distributed across a business sector. There are several reasons: one, the people they are addressing share the same immediate context; two, should they not understand, they can always ask.

This definition of situational ellipsis is not perfect as, again, spoken utterances are being compared to written language; and because there are obviously 'rules' as to which elements can be omitted and which cannot. The 'elliptsed' elements above occur generally at the beginning of the clause, and they involve the omission of a pronoun in subject position (*I*), auxiliary verb (*do*) and determiner (*a*). The ellipsis of *I* before *think* is illustrative of a tendency for speakers to omit the subject pronoun before 'mental process verbs' such as *like*, *hope*, *think*, *guess* and so on. However, other omissions would be impermissible in speech. People do not tend to say 'Do fancy one?' or 'a cup coffee' – although these are words that could also be retrieved from the context.

To this extent, ellipsis in speech is in fact more constrained than in texting, where we see different types of ellipsis – that which we would expect to see in spoken language (again, with apologies for the mixed metaphor) and that which more readily resembles written notes. This reflects the pattern described above for the combination of clauses in texting, and suggests again that texters are only sometimes concerned with sounding speech-like. What the different forms of ellipsis also highlight is the fact that spoken ellipsis is to an extent arbitrary – why can some elements be omitted but not others?

Speech-like patterns of ellipsis occur across the text messages in CorTxt. What elements are missing from these examples?

4.20   Dunno, haven't spoke to NAME10 about it yet.

4.21   Easy mate, guess the quick drink was bit ambitious.

4.22   What u wearing?

4.23   What u up to?

4.24   Hi- seems a small group will be going out on fri

4.25   Just checked.

4.26   yes. . . staff-room can be pretty unbearable sometimes!

The subject pronoun *I* is omitted from the first two text messages (twice in 4.20) – note that *I* precedes a verb of mental process: *dunno* and *guess*.

In the following two examples, the verb *are* is missing from the questions. The subject pronoun omitted from 4.24 is *it*. In 4.25, both the subject (*I*) and the auxiliary verb (*have*) are missing. Finally, the determiner (*the*) is omitted from 4.26.

We might suggest two reasons for this speech-like ellipsis in texting. Firstly, there is the need to abbreviate. The tendency to abbreviate in text messages for reasons of time, effort and space is an obvious possibility, and widely documented (e.g. Hård af Segerstad, 2002). However, if I can convince you that other forms of ellipsis also occur in texting – forms which are not speech-like – then this factor alone does not explain the choices texters make as to how they abbreviate. Secondly, then, we must assume that the speech-like ellipsis forms part of an attempt to create a sense of informality and closeness by drawing on features of spoken interaction.

'Dont worry is easy': the verb 'be' without the subject

Why does the following spoken utterance sound wrong?

A: Where's Hillary?

B: Is coming.

It is difficult to say why it sounds wrong; it's just not what people tend to say. *She* and *he* tend not to be ellipted as much as *I* and *you*, and where any of these pronouns are ellipted before the verb 'be', that would have to go too, leaving:

A: Where's Hillary?

B: Coming.

In texting, however, this unspeech-like pattern of abbreviation can and does occur, with nearly all forms of the verb be: *is*, *am* and *was*. What is omitted from each example? Do you agree that these do not sound speech-like? What would a more speech-like way of ellipting be? (Asterisks mark the missing elements.)

4.26   Don't worry, * is easy once have ingredients!

4.27   NAME232 came to look at the flat, seems ok, in his 50s? * Is away alot wiv work. Got woman coming at 6.30 too.

4.28   * Am on a train back from northampton so i'm afraid not!

4.29   No * am working on the ringing u thing but have whole houseful of screaming brats so * am pulling my hair out! Loving u

4.30   * Was thinking about chuckin ur red green n black trainners 2 save carryin them bac on train

With the exception of *was*, a more speech-like alternative for the above forms would reasonably be a contracted form: *it's, he's, I'm*. One possibility might be that people are avoiding having to access and type the apostrophe, on the assumption that this might be seen as involving extra time and effort. But is saving time and effort the only motivation? Have another look at the two examples of *am*. In 4.28, *am* occurs alongside the contracted form of *I am*: *Am on a train back from northampton so i'm afraid not!* The two forms might be arbitrarily chosen, or the choices motivated by the immediate context; the rhythm or sound of *i'm afraid not* somehow requiring the contracted form. In 4.29, the ellipted form occurs within an otherwise lengthy and expressive message: *No am working on the ringing u thing but have whole houseful of screaming brats so am pulling my hair out!* Can brevity be the dominant motivation here?

A similar ellipsis occurs with other verbs. Which of the following seem speech-like?

4.31   * Will have two more cartons off u and NAME262 is very pleased with shelves

4.32   Aye- * will do my lover!

4.33   * Will be september by then!

Will do is a speech-like phrase. However, in the other two examples, *I'll* and *it'll* appear less naturally speech-like.

'Wine good idea': medial ellipsis

We now return to the text message you saw at the beginning of the chapter. Seen now in the context of other types of ellipsis, can you describe the linguistic features of medial ellipsis?

4.35   Evening * v good if somewhat event laden. Will fill you in, don't you worry . . . Head * ok but throat * wrecked. See you at six then!

4.36   Hi. Hope ur day * good! Back from walk, table booked for half eight. Let me know when ur coming over.

4.37   R u sure they'll understand that! Wine * good idea just had a slurp!

In these examples of medial ellipsis, the verb 'be' is omitted following the subject (which in each case is a noun not pronoun) and before the adjective (or adjective + noun) that describes it. (The use of 'be' to link nouns and adjectives is known as the copular.)

Again, the above are not what you would expect to hear someone say. As we saw in earlier examples, in speech, the subject *and* the verb 'be' may be omitted, as in *Coming!* (or, in CorTxt, *Just checked*), but it is unusual for the subject to be present in speech without the auxiliary, particularly where the subject is a noun rather than a pronoun. The nearest speech-like form, according to Carter and McCarthy (2006, p. 182), is the omission of auxiliaries in questions.

> The dog bothering you? Shall I throw him out?
>
> (Carter and McCarthy, 2006, p. 182)

If neither medial ellipsis nor use of copular *be* without its subject is typical of speech-like language, this suggests that texters are not consistently engaged in constructing speech-like informality; and that ellipsis must be explained with reference to other factors – such as the need to abbreviate. Abbreviation cannot however constitute the full picture, not only as it fails to explain choices in how people abbreviate, but also because it does not clarify why some elements are omitted and others not. To take the last instance above, in *Wine good idea just had a slurp!* the auxiliary is omitted, as is the article before *good idea* and the subject in the second clause (presumably *I*), but the article in *a slurp* retained. We also saw above that these ellipted forms can occur in otherwise length and expressive messages: *No am working on the ringing u thing but have whole houseful of screaming brats so am pulling my hair out!*

Could another explanatory factor be that ellipsis is guided by consideration of which elements are necessary for communication in any given situation, as Carter and McCarthy (2006, p. 181) suggest with reference to speech? Carter and McCarthy's description of written language as a necessarily elaborated version of a streamlined spoken variety is an attractive one, as it reverses common notions that spoken ellipsis is simply an abbreviated version of a fuller and richer written structure. However, Carter and McCarthy's argument that what is omitted is 'unnecessary' or surplus to what is needed to fulfil 'the purposes of communication' also fails to explain why some elements are omitted and others typically *not*. For example, as Carter and McCarthy (2006, p. 182) point out, pronouns tend only to be omitted in statements when they occur with auxiliary and modal verbs, or verbs such as *hope* or *wonder*, and not in such cases as the one we saw earlier.

> A: Where's Hillary?
>
> B: Is coming.

Nevertheless, as *she* in the above example is easily retrievable from the previous turn, the fact that it could be omitted in texting but not in speech challenges the idea that ellipsis is solely determined by what is necessary for understanding the overall message. In other words, these non-speech-like forms are only in part driven by consideration of what is necessary for communication, as they are by technological limitations. The argument that I shall put forward later in this book is that these forms contribute in more complex ways to the identities that people construct and convey through texting.

4.6 Deixis

Read this text message. To what extent do you know which bus the texter is on, where he is going and who is likely to beat him there?

4.38   Man this bus is so so so slow. I think you're gonna get there before me

If you don't, that is because of the extent to which the text message relies on references to the context in which the exchange took place. **Deictic references** are words or phrases which speakers use to refer to people, places, objects and so on within the immediate context. Deixis is therefore particularly likely when people are doing things together and as such tends to be more frequent in spoken than in written language. Deictic reference is realized through three main word groups: adverbs of time and place (*here*, *now*, *then*), pronouns (*it*, *we*, *him*) and determiners (*the*, *that*). Investigation of CorTxt reveals similar deictic uses made of these words, as illustrated in the text message above. Can you categorize the deictic words (underlined below) into the three word groups?

Man <u>this</u> bus is so so so slow. <u>I</u> think <u>you</u>'re gonna get <u>there</u> before <u>me</u>

The following overview of deictic reference in texting focuses, as does Carter and McCarthy's investigation of spoken deixis, on the determiners *this* and *that* which occur, respectively, 427 and 229 times throughout the corpus. The investigation reveals that determiners are used in texting to refer to a shared time framework, but not so much to shared space beyond the 'virtual space' created through the medium and the 'future space' which texters plan to share. You will also see that, as in speech, deixis in texting is another resource for evaluating, heightening intimacy and expressing disapproval.

Reference to time

Explicit reference to periods or points of time is made by over three-quarters (315) of the 427 occurrences of *this*, including the following:

this weekend (62)
this week (48)
this morning (46)

this evening (28) and *this eve* (6)
this afternoon (21)
this time (15)
this year (12)
this Saturday (4)
this Christmas (3)

this can refer to present, past or future time. Reference to a present, ongoing period is the least frequent reference of the three categories, accounting for around a fifth of occurrences.

4.38   Rightio. 11.48 it is then. Well arent we all up bright and early <u>this morning</u>.

4.39   Bognor it is! Should be splendid at <u>this time</u> of year.

4.40   I take it we didn't have the phone callon Friday. Can we assume we won't have it <u>this year</u> now?

Past-time reference is to the recent past, or to events that happened at an earlier point in an ongoing period, as illustrated in the following examples. These recent-past references make up around a quarter of all *this* time references.

4.41   Have you heard from NAME159 <u>this week</u>?

4.42   Will do. Was exhausted on train <u>this morning</u>. Too much wine and pie. You sleep well too x

4.43   . . . we r stayin here an extra week, back next wed. How did we do in the rugby <u>this weekend</u>? Hi to NAME281 and NAME159 and NAME79, c u soon xx"

Most time references are to the near future (just over half of all occurrences). These, perhaps unsurprisingly, suggest a role for texting in making future plans or arrangements.

4.44   Bbq <u>this sat</u> at mine from 6ish. Ur welcome 2 come

4.45   <u>This weekend</u> is fine (an excuse not to do too much decorating)

4.46   I'm really sorry i won't b able 2 do <u>this friday</u>.hope u can find an alternative. hope yr term's going ok:-)

That, in contrast to *this*, is not used predominantly with reference to time or place. However, like *this*, where it was used with reference to time (17 out of 150 occurrences), it referred mainly to future plans or arrangements. (Note that, for the purposes of this study, only 150 of the total 229 occurrences of *that* were categorized.)

4.47   Yeah confirmed for you staying at NAME150's <u>that weekend</u>

4.48   Unfortunately i've just found out that we have to pick my sister up from the airport <u>that evening</u> so don't think i'll be going out at all. We should try to go out one of th

4.49   NAME87's gonna let me know cos comes bak from holiday <u>that day</u>. NAME125 is coming. Don't4get2text me NAME498's number. Xx

that time can also refer to present or general points in time. In the following examples, it is used to appeal to a shared understanding of the significance of a particular time.

4.50   Cheers for the card . . . Is it <u>that time</u> of year already?

4.51   Our ride equally uneventful – not too many of those pesky cyclists around at <u>that time</u> of night ;).

4.52   Need a coffee run tomo? Can't believe it's <u>that time</u> of week already

The frequent uses of *this* and *that* in referring to shared, present or future, time can be explained by the near-synchronous nature of texting (i.e. texters share a time frame if not physical space) and to the interpersonal functions of arranging and coordinating future plans.

Reference to place

References to place were low, with only 21 (of 427) occurrences of *this*. These include references to transport such as the following.

4.53   twenty past five he said will <u>this train</u> have been to durham already or not coz i am in a reserved seat

Unlike face-to-face interaction, texters are unlikely to be sharing physical space. In the text message above, for example, only the texter is on *this train* and not the person she is writing to – her sister, who is waiting for her to arrive. Other references to *world* or *country* do not necessarily indicate close proximity.

4.54   It's reassuring, in <u>this crazy world</u>.

4.55   Can not use foreign stamps in *this country*.

In fact, texters may not even know where their interlocutors are.

4.56   R u in <u>this continent</u>?

References to place with *that* (11) mainly comprise directions to or suggestions about places of entertainment with the implication that texters have been there and/or will go there.

4.57   Golly, poor u! Will aim to be at urs for just bfore 9. No idea wher <u>that</u> pub is.

4.58   Can u meet me at <u>that</u> corner shop at half 2 plz? Tb 2 me x x

The apparent lack of reference to actual shared space in texting would seem to distinguish it from face-to-face interaction where speakers are in the same place. Spoken utterances such as *I'd like to pop in to that little shop over there before we leave* (Carter and McCarthy, 2006, p. 179) would probably only occur in texting if the people involved had become separated while on their day trip – and even then the reference to *little shop over there* could be unhelpful.

Reference to the medium and the interaction

Another 27 uses of *this* refer to the medium itself, either to *this text* (8) or *this message* (3), *this phone* (4) or *mobile* (1) or *this number* (5). Most references to *this message* or *this text* refer to the one being written (with some references to text messages just received). Similarly *this number* and *this phone* can refer either to the texter's or their interlocutor's phone.

4.59   Hi hope u get <u>this txt</u>~journey hasnt been gd,now about 50 mins late I think.

4.60   Only just got <u>this message</u>, not ignoring you. Yes, i was. Shopping that is

4.61   Realy sorry – i don't recognise <u>this number</u> and am now confused :) who r u please?! NAME12 x

4.62   Wrong phone! <u>This phone</u>! I answer this one but assume the other is people i don't know well

Sixteen of 150 occurrences of *that* refer to the medium, either *that message*, *that text* or, less frequently, *that call*. The difference between *that* and *this* in referring to the medium is that *that* refers not to the current text message but to previous text messages, either sent or received by the texter.

4.63   Mm not entirely sure i understood <u>that text</u> but hey. Ho. Which weekend?

4.64   did u get <u>that message</u>

4.65   I didn't get the second half of <u>that message</u>

References to <u>that call</u> refer to interaction between the texters beyond the texted exchange:

4.66   1.20 <u>that call</u> cost. Which i guess isnt bad. Miss ya, need ya, want ya, love ya

4.67   Hello- thanx for taking <u>that call</u>. I got a job! Starts on monday!

The above examples show texters referring to the medium as they organize their interaction (texted and otherwise) through texting.

Deixis in an evaluative role

How do you think these two spoken utterances differ in meaning, if at all?

Now tell me what you think of this new girlfriend he's got?
Now tell me what you think of that new girlfriend he's got?

(taken from Carter and McCarthy, 2006, p. 180)

Carter and McCarthy suggest that in such cases *this* and *that* refer not to physical space but to psychological proximity or distance. *This*, they suggest, can indicate importance, immediacy and familiarity, as well as a speaker's positive stance – in this case, their approval of the new girlfriend. In contrast, they argue that *that girlfriend* implies a more detached, critical and disapproving tone.

In CorTxt, an evaluative meaning frequently attaches to the use of *this* (51 occurrences) and *that* (85 occurrences), as texters indicate familiarity or immediacy through reference to shared experience, knowledge or background.

4.68   That's ok. I popped in to ask bout something and she said you'd been in. Are you around tonght wen <u>this girl</u> comes?

4.69   Hey chief, can you give me a bell when you get this. Need to talk to you about <u>this royal visit</u> on the 1st june. NAME182

4.70   I've got an interview for <u>that job</u> in Exeter!

Such references are often critical rather than affirming (in contrast to Carter and McCarthy's observations of speech), as illustrated by the following.

4.71   Hello. Damn <u>this christmas thing</u>. I think i have decided to keep this mp3 that doesnt work.

4.72   Think I might have to give it a miss. Am teaching til twelve, then have lecture at two. Damn <u>this working thing</u>.

4.73   Not getting anywhere with <u>this damn job hunting</u> over here!

4.74   what I meant to say is cant wait to see u again getting bored of <u>this bridgwater banter</u>

4.75   Gosh <u>that NAME62</u>, what a pain. Spose I better come then.

4.76   Sorry im getting up now, feel really bad- totally rejected <u>that kinda me thing</u>.

This is not to say that the deictic references were always critical; <u>that</u> in particular also implies affection or approval.

4.77   hiya hows it going in sunny africa? hope u r avin a good time. give <u>that big old silver back</u> a big kiss from me. X

4.78   Love <u>that holiday Monday feeling</u> even if I have to go to the dentists in an hour

Looking back at the examples of a negative framing, a distinctive pattern emerges. The pattern is one seen also in spoken English and comprises *this/that* + noun + *thing*, which is used (as in spoken English) in an apparently derogatory or dismissive way. The pattern extends to use of *malarky* and *shit*, as well as *thing*.

4.79   Mate. I misunderstood. NAME127 can't drive on saturday to <u>this training thing</u> cos her car has broken down and is sitting in a garage. Please could i use your car otherwise we're stuck. I'll be claiming back petrol so will leave him full up

4.80   Hello. Damn <u>this christmas thing</u>. I think i have decided to keep this mp3 that doesnt work. May sound odd but i can explain.

4.81   <u>This pen thing</u> is beyond a joke. Wont a Biro do? Don't do a masters as can't do this ever again! X x

4.82   What with all <u>this working malarky</u> and your commitee meetings, when am i going to find the time to corrupt you

4.83   Wot rubbish. And dont try using any of <u>that whacky science shit</u> to prove it! X

One interesting thing about the use of this structure in texting is its length. *Damn this christmas thing*, for example, could feasibly be paraphrased as *damn christmas* and so the choice of the longer phrase again suggests that texters are more concerned with how they express themselves and how they feel than with cutting down on words.

Two conclusions can be drawn from the above study of *this* and *that* in CorTxt. Firstly, these deictic references highlight texters' assumption that they and their interlocutor are working within the same time framework, while frequent references to future time indicate the role of texting in making arrangements or securing future interaction. However, they also remind us that texting does not take place face-to-face, and thus the extent to which texters refer to what is physically around them through deictic reference is limited. The context that texters do share is 'virtual space', and *this* and *that* are used to refer to the ongoing interaction itself and to places where they plan to meet. Secondly, the fact that texters tend to have intimate relationships which extend beyond texting means that reference can be made to shared knowledge of current events and situations through *this* and *that*. What is interesting about this is the role of the determiners in evaluating these events and situations, often in dismissive or critical ways. Evaluation – the marking of opinions and attitudes – is something we shall return to in Chapter 7's discussion of creativity. It is interesting to see how users adopt and adapt strategies for making evaluative statements, within the particular context of texted interaction.

4.7 Chapter summary

Towards the start of this chapter, I cited an online article from the *Daily Observer* which claimed in 2010 that 'Texting encourages bad grammar'. Debates over the effect of texting on grammar are rife, and they reflect real concerns about children's literacy and education standards, often based on teachers' classroom observations. I don't wish to dismiss these claims out of hand, and I am not able to; the text messages I have explored in this chapter were not written by children but by literate, educated adults. However, my research lends some support to counterarguments which suggest that texting *per se* is not damaging to literacy; it can either be seen as beneficial (in that it gives children and other people the opportunity to write in motivated and purposeful ways); or it is at worse neutral (the fact that children text out of school need not affect how they learn to write in school).

My research rests on an understanding of grammar not as a series of rules which must be followed regardless of the situation in which we find ourselves; but as a mechanism underlying all language use and which responds differently to different contexts. What we have seen in the course of this chapter is how a particular group of adult texters drew on their awareness of spoken grammar and the grammar of written notes in order to create certain effects through texting – at times, heightening intimacy and creating a sense of speech-like informality. This suggests that these texters are active producers of 'texted grammar', able to respond to the communicative and technological demands of texting through their grammatical choices. In other words, their grammar is *appropriate* to the particular situation. I can only speculate on the practices of other groups of texters, but such speculation can proceed from the assumption that all texters can use grammar to respond in communicatively appropriate, flexible ways to the text messages they receive. Keep an eye on text messages you receive, and see what you think about the grammatical choices made by the people texting you.

Answers (p. 85)

2.

No	Clauses
1	*Thankyou for ditchin me*
2	*i had been invited out*
	but
3	*said no coz u were cumin*
	and
4	*u said we would do something on the sat*
5	*now i have nothing to do all weekend*
6	*i am a billy no mates*
7	*i really hate being single*

3.

	Hi-
1	*Seems*
2	*A small group will be going out on fri-*
3	*I'll book a table for a meal at 7.30-*
	so
4	*try to get the earlier train*
	and
5	*pack light*
6	*If possible*
	X

CHAPTER FIVE

Discourse markers in texting

5.1 Introduction

5.1 Hey bird. i'm gonna email you my very almost completed diss in a min. do what you can and give me a shout when you're returning it. thanks. **oh and** how are you anyway

Darcy, in his early twenties

There are a number of interesting features in the above text message, but I'd like to start this chapter by focusing your attention on the use of *oh and*, which I've emboldened above. Like *well*, *now*, *right* and so on, *oh* is an example of what is known as a **discourse marker** and as such plays a role in organizing what a language user has to say (more on this later). The background to the above text message is that the texter's sister had agreed to proofread his university dissertation, and his text message alerts her to the fact that it is *very almost completed*. (One of the features of interest here is the integration of media, as the text message is sent to announce the imminent arrival of an email.) As an apparent afterthought at the end of the text message, the texter asks how she is. Why does he mark this postscript with *oh and*? There are two possible ways to interpret its use here.

Perhaps your immediate reaction is that the texter has realized, towards the end of his text message, that he has launched rather bluntly into the purpose of his text message and, given that he is expecting a favour, he decides to engage in some interpersonal niceties. *Oh and* marks the fact that he has stopped one topic and shifted his focus to another. You can imagine the same thing happening in speech. Indeed, Carter and McCarthy (2006) give some spoken examples of *oh* used to indicate a diversion in topic (the *oh* of interest is in bold below). (Below, + indicates overlapping speech.)

A: So you get the prestige of working for the University of Bristol with living in the country in a nice big open environment which is +

B: Yeah.

A: + more appealing when you're a bit older isn't it?

B: Suppose so.

A: That's my theory anyway.

B: Never really thought about it like that. **Oh** I forgot. Your washing up's there. Sorry just noticed it.

A: Oh you've not even put it out or anything.

B: Sorry, I forgot about it.

(Carter and McCarthy, 2006, p. 219)

It is perhaps unsurprising that this speech-like practice would also occur in texting, given the ways in which texting resembles spoken interaction, not only in terms of its intimacy and informality but also the occurrence in texting of a range of other features of spoken grammar (see Chapter 4). In this sense, the use of discourse markers such as *oh* would seem to bolster arguments that texting is in many ways 'like' speech.

On the other hand, we have also seen in other chapters of this book that texting is not completely like speech. Three differences relevant for present purposes are, firstly, that texting is not necessarily produced in real time, and it certainly isn't produced as quickly as speech; secondly, that texters are able to reflect on what they've written and potentially to alter it rather than, in this case, add an afterthought (they may not; but the possibility – the affordance – is there); and, thirdly, that texting is written and so the transfer of speech-like features from spoken language to texting implies a degree of awareness. To elaborate on this last point, the argument is not only that writing is a conscious activity but that the act of transfer itself requires cognizance: if texters are not aware that they use certain features in speaking, they cannot reproduce them in a text message.

Bearing these three points in mind, if the texter had solely wanted to correct the blunt way in which he put forward his request, then he had recourse to another possibility: he could go back and insert *how are you* at the beginning of the text message. The fact that he didn't implies the quite deliberate stylization of his utterance. The overall message that he conveys to his interlocutor may be that he is focused intently on his work and that the text message is chiefly a business-oriented one, but that he can nonetheless find time to express some concern for his interlocutor. The afterthought also injects humour into an otherwise officious text message – an element that would be lost in a more straightforward *Hey bird, how are you? I'm gonna . . .*, and it marks a certain relationship between the two: close, teasing, relaxed. This relationship is also marked by a range of informal features: *Hey bird, gonna, in a min, diss, give me a shout*. In the light of this configuration of speech-like features, the text message can be seen as a brief oral performance enacted through writing.

Alternatively, of course, you may argue that the texter simply did not have time to go back and rework the text message, and that *oh and* may indeed fulfil a function similar to that in speech, a repair strategy in fast interaction. But whatever the actual motivation, the example sheds doubt on any simple analogy between speech and texting. In speech, discourse markers such as *oh* – and *well, so, right, okay, now, you see* and so on – may be used unconsciously as speakers search for words or organize what they want to say. Their use in texting is, to some extent, contrived – in the sense that texters consciously reproduce these features of speech as they construct close relationships through texting. In other words, the discourse markers do not emerge as the result of texters' struggle to produce language in real time; they are used to indicate how a recipient should interpret the message – is it to be understood as an afterthought, as in the text message above: *oh and how are you anyway?* Or, as signalled by *oh ok* below, is the message to be interpreted as acknowledging an unexpected and possibly unwelcome piece of information?

5.2   Chloe: Guess ur back now. Do u want to come here for around four?

       Jo: **Oh ok**. I had visions of your coming here! But ok, see you then.

       Chloe: Oh sorry, hadn't thought of that.

Or, as signalled by *oh sorry* in the same exchange above, is the listener to understand a sympathetic response (a 'negative subjective orientation' towards the preceding text message)? Lastly, to take an example of another discourse marker, *right*, is the message to be interpreted as final confirmation of a decision, as marked by *Right* below?

5.3   **Right** i can confirm that i an on the train so eta the same in bw. Goodnight and i hope to wake to see you there

This interactional or pragmatic use of discourse markers in texting (whereby they are used to create a certain effect for recipients) in turn has implications for how we understand discourse markers in speech. To what extent should they be seen as aiding speakers' cognitive processes, and to what extent understood as signalling to listeners how the message is to be interpreted?

In this chapter, I look in more depth at the use of *oh* as an example of a frequently occurring discourse marker in CorTxt, as well as considering occurrences of *you know* and *you see*. Before this, however, I look more closely at what spoken discourse markers are, what they do and why they are used, not only in spoken but also in written discourse.

5.2 What are discourse markers and what do they do?

Using if necessary the discourse markers emboldened in the following spoken conversation, what can you say about discourse markers as a category of linguistic items?

A: **Right** that comes to er seventy three eighty six. Thank you. **Right** I just need you to sign there.

B: Thank you.

A: **Well** the weather's turned up today anyway.

B: Mm, it's nice isn't it.

A: It's breezy though.

B: [laughs] Dick said it's been going on forever. He said it's been raining for about =

A: It's been raining, we had a snow blast, we had a snowstorm last weekend there.

B: Mm.

A: Amazing stuff.

B: **Great**. Thanks.

A: **Good**. I'll give you a receipt for that. **There you go.**

B: **Great**. Thanks. Thank you.

(Carter and McCarthy, 2006, p. 212)

Discourse markers can be defined according to form, position or function. With respect to form, discourse marking is carried out by a set of various words and phrases. These include *right, well, great, good* and *there you go* in the above exchange, as well as:

> *anyway, because* (or *cos*), *fine, good, great, like, now, oh, okay, so, now, then, and, but, so, you know, I mean, as I say, for a start, mind you*

The set is by no means a fixed or clearly demarcated one. Firstly, linguists disagree over which words to include – Schiffrin (1987), for example, suggests that discourse markers could also include paralinguistic features and non-verbal gestures, items which other linguists would not include. Secondly, we could argue that words not usually used as discourse markers can idiosyncratically be used as such, or that novel forms could emerge in new contexts. For example, I will go on to suggest that emoticons fulfil a similar role as other discourse markers in texting. Despite this flexibility and variability, however, there is a set of core and recognized forms that include those listed above.

Whether a word is classified as a discourse marker rests in part on its position in an utterance and on its use. Discourse markers tend to be positioned outside the clause; they are non-clausal elements (see Chapter 4 for discussion of the clause and its elements).

Ultimately, however, discourse markers are best defined as a category by their functions. In general terms, discourse markers reflect a speaker's engagement with, and construction of, the unfolding interaction. In practical terms, this means that they are used by speakers to organize their talk. On the one hand, discourse markers link utterances and ideas together – that is, they organize the informational content carried in each clause – and, on the other, they indicate a speaker's position in relation to what is said and are used to monitor or direct the understanding of the listener – that is, they determine how what is said is to be understood by a speaker's interlocutors. As such, discourse markers play an interpersonal role in indicating formality and power relations between speakers and highlighting their evaluations of the interaction. More specifically, their functions include opening or closing interactions, sequencing interaction and marking topic boundaries and shifts, focusing attention and monitoring shared knowledge. So, what this means is that discourse markers operate on a number of levels: interpersonal (smoothing relations between interlocutors), referential (organizing the world through discourse), structural (organizing and sequencing the discourse) and cognitive (making cognitive processes explicit, verbalizing hesitations and doubts and so on) (Fung and Carter, 2007a, pp. 414–15).

I have been talking about 'spoken' discourse markers and 'speakers', in part because of their different distributions across spoken and written varieties. Discourse markers such as *so* and *now* do of course occur in sentence-initial position as a normal feature of written texts, at least in some genres. However, even the use of these discourse markers is more restricted in written than in spoken texts. Other discourse markers – *you see*, *you know*, *oh* – occur much more frequently in spoken texts and are very rare in written texts. Where they do occur in writing, it appears that they are used as spoken discourse markers, in order to project a sense of orality or conversational intimacy into the written text. In other words, these discourse markers seem able to evoke speech.

McCarthy (1993, p. 171) highlights a relevant distinction here, between **medium** (referring to 'how the message is transmitted') and **mode** ('how it is composed stylistically'). Crucial to this distinction is the fact that there exists a prototypically speech-like mode of communicating and a prototypically writing-like mode. (This McCarthy shows by asking people to label decontextualized extracts as having been spoken or written, which they do through recognition of stylistic features, including discourse markers.) However, there need not always be a convergence between a typical spoken mode and the spoken medium; or between the written mode and a written text. So, a written text may include varying numbers of speech-like features, and vice versa. (Although 'informants' in McCarthy's study tended to correctly identify extracts as being from texts that had originally been spoken, they were also happy with the idea that certain genres – literacy and advertising – would also use spoken discourse markers and they correctly identified these texts as written on the basis of other factors.) However, as I suggested above, where a written text contains discourse markers, it is often with the intention of purposefully evoking a conversational style (just as we shall see in texting).

One important point is that the use of spoken discourse markers in writing is not new; its use in online texts or in texting can be seen as an extension of practices that have always been engaged in by writers trying to engage with readers, or create the impression of engaging with them. McCarthy (1993, p. 175) gives the following example of a written advert from The Guardian (15 September, 1987).

UNIVERSITY OF BIRMINGHAM OPPORTUNITIES IN SPACE: Well, not strictly in Space, but Space Research.

You may recall more recent examples – if not, keep an eye out for them in newspapers and literary texts.

5.3 Discourse markers in CorTxt

The first thing to note with respect to texting is that discourse markers typically associated with speech are used by texters – at least in CorTxt. They were not all particularly frequent, as the figures in Table 5.1 show.

Table 5.1 Discourse markers in CorTxt

Frequent in CorTxt	Not frequent in CorTxt
well (166)	now (3)
Anyway (64)	mind you (3)
So (56)	I mean (1)
oh (oh and, oh wait, oh yeah) (21)	you see/u c (3)
right (19)	you know/u no (3)

However, as McCarthy notes of the literary texts he examined, this inconsistency 'only serves to foreground [the use of discourse markers] even more when it does occur' (p. 178). In other words, discourse markers in texting remain marked and meaningful features. Table 5.1 suggests a division between more commonly used discourse markers in CorTxt and those which occurred very infrequently.

The table shows that the spoken discourse markers *well*, *anyway*, *so*, *oh* and *right* were much more likely to be used by this texting network than others, including *now*, *mind you*, *I mean*, *you know*, *you see* (as well as sequence markers such as *firstly* which did not occur). How can this be explained and what does it tell us about discourse markers in texting?

Various factors can be suggested to explain the preference in texting for certain discourse markers over others. Given the space constraints of a text message, one factor may be word or phrase length, and in support of this argument we can cite the infrequency of phrases such as *I mean* and *you see* (while *I say* did not occur at all) and the use of short words such as *oh* and *okay*. However, this argument hardly explains the frequent use of *anyway* in contrast to the infrequency of *now*. Another factor may be that the discourse markers used in texting tend to be involved in organizing and managing discourse, marking topic boundaries, focusing attention and diverting (*oh*, *well*, *so*, *anyway*), but not as much in monitoring the interlocutor's involvement and understanding (*you know*, *you see*). Again, although this may be a factor, it is not consistently deployed, given that sequence markers such as *firstly* are absent.

A third argument lies with the particular texters who contributed text messages to this corpus. It may be that those discourse markers frequently used in CorTxt are simply those which this group of texters tend to use more often in speech – an argument difficult to follow up without spoken data. A more compelling argument lies not so much in how this group uses discourse markers, but that these texters perceive and value certain discourse markers differently from others. I noted above that the transfer of discourse markers from speech to texting implies that texters are to varying extents aware of them (even if they could not voice this awareness or explain the feature) and that they perceive the markers to fulfil certain functions. So, a conscious or semi-conscious decision is being made whenever a texter uses a discourse marker, based on the fit between what the texter wishes to convey and the social meaning he or she feels the discourse marker carries.

Whether a texter uses a particular discourse marker may also be shaped by how they value the particular feature. As noted in Chapter 1, people's language use is shaped by their **values**. If speakers negatively value a certain feature – such as the dropping of /h/s in British English or the dropping of /r/s in New York – then they are likely to avoid it in their own speech, criticize its use by others and/or distance themselves from it by denying that they use it. Although people may genuinely believe their denials, linguistic researchers often find that people use features in interview even as they deny using them (Asprey, forthcoming).

My point is that another way in which people might react to a negatively valued feature would be to avoid it in written forms of conversation, such as texting, and that this might explain the avoidance of *you know* and *I see*. Whether this holds up in relation to the infrequently or never-used discourse markers can only be determined by gauging the values of the texters in question. However, what is your feeling? Might people around you avoid the features in the right column of Table 5.1 (or others) because they see them as sloppy, uneducated or lazy features of speech?

In the rest of this chapter, I look at three discourse markers particularly associated with speech. I start by looking at the monitoring discourse markers *you know* and *you see* that occur infrequently in texting, before moving on to the investigation of *oh*, an organizing discourse marker that occurs frequently in CorTxt. I then turn to the use in texting of emoticons, the representations of laughter and *lol*, and argue that these can be seen as fulfilling discourse marker functions.

5.4 *you know* and *you see*: monitoring discourse markers in CorTxt

According to Carter and McCarthy, shared knowledge is commonly monitored in speech by two markers: *you know* and *you see* (or *see*), which 'signal that speakers are sensitive to the needs of their listeners and are monitoring the state of shared knowledge in the conversation' (Carter and McCarthy, 2006, p. 221). *You know*, they continue, 'projects the assumption that knowledge is shared or that assertions are uncontroversial, and reinforces common points of reference, or checks that the listener is following what is being said'. *You see*, on the other hand, 'projects the assumption that the listener may not have the same state of knowledge as the speaker'. Carter and McCarthy's spoken examples include:

> **You see,** since I've damaged my back in that fall, I find it difficult to climb the stairs without help.

> If you got the earliest train in the morning and then, **you know**, like, got the last train back at night, it might be cheaper that way.

> (Carter and McCarthy, 2006, p. 221)

In CorTxt, however, the phrases *you see* and *you know* occur only infrequently, and of the 6 occurrences, half are used in exchanges between the same two participants. These participants use the phrases within what appear to be stylized representations of certain ways of speaking and as part of light-hearted and jocular interaction. In other words, the discourse markers seem to index an element of the texters' social identities that is assumed or foregrounded during playful interaction, and they may not be forms which the texters would adopt in more 'serious' exchanges. This first texted conversation took place before Christmas 2006 and centres around an idea for a Christmas present for 'NAME46'.

5.4   Jo: Do you have any ideas for NAME46?

        Laura: All he has said really is clothes. Why? Got some for me?

        Jo: Clothes?

        Laura: **You know**, wot people wear. T shirts, jumpers, hat, belt, is all we know. We r at Cribbs

Jo's query – that is, *Clothes?* – is presumably intended to elicit the type of clothes that NAME46 would like for Christmas, but Laura responds humorously with a definition of clothes as *wot people wear*. The humour is marked not only by unconventional spelling (<wot>), but by the discourse marker, *you know*. If we see both as intended to imply a coarse and somewhat blunt speaker – the type of person who would give such an elementary definition – we can argue that Laura is putting on a particular voice in order to tease Jo. She does, however, go on to answer the question, confirming (if confirmation is needed) that the initial response was an ironic one.

This second exchange between the same participants is equally humorous (and again includes discussion around language). Laura texts to say good morning, and the following discussion about how nice the morning is and what Laura is eating ensues.

5.5   Jo: It's a nice one. . . Ok have a good day xx

        Laura: Not such a nice one. Just got rained on, but now it is sunny. Typical. Just about to have hops bilate, Yummy. X

        Jo: Just about to have hops bilate? Even my phone doesn't recognise that.

        Laura: Ah **you see**. You have to be in the lingo. I will let you know wot on earth it is when NAME50 has finished making it!

In this case, *you see* is part of a performance aimed at coming across as smug and knowing. Ultimately, it is ironic – Laura does not in fact know what the dish is either. Again, Laura uses <wot> to contrast her smug knowingness with acknowledgement of her ignorance (*I will let you know wot on earth it is when NAME50 has finished making it!*).

The third use of these phrases by Laura in conversation with Jo is the following (Jo's turns are not included in the corpus). It appears from Laura's turn below that Jo may have previously commented on a 'Txt-like' feature of Laura's previous text message. Laura then elaborates on her performance of 'Txt', that is, she uses more linguistic features associated with Txt to humorously argue that she too can 'speak' it, and she also marks the performance with the discourse marker *u no*.

> 5.6   Oh yes I can speak txt 2 **u no**! Hmm. Did u get NAME12s email?

What conclusions can be drawn from the above? Only cautious and limited ones – we can only talk about the practices of one person and there are too few occurrences even to suggest that these uses are typical or indicative of her general practices. However, bearing this firmly in mind, it is interesting that the two phrases are not only infrequent across CorTxt but that, where they are used, they tend to be used in acts of parody and humour, in which the texters are performing particular stances towards their own linguistic practices; performances that often seek to suggest a derogatory character (through eye dialect or forms associated with Txt). I should at this point note that the other occurrences of these discourse markers (such as 5.7) appear to be straightforward attempts to monitor the level of the interlocutor's understanding.

> 5.7   Hiya NAME196, have u been paying money into my account? If so, thanks. Got a pleasant surprise when i checked my balance *–u c*, i don't get statements 4 that acc

Given the scarcity of examples in CorTxt, it would be interesting to look for more examples among the text messages you send and receive – or to ask people whether they would use such discourse markers in speech or in text messages.

5.5 *oh* in CorTxt

Look at the following spoken utterances. Are these two uses of *oh* the same? How, if at all, do they differ?

> Oh! That hurts!
> Oh, did he really say that?

The difference between the two is captured by linguists in that the first is an **interjection** and the second a discourse marker. *Oh* the interjection is an exclamatory word used to express pain, shock, surprise, disappointment and so on. Traces of *oh* as a marker of emotional responses can be found in *oh* used as a discourse marker – you can probably see that *oh* in *Oh, did he really say that?* indicates surprise. How then does it differ from the interjection?

It differs firstly in that it constitutes a response to something that has been said, rather than a reaction to a hammer being dropped on a toe. *Oh* as a discourse marker is used in various ways to respond to new or surprising information; in Carter and McCarthy's (2006, p. 115) words, 'to respond to new information or to indicate that a speaker has just discovered something surprising'. Secondly, *oh* as a discourse marker indicates how the response, and in particular the utterance following *oh*, should be interpreted. In Schiffrin's (1987) words, *oh* prefaces the evaluation of information or 'shifts in subjective orientation' (p. 95). We can imagine the speaker in the second utterance above who says *oh, did he really say that?* being shocked by the information she has just received. Finally, *oh* as a discourse marker also serves to indicate the status of a piece of information within a conversation. That is, *oh* draws attention to an utterance, signals whether a piece of information is new or old and, if old, whether it is newly the focus of attention. In Schiffrin's (1987) words, '*oh* pulls from the flow of information in discourse a temporary focus of attention which is the target of self and/or other management'. We can see this in the *oh and how are you anyway* example.

5.8   Hey bird. i'm gonna email you my very almost completed diss in a min. do what you can and give me a shout when you're returning it. thanks. **Oh and how are you anyway**

It should be noted, however, that there is no clear line between the two roles of *oh* as discourse marker or interjection. In CorTxt, *oh* appears to occur solely as a discourse marker – it in some way responds to or organizes the surrounding discourse – but you shall see, particularly in some examples below, how *oh* (the discourse marker) is influenced by the meaning of *oh* (the interjection).

According to Biber et al. (1999, p. 1083), *oh* is the most frequently occurring interjection in speech: it occurs 5052 times in a million words of the spoken part of the British National Corpus (or around 1000 times per 200,000 words) (its use as discourse marker and interjection is conflated). In comparison, *oh* occurs 262 times in the 190,052-word CorTxt – so, somewhat less in this data set than the spoken one. Its uses in CorTxt can be categorized into the categories suggested by Schiffrin (1987) in relation to its use in speech, all of which show language users responding or readjusting to information, old or new.

- in repair initiation and completion;

- to preface requests for elaboration, suddenly remembered questions and unanticipated answers;

- accompanying the receipt and recall of information; and

- marking shifts in subjective orientation.

If those categories seem a little opaque, not to worry – each use is illustrated below with examples. What the examples reveal is that, as with other features of spoken grammar, the occurrence of *oh* in texting highlights the importance of interpersonal considerations over the constraints of the medium, and how speakers draw on spoken language to achieve this. It also, as I shall discuss further below, marks the use of *oh* as pragmatic rather than primarily cognitive – that is, designed to impact on the hearer rather than to ease the speaker's processing burden. It is also evident that, as in speech, *oh* clusters with other discourse markers to form phrases such as *oh yeah* and *oh yeah*, *oh and*, *oh ok* and *oh right*, *oh well*, *oh sorry*, *oh no* and *oh my god*.

The use of oh *in conversational repairs*

The following examples show *oh* being used in the initiation and completion of conversational repair. That is, the texters are engaged in correcting something that they or their interlocutors have said. There are six occurrences of self-repair using *oh* in CorTxt. The background to the following example is that the first texter is based in the UK, while her interlocutor is currently in a sunnier, French-speaking country.

> 5.9   How would you tell someone: have a good time practising your french, in french?
>
> Amuse-toi pendant que tu t'exerce a parler a francais. Thats how id say it anyway, and strictly speaking thats wot u asked. I have a stinkin cold
>
> Oh what crap luck. You need to spend some time in a warmer clim- **oh** how lucky! Ta for translation, perfect x

The example is illustrative of others in the corpus in that the use of *oh* can be seen as a stylized attempt to amuse and engage, rather than a genuine effort to correct what has been said. In the context of this informal and intimate exchange, we can see the self-repair as an interpersonal strategy to acknowledge the problem being expressed, and to do so with a humour that also achieves significant relational work.

In the following example, *oh* is used not in self-repair but to initiate the repair of another's utterance. The topic of the exchange is the arrival of a birthday card, and the text message missing from the corpus presumably involves the confirmation of the sendee's address, which the first texter corrects with *Oh no its POSTALADDRESS* (thus explaining the card's failure to arrive).

> 5.10   No still no sign of the card. and yeah there is someone running against me. hopefully in for a good competition now. bit sacred though
>
> *[text message not in corpus]*
>
> **Oh no.** its POSTALADDRESS

In 5 further occurrences, *oh* is used to complete a repair made by others. In other words, *oh* occurs in response to a correction. In each case, *oh* is followed by *sorry*. The texters in the following exchange are organizing a night out with other teachers in the school where they all work.

> 5.11   Bonsoir, ca va? Have you organised the boys for this evening?
>
> Hiya. No i've been rubbish and disorganised! Can u tell them we'll meet in moseley at 8pm in pat kav's. X
>
> Not easily, i'm at home... I'll text NAME117 for you, just this once! Hopefully see you there but might not make 8...
>
> **Oh sorry** i forgot that you're not at school! Ok cool see u later x

Requests for elaboration, suddenly remembered questions and unanticipated answers

Questions prefaced by *oh* are those that request information while also acknowledging or responding to old information. One example of this is a request for elaboration of a previous point, which indicates that information has been received while soliciting new or further information. Two requests for elaboration are made in CorTxt with *oh*.

> 5.12   Theres a great beaming photo of NAME504 in the times today!
>
> **Oh gosh** what did he do this time?
>
> Just being cute i think. In the travel section cuddling a baby gorilla!
>
> Sounds like cutting edge breaking news. 'NAME504 still cute'.
>
> Its reassuring, in this crazy world
>
> 5.13   What's your address? I can't find it! Xx
>
> **Oh why?** she asks innocently. POSTALADDRESS.
>
> Lol. How many times have you said that recently?

Again, both uses appear to be carefully stylized. In *Oh gosh what did he do this time?* the use of *oh gosh* signals an ironic response to the announcement that somebody they know is in the paper, while eliciting further information. In the second text message, an address is requested so that a birthday card can be sent. *Oh why? she asks innocently* is an ironic, humorous pretence of ignorance as to the interlocutor's motivation. The intended effect is achieved firstly by *oh*, which marks her question *why?* as genuine, wide-eyed surprise at the unexpected request; and then by *she asks innocently*, which reflects ironically on her question. *Lol* in the final response shows that the question has been interpreted as humorous.

Oh is also used to preface suddenly remembered questions. As these examples show, here *oh* clusters with *and*. (If you remember, the text message at the start of this chapter – *oh and how are you anyway* – also fits into this category.)

5.14 **Oh and** are you and NAME324 coming to NAME117's housewarming on Saturday?

5.15 Hiya can we make it 15 min later gotta in buy a tax disc! **Oh and** do you have a video camera?

5.16 Hiya, ru getting a train down on sat? Do u need me to pick u up? Any idea of time yet? Ru staying at mine? Just checking! **Oh, +** how is new job – any nice men?

Oh is also used in the acknowledgement of unanticipated answers (with 9 occurrences), which the following example nicely illustrates.

5.17 What day is it today?

Thursday.

Oh, i thought it was weds

Recall of information

Another category is the recall of information. In 7 cases in CorTxt, the recall is prompted by an interlocutor, as illustrated in the following example. (The capitalization is typical of this texter at the time.)

5.18 Hello! How's you and how did saturday go? I was just texting to see if you'd decided to do anything tomo. Not that i'm trying to invite myself or anything!

HELLO! **OH BUM** I COMPLETELY FORGOT. WILL LET YOU KNOW EITHER LATE TONIGHT OR EARLY TOMORROW. I AM GOOD, LOOKED LIKE A COMPLETE TART ON SATURDAY AND I LOVED IT.

Ha ha! Don't feel obliged to organise anything just to entertain me ;) as for the singing – next stop, wembley stadium?

In 22 other cases, the recall is self-prompted. These uses are similar to those which preface suddenly remembered questions, and those which initiate self-repair. As with those other uses of *oh*, self-prompted recall is often prefaced with *oh and*.

5.19 Hi entering u for race for life! Put my pa down as emergency contact. Hope u don't mind but cldn't get hold of u. **Oh** just remembered, ur meeting that guy from last wk. Hope ur having fun! X

5.20   Laura: Hey bruvver, Hows things? Got any further on checkin out digi cam prices? I can do anything online if u want, and can be in for deliveries. Any ideas for NAME36?

      Laura: **Oh and** if you get a camera, get one that uses SD card, so its compatible with the mp3. Cheers bud. X

Acknowledgements of the receipt of new information are often prefaced in CorTxt by *oh*. Again, this category has similarities with the acknowledgement of unexpected answers.

5.21   **Oh** is that so, well if i do get the tickets then i know not to invite you! hehe! yeah awesome film, a guaranteed tear jerker! is spoons busy

5.22   Hi- text me if delayed- otherwise i'll be at station 2 collect at 12

      Twelve twenty five. Okay, see ya then, national rail permitting. . . Looking forward already xx

      As you well know i like to plan my day with military precision- therefore it amazes me that you gave your arrival time as 12.25 when it is clearly 12.27- for a busy professional like myself those 2 mins could make a lot of difference! I am now with- holding info about my disguise and will watch with delight as you struggle to find me!

      suddenly appears we are ten minutes late. Sorry!

      Oh- and it gets worse

Shifts in subjective orientation

A final use of *oh* is the intensification of how a texter feels (i.e. the emphasis of their stance), expressed in CorTxt with such clusters as *oh dear*, *oh crap*, *oh well*, *oh my god*, *oh yes*, *oh no*. These occur either in response to a previous text message or to introduce new information. As mentioned previously, given the function of the discourse marker in expressing emotional stance, *oh* is here closest to its role as an interjection.

In 11 occasions, *oh* is followed by a name or vocative which together express, or appeal for, sympathy or apology. In the first example below, the first texter has a bad cold.

5.23   Do you think that you can have nose transplants? I need one big time! Xx

      Oh honey u will feel better soon x x

      Hopefully! Bastard germs! Nasty little bleeders!

In this other example, the texter appeals for (rather than expresses) sympathy, using *oh*.

5.25   Hi, are we on for lunch today, i've asked NAME296 and NAME408 to join.

What time?

12.30, hope you don't mind me taking the liberty of inviting them!

Oh NAME176, i'm sorry but i don't think i can come. I don't feel too good and even the walk to campus seems daunting. Do you mind?

No, not at all, hope you feel better soon!

In 83 further cases, *oh* is used to respond to unpleasant or unfavourable situations. These include the expression of sympathy in phrases such as *oh dear* and *oh sorry*, as in the following examples.

5.26   Hello. How was your weekend then? The bird behaving itself?im listenin to the new Robbie album- bday pressie!

Cool! An early present! The birds behaving itself, can't say the same for NAME281!

Oh dear, what has he broken now?!

Oh is also used to express resignation, as in *oh well* below from someone texting from a fairground.

5.27   yep, as a matter of fact i am :) it wasn't bad. i'd like to go on the rides but no-one dares. **oh well.**

Shock or surprise is expressed with *oh no* or *oh my god*.

5.28   **Oh my god** I just realised I'm going to miss strictly come dancing on Saturday

5.29   **Oh no** im on second bottle of wine and 5 bottles of breezer!

Responses to more positive pieces of information include the following news of a friend's election onto the student union. Twenty-eight occurrences of *oh* appear to respond in this fashion to good news.

5.30   He won!

Oh good. er..remind me what post he's won..?

Something like communications and campaigns i think

Ah, she says as if it means something.been thinking, speak to you later.

Okay. I an gardening

Finally, in 3 cases in CorTxt, *oh* is used to preface wishes or desires.

5.31   Excellent still drunk on Tuesday from Sunday, **oh** I miss those days with him!! Tell him I got a new phone so my best friend can be kept in the loop!! NAME192 is away working and NAME289 is here as he has lost his door key and he has no where else to stay, haven't seen him 4 ages and he's quite cute but beer goggles mite b helping that!? X x

5.32   **Oh** I so hope so bit bizarre really but think he is really great. Quite surprised I think that but it's good 2 learn new things about yourself! Glad we r cool was a bit worried I had been replaced by NAME156! Xxx

5.33   Well, i envy you greatly as i am on my tod with a glass of wine watching boules waiting for everyone to turn up! **Oh** for hot choc and duvet.. How sad i look! See you soon and sleep well! Xx

Finally, in 10 text messages, *oh* is used to indicate discrepancies between texters' perspectives, a use noted of *oh* in spoken interaction (Schiffrin, 1987, p. 97). In the following exchange, for example, two texters discuss finding a drummer for the second texter's band – their interlocutor has suggested a drummer she knows (but who doesn't have his own drum kit), and *oh* is used in the phrase *oh details details* to dismiss concerns over the validity of a drummer unable to supply his own drum kit. As in other examples, the use of *oh* may be somewhat ironic, if we assume that a drum is more than just a detail to a drummer and in the light of the jokey warning made regarding the ex-drummer: *by definition they don't drum any more.*

5.34   Should i take your silence to mean you're not interested in my drummer? Have you already found one? It was the drummer you were missing, wasn't it? These and other questions. . .

Might be starting something with the exdrummer. Thanks for saying but it doesnt sound much good ifhe doesnt have his own kit?!

Oh details details. Well, I shall give up on the match marking then. Watch out for hte exdrummer mind – by definition they don't drum any more.

These examples of *oh* bring us back to the argument outlined at the start of this chapter, regarding the way in which its functions should be understood, both in texting and (by extension) in spoken interaction. *Oh* is generally seen, by analysts of spoken discourse markers (Aijmer, 2002; Schiffrin, 1987), as fulfilling both a cognitive and interactive role. The cognitive task that *oh* is seen to fulfil is that of helping speakers to organize the content of their utterances (and to indicate the relative importance of items of information), in order to free the speakers up to focus on content. In other words, *oh* eases the cognitive burden demanded of speakers.

The use of *oh* in the text messages above, however, shifts attention from its cognitive role towards its pragmatic function – that is, its role in indicating to interlocutors how a message is to be received. As I argued above, in texting, *oh* cannot easily be described as a strategy for coping with the real-time demands typical of fast spoken interactions. Instead, it can be seen as a semi-conscious attempt to convey in writing a particular orientation towards a (texted) utterance, and in a way that indexes the kind of informality, intimate relationships, and close attention which are associated with spoken encounters. I can imagine someone receiving a text message which makes them say to themselves 'oh!' and they then carefully compose a message which incorporates a written representation of their initial spoken response. *Oh* in such a situation creates an effect – or is part of a range of resources drawn on in creating a certain effect – intended to be received by a texter's interlocutor.

One way to appreciate this is to think about your own use of *oh* – if you use it – in text messages. Do you use it in an almost automatic reaction to what has been said? Or are you aware of how you want your interlocutor to interpret what you write? If the latter, it is interesting to speculate on the implications for the use of *oh* in spoken interaction – to what extent does it relate to a speaker's cognitive burden or their handling of their relationship with an interlocutor?

5.6 Emoticons as stance markers

In this final section, I look briefly at one emerging type of discourse marker associated with internet and texting discourse. Emoticons are 'paralinguistic restitutions' (to use Thurlow and Brown's 2003 term), images of faces formed through combinations of punctuation symbols, such as the following from CorTxt.

> 5.35 Whiskey was called bulleit bourbon...u will make NAME321 a very happy man if u can find some:) enjoy the sales! Xxx

Other forms which occur frequently in CorTxt are a smiling face complete with nose :-), the sad faces :(and :-(and the winking faces ;) and ;-(.

In CorTxt, emoticons can be described as **stance markers**: items that operate outside (and serve to frame) a clause, in order to explicitly indicate people's attitude towards, feelings about and evaluation of the proposition they are putting forward (Carter and McCarthy, 2006, pp. 222–3). Emoticons in CorTxt can be seen as fulfilling two of the three main functions identified of spoken stance markers: attitudinal markers and indicators of speaking styles. There is less evidence in the corpus that emoticons express **epistemic** stance, that is, in marking certainty and doubt, precision, or limitation; and source or perspective of knowledge through the use of markers such as: *in fact, sort of, I know, I'm not sure* and might.

- **attitudinal**—that is, signalling both evaluations and personal feelings, generally by introducing clauses with (for example) *I wish, I prefer, It's amazing what*. According to Biber et al. (2001, p. 974) attitudinal stance markers are less common in most discourse types than epistemic markers.

- **style of speaking**—which involves 'presenting speaker/writer comments on the communication itself' Biber et al. (2001, p. 975) expressed largely through stance adverbials such as: *honestly, to tell you the truth*, and *I swear*.

Biber et al. (2001, pp. 972–5)

Attitudinal uses of emoticons

Most emoticons in CorTxt are concerned with expressing a texter's personal feelings. The extent to which the texter relies on the emoticon to indicate their attitude varies, as you shall see. Firstly, in some text messages, emoticons occur in conjunction with lexical stance markers. In the examples below, the emoticon :) can be seen as reinforcing the sentiments expressed by *Glad, sorry* and *no worries*.

5.36   **Glad** it went well:) come over at 11 then we'll have plenty of time before Claire goes to work.

5.37   Hi mate hows things, **sorry** I didn't make it over to c u ;-(, going to be working over torquay mid feb, so should make it over to c u ok buddy text soon xxx:-)

5.38   After lunch on the sunday. . . **No worries** about lifts :-) Xxx

In other messages, an emoticon is used at the end of a message which is generally upbeat – that is, it contains several positive sentiments marked by lexical stance markers (*good, great* and *hope* in the first text message).

5.39   Was **good** to see you. **Great** to go to tapas **hope** you got train ok. :-)

5.40   **Good** to hear from you. Sorry to hear you're not great. **Hope** you feel better soon. Would be **nice** to meet up, seems ages since I last saw you. 1/2 term next week if you are around. :-)

Elsewhere, the emoticons do not occur with other stance markers, but they still occur alongside the expression of positive or negative feelings, as if to reinforce the already explicit attitude statements.

> 5.41   Stuck in a bit of a rut with the work unfortunately but getting on slowly. **Other than that i'm doing ok:)**

> 5.42   Hey honey! How was the meal? **I'm bored and alone** :(give me a call if u ain't busy. Hope ya having a good night xxx

In the first example, the texter is explicit about their mood with *Other than that I'm doing ok* and the emoticon supports what has been said (although not necessarily what is really the case – in this example, one can imagine a concerted effort to appear cheerful). The second example is similar, but the mood which is reinforced is negative.

In other examples where emoticons are used, the texter's mood or attitude is otherwise not explicitly expressed. Instead, it is the emoticon that primarily indicates the speaker's feelings towards the proposition.

> 5.43   C u at the airport 2moro! Dont forget ur bikini-**its about 30 and sunny right now :)**

> 5.44   R u coming 2 alesoc ale evnt? **£50 behind the bar at the welly :-)**

> 5.45   Apparently there's a huge queue :-(

In the first example, the texter is advising her interlocutor as to what clothes to bring on holiday, and addresses the need to bring a bikini by explaining *its about 30 [degrees] and sunny right now.* How the texter is likely to feel about the clement weather may be easy for her interlocutor to guess, but it is only made explicit by the smiling emoticon. The second example is similar, in that the texter exhorts its interlocutor to come to the *alesoc ale event* (i.e. organized by the university ale society) because there is *£50 behind the bar at the welly* (a pub called the Wellington) and how the texter feels about the £50 is made explicit by the emoticon (presumably, how generous a gesture the £50 was would presumably depend on the number of Ale Soc members attending and, without the emoticon, the statement could, for example, be intended to indicate disappointment). What these two examples have in common is that the emoticon provides the evaluative frame for the informational content of the message, rather than simply reinforcing the stance expressed in the clause.

Style of speaking

In other cases, emoticons serve to comment on the preceding proposition. Rather than showing the texters' personal feelings or evaluations, the emoticons in these cases show how a statement was intended to be received. While the majority of emoticons in CorTxt that fulfil this function represent smiling faces, serving to lighten an otherwise accusing, direct or insulting statement, sad faces also fulfil a contrasting role – indicating that a texter is displeased or that a statement is to be taken as accusing.

In the following, the smiling emoticons serve to lighten the tone of the preceding statement, or to make it less direct. For example:

> 5.46   Hiya. Can I just check when the Badger is coming back from yours? Presume
> the offer was both ways . . . ;)

In this example, the texter is checking that the lift they have been promised (with 'Badger') includes a lift back home, and at what time this would be. The question is presumably sensitive, in that the texter is negotiating a favour – and perhaps challenging her interlocutor's ability to organize the lift properly. This is offset by the emoticon that appears to lighten the demand. Other examples include the following:

> 5.47   Yeh do u like it and no u cant lend borrow or pinch it ! :)

> 5.48   Lessons were fine – nice groups. We'll have to meet up Friday or sometime
> to do your holiday snaps – hope you took some . . . And hope your Japanese
> was up to it;)

> 5.49   Are u home? If so,what door number & **put the kettle on! Ta :-)**

Indicating irony

In other examples, the emoticon does not soften an assertion or demand but either contradicts it (indicating irony) or indicates what is to be implied by a statement in the text message. In the following two examples, the emoticons suggest an ironic tone.

> 5.50   Ahhhh. . .just woken up! **had a bad dream about u tho, so i dont like u
> right now:)** i didnt know anything about comedy night but i guess im up
> for it.x

> 5.51   Hm good morning, headache anyone?:-)

In the first, the smiling emoticon contrasts with the verbal content: *i don't like u right now* which suggests that the statement should not be taken seriously. In the second example, assuming the message to have been texted the morning after a night out, we can see that the query – *headache anyone?* – is ironic in that the texter is assuming that the people who are being texted will all have headaches (*anyone* suggests that this text message was sent to more than one person).

These emoticons are interesting on the one hand because they show how texters compensate for the lack of paralinguistic cues – the fact that they cannot see whether their interlocutors are smiling or frowning or deduce how they feel from their body language and gestures. On the other, it is evident in the examples that their use must be seen as more sophisticated than simply the representation of facial expressions. Emoticons can be used to soften otherwise very direct or accusatory statements and they can be used to indicate irony, subtly changing how an utterance is to be interpreted. Similar graphic resources which you could investigate – but which I do not have the space to discuss here – include the representation of laughter with *ha ha*, *tee hee* and *lol*.

5.7 Chapter summary

In this chapter, you have seen how at least one network of texters draws on discourse markers typically associated with spoken interaction, and that they do so in order to recreate the kind of informal and close relationships that the spoken mode implies. That is, they are recreating the spoken mode through what is a written medium. However, texting in this respect is more than simply speech written down. Firstly, the transferral of spoken features to the written medium implies a degree of conscious decision-making, and the choices made as to what features to use in texting and which to avoid are likely to be determined by texters' judgements regarding the function of the discourse marker and the way in which the item is valued – discourse markers associated with overly sloppy, uneducated or regional speech may be avoided. Thus, we may see in texting what may be a more filtered production than in spoken language; and the use of certain markers (such as *you know*) as part of deliberate performances of a particular persona. Secondly, given the lack of access to paralinguistic features such as facial expressions and so on, texters also draw on a set of emoticons to indicate their stance in relation to the content of the text message, and how it should be interpreted.

CHAPTER SIX

Frequent words and phrases in text messaging

6.1 Introduction

6.1   Bob and Charlotte. Just to let you know that Lou and I have just enjoyed
      your bottle of English Rose with home made fish and chips. It was delicious!
      Many thanks Dave

In terms of its informal and friendly purpose, Dave's text message to Bob
and Charlotte is typical of many in CorTxt. His text message functions
ostensibly to show his appreciation for the gift of a bottle of wine – an act
of communication that reflects written 'thank you' notes. The text message
thus fulfils a largely interpersonal function – that of acknowledging and
consolidating a social relationship. As well as thanking his friends, Dave also
makes it clear that they enjoyed the bottle, and he tells them that they drank
the wine with *home made fish and chips* – an odd detail which we could
speculate may refer to a liking that the texters share of local produce and
home cooking. The interpersonal focus of the text message is reflected in the
kind of formulaic phrasings that characterize phatic talk – *Just to let you
know that . . .*, *It was delicious!*, *Many thanks*. It is unsurprising that such
phrases are used, given the intimate and informal nature of the text message.

However, I'd like to consider the relative *length* of some of them. In
Chapter 1, I noted that although texters may in part be concerned with
abbreviating their text messages, they balance this need for brevity with

their desire to express themselves and to interact in preferred ways with their interlocutors. We could argue that *Just to let you know that . . .*, for example, chiefly reflects a concern for the interlocutor: the phrase pads out the text message and makes it less abrupt. Brevity is not an issue.

I suggested above that this text message was 'typical' of CorTxt and this is also true of the language used, as these formulaic phrases are repeated throughout the corpus. The above phrase, *Just to let you know that* occurs just six times; but the smaller, embedded chunk, *let you know* occurs 63 times in a variety of lengthier phrases, such as *let you know if . . .* or *let you know when . . ..* The most frequent 3-word phrase in CorTxt is *have a good . . .* which occurs 231 times in the corpus. On eight occasions, it occurs in the longer phrase: *did you have a good time* – other phrases include *hope you have a good time.*

6.2   lhey, did you have a good time in porague? I'm in ireland at the mo with the in laws! Going ok.\\yes love being on hol 2!

So, a large part of the text messages in CorTxt is made up of these recurring chunks.

However, my argument is not that texting as a discourse is uniquely formulaic, nor that the recourse to repeated phrases renders it uncreative. Firstly, these phrases can best be seen as **frames**, into which people are relatively free to slot different words in order to express what they wish to say. For example, *have a good . . .* can be followed not only by the word *time*; texters wish each other *a good day, journey, week, night, evening* and so on. Furthermore, such frames can be a springboard for a more individual creativity. For example, one texter tells her interlocutor to *Have a good strike!* in anticipation of a union strike the next day, juxtaposing the inconsequential, phatic expression with a serious event that you would not expect to see in such a construction. Perhaps the incongruity of the phrasing hints at the possibility that the interlocutor may indeed, for whatever reason, enjoy the strike, while suggesting that this is odd.

The second point is that *all* language use may be characterized to some extent by the repeated use of phrases – that is, texting is not *particularly* formulaic. Although it is traditional to think of language as comprising words which in turn combine into clauses and sentences (see Chapter 4) more recent analyses suggest that language users do not always communicate by selecting and combining words, but that they draw on ready-made chunks of language, so that when they speak or write the first word, this already predicts the rest of the phrase. These chunks of language may include idioms such as *at the end of the day*, formulaic expressions such as *have a good time!* and also commonly used strings of words – such as *a bit of a* or *at the end of*, which language users themselves may not recognize as single, holistic items. Corpus linguistics – the study of language through the investigation of large, electronically stored corpora or text databases – is strongly bound up with this way of conceptualizing language use (see Chapter 2).

In the rest of this chapter, I discuss this conception of language use and go on to exploring the words and phrases that recur in CorTxt. My starting point is word frequency, that is, the most frequently occurring words in the corpus, and I shall go from there to look at the phrases in which these words occur. In particular, my investigation will highlight the unexpected frequencies of two words – *a* and *the* – and then explore the extent to which this can be explained through the phrases that characterize CorTxt. In other words, the investigation is to some extent **data-driven**, in that initial findings drive the subsequent direction of the research – other studies, as I point out later, may take very different directions.

6.2 Words and phrases

As Stubbs (2001, p. 27) points out, texts can be analyzed into meaningful units which are both smaller and larger than the 'word'. My main concern is with the phrase – the larger unit – but it's useful to look briefly at the smaller – the **word form**. The argument behind use of the term 'word form' for text analysis, as outlined by Stubbs (2001) and Sinclair (1991), lies in the observation that a traditionally defined 'word' (such as *go*) is in effect an abstract lexicographical category, encompassing as it does a number of forms (*go, goes, going, went*). That is, the typical dictionary entry (e.g. *go*) has already gone through a stage of interpretation, of categorization, and such abstraction is to some extent arbitrary. Dictionaries, for example, vary as to whether they include particular forms under one 'word': *ing* forms such as *confusing* may be listed as a form of the verb (*confuse*) or separately as an adjective (Stubbs, 2001, p. 25).

Furthermore, definitions based on semantic meaning fall down once, driven by corpus data, meaning is seen to emerge from usage patterns. *Consuming*, for example, is widely used in phrases such as *consuming passion* and *time-consuming* in which *consume* and *consumed* do not appear (Stubbs, 2001, p. 27) – we do not, for example, tend to say that something has been *time-consumed* or describe an emotion as *consumed passion* (unless we are being playful). Similarly (although here the distinction is not absolute), *decide* tends to collocate with a wh-word, and *decided* with *that* in referring to open and resolved decisions, respectively (Hunston, 2003, pp. 36–40) – we *decide whether to have that last piece of pie* but we have already *decided that the answer is no*, for example. In contrast, a word form is identified solely according to features of its form, that is, as an 'unbroken succession[s] of letters' (Sinclair, 1991, p. 28). So, while 'words' may be relevant units of vocabulary, word forms are more useful, objective units of text or corpus analysis (Stubbs, 2001, p. 25). In the word frequency count reported on in this chapter, I use *word* when what I actually mean is 'word form' – for the practical reason that the latter term is a little clumsy.

Respelt word forms

Generating a list of words ('word forms') for CorTxt using *Wordsmith Tools* (Scott, 1996) is complicated by the respellings that characterize texting (see Chapter 3). That is, what is usually a word form can, in CorTxt, take variously respelt forms. Should *you*, *ya* and *u* be characterized as different word forms or, at the risk of invalidating the point of the word form entirely, variants of the same form? For practical purposes, arguments can be made for either decision – if, as argued in Chapter 3, respellings carry the potential for social meaning, then they should be treated as different forms; at the same time, the referential meaning is the same and treating them as separate may give a misleading picture as to how often, for an example, an interlocutor is addressed (using *you*, *ya*, or *u*). Actually, for the purposes of compiling the word frequency list, the two options did not entail significant differences, so my decision to consider respelt words as variants of the same word form was largely unproblematic – but the questions raised here remain.

A related issue is the omission of spacing between words, and the forming of alphanumeric sequences such as *looking4ward 2seein u* soon. Is this string comprised of four word forms (*looking4ward, 2seein, u* and *soon*) or six? *Wordsmith Tools* works on the basis that a word form is separated by spaces, and so *looking4ward* would be treated as one word form. Any breaking up of this unit would indeed presuppose the existence within it of 'words' – however common sense a notion that may seem – and thus invalidate the notion of a unit based solely on orthographic form. In general, although these issues are resolvable, the text message data problematizes the notion that the word form – an 'unbroken succession of letters' – is necessarily a straightforward and non-arbitrary unit of analysis.

Meaningful units of text are often larger than word forms, and this is where we come to the significance of language phrases. **Phrases** are chunks of language that for various reasons – frequency of occurrence or the way in which they seem to be processed – can be treated as one linguistic item. The following (invented) uses of *by the way* show how meaning can reside in the phrase as a whole (example **a**), rather than as a string of words (example **b**).

a. By the way, we're meeting at 2.

b. I knew it was him by the way he was walking.

That language 'chunks' in the way it does in example **a** is by no means a new observation in linguistics, but it is one that was sidelined somewhat in the mid-twentieth century by the prominence of Noam Chomsky's ideas about grammar, which prioritized a 'slot-and-filler' model of language – the conception that language comprises a sequence of slots into which speakers place words in various combinations (with some constraints, of course, largely those of word class in that a word can fit in a slot only if it is a noun, or an adjective and so on). Given this focus on word combinations, idiomatic language has tended to be relegated to a marginal role in dictionaries and is often tacked on to the end of an entry. Chomsky's grammar model is often criticized for focusing on what he called speakers' competence – that is, on an abstracted model of language in a person's head – and rejecting their performance – which would diverge from the idealized model because of extra-linguistic factors such as memory, stress and other limitations of a real-time performance. (Note that Chomsky's use of 'performance' is different from my use of the term elsewhere in this book; see Chapter 8.) In practice, what this focus entails is a model of language based on decontextualized sentences that are deemed 'correct' by 'native' speakers (both problematic terms).

However, in corpus linguistics and across many linguistic disciplines, value is now placed on what Chomsky called 'performance' – that is, on understanding language in use, often using attested data. What becomes evident when looking at naturally occurring data is that although it may be *possible* for people to generate infinite numbers of sentences by slotting words into grammatical structures, in practice they do not: each choice of word constrains and is constrained by those around it (Sinclair, 2004). That is, people resort to ready-made chunks of language. So, as illustrated above with *by the way*, it seems that there may be two ways of producing and understanding language – as a series of words or as prefabricated chunks. Sinclair (1991) labels these two approaches, respectively, the **Open Choice principle** and the **Idiom principle**. These two principles are often exploited in jokes, using a stretch of language – like *by the way* – that can be interpreted either literally (word-by-word) or figuratively (as a chunk). Take for example the humorous newspaper report that:

> The misguided prophet who predicated the apocalypse was of course disappointed that it has failed to occur, but told reporters that it wasn't the end of the world.

The two principles may occasionally be the cause of misunderstanding. On our walk from the car park to the starting line of a half-marathon, a conversation with my Dutch friend and I went something like this:

My Dutch friend:	Oh, I'm getting cold feet.
Me:	Oh no, you can't back out now!
My Dutch friend:	What? I won't back out now. But my feet are freezing.

According to Sinclair, the 'default' processing is the Idiom principle. If we have no reason to think otherwise, we assume a chunk is to be read as a phrase – so that I interpreted my friend's *getting cold feet* as meaning she was having second thoughts. However, should this reading fail, we then resort to the Open Choice interpretation and break the chunk down – which I did following my friend's response.

But what exactly a phrase is and how they can be identified remain a matter of debate. This is evident in the number of different terms used to describe them. You may be familiar with some of the following. To what extent do you find any of them to be synonymous?

clichés, stereotypes, collocations, formulaic sequences, idioms, proverbs, frames, n-grams, lexical bundles, metaphors, fixed expressions, chunks, recurrent clusters

(See, e.g. Wray A., 2002, pp. 8–9)

As Wray suggests, different terms do not map neatly onto different aspects of the same phenomenon but instead mask overlapping or conflicting interpretations and theoretical priorities. For example, most people would recognize those non-technical terms that are widely used outside linguistics such as *cliché* or *stereotype* (both generally with negative connotations), but they may be less familiar with discipline-specific terms such as **collocation**, which is now established within corpus linguistics as referring specifically to statistically significant word co-occurrences (Sinclair, 1991), or **formulaic sequence**, used in psycholinguistics to refer to holistically processed word strings (Wray A., 2002). I shall discuss the significance of differences between these two disciplines presently.

Other distinctions include how fixed or fragmented the units are; and the extent to which they are meaningful wholes. Some terms refer to unbroken, contiguous phrases – *lexical bundles* are recurrent sequences of words (Biber et al., 1999) and *n-grams* are sequences of *n* items (where items are, in this case, words). Other terms, however, allow phrases to be characterized by variation, where words are either moved around or inserted into a phrase. These terms include **frames** such as *a + ? + of* (Sinclair and Renouf, 1991), which explicitly provide slots within otherwise fixed expressions, and *concgrams* (Cheng et al., 2006). These concepts allow for the fact that even fixed phrases, such as *Don't burn your bridges*, are regularly manipulated in utterances like *The words 'burning' and bridges' come to mind* (Carter, 2004, p. 138).

Moving on to the next distinction, some terms describe phrases which are meaningful 'wholes' – these include idioms and fixed expressions as well as formulaic sequences – while others do not. Chunks, for example, tend to be pragmatically complete – they are **pragmatic** in that they fulfil an interpersonal or interactional function – but are otherwise fragmented. O'Keeffe et al. (2007, p. 71) give the example of *a bit of a*, hardly a semantic whole but which functions as a frame with the pragmatic purpose of downplaying criticism. Note that, according to O'Keeffe et al. (2007, p. 71), it tends to occur before negatively oriented nouns.

	mess
	problem
a bit of a	performance
	hassle
	nuisance
	bargain

One important distinction within approaches to understanding language phrases is whether they should be defined by frequency of occurrence or through the way in which they are seen to be produced. The former is an approach adopted by corpus linguists; the latter lies in the domain of psycholinguistics (the study of how language is processed in the mind). For psycholinguists, a phrase or 'formulaic sequence' differs from any non-formulaic string of words in that it is 'stored and retrieved whole' (Wray A., 2002, p. 9). In other words, when speakers search in their minds for a phrase, they do not need to retrieve it word-by-word – it comes out whole. The obvious function of formulaic sequences is, then, that it reduces the effort that goes into producing or understanding language.

When it comes to reconciling these 'holistically produced phrases' with a corpus linguistics approach, the question is the extent to which these phrases are also the most frequently used. They may often be because, firstly, frequently co-occurring words may come to be processed holistically through repeated use and, secondly, we might imagine that holistically produced phrases would be frequently used for ease of processing (Wray A., 2002, p. 25) – if you have to communicate in real time (as we do in most spoken interactions), why not rely on ready-made phrases? However, the two – frequently occurring phrases and holistically produced formulaic sequences – do not map exactly onto each other. Empirical study shows that fixed expressions intuitively felt to be part of the language are not always particularly frequent (Moon, 1998) and therefore not reflective of typical language use. That is, many idioms which are very prominent in people's awareness (*it's raining cats and dogs* or *as dead as a dormouse*) in fact occur very infrequently in most corpora, and others may be contextually constrained (*God save the Queen*, for example, would be used only in certain contexts at certain times).

At the same time, it is very difficult to prove how an item is stored and received (Wray A., 2002, p. 19), despite research into eye-movement and phonetic production and experiments such as cloze tests where people are given texts with words blanked out which they are asked to fill in (Kuiper, 2004, p. 869). As Read and Nation (2004, p. 25) suggest, how language is stored and retrieved varies between individuals and communities, and as communicative purposes and processing demands shift. Formulaic sequences must therefore be extracted in part by recourse to intuition –the researcher must select sequences which they can argue may be holistically processed.

Corpus analysis (such as in this study) therefore has the practical benefit that its target – frequently occurring phrases – can be identified and retrieved using corpus methods. Furthermore, the process is driven by the data, in so much as the computer uses statistical frequency to identify recurrent strings which may not be evident to speakers' intuition and are thus neglected in lists determined through introspection. Indeed, it appears to be the case that speakers lack accurate awareness of the frequent patterns of language use which corpus analysis reveals (Sinclair, 1991; Stubbs, 2001). As Wray A. (2002; 2008) points out, speakers do not tend to break down longer units of meaning for analysis into their constituent parts, which explains why they may then be unaware of frequent patterns of use. For example, she cites an interesting study in which people failed to identify what the breakfast cereal *Rice Krispies* is made of. (This is of course also the case with researchers, which makes the intuitive identification of formulaic phrases problematic.)

Strings identified initially through frequency are distinguished from *formulaic sequences* by Schmitt (2004) as *recurrent clusters*, and it is essentially these recurrent clusters that this study calls 'phrases'. These are strings of two or more words which recur in CorTxt, often as frames to which new content can be added. Some variation is thus recognized, although the approach can be criticized for not allowing for the full range and degree of internal variation which appears to characterize 'fixed' phrases. Another limitation is that a corpus analysis cannot determine how these are being processed or how salient the phrases are for them. Hopefully, this section has provided a brief overview of the varied approaches that characterize the study of formulaic language, against which you can evaluate my study of CorTxt.

6.3 Word frequency in CorTxt

The study of CorTxt began with an analysis of word frequency. The value of word frequency lies in the observation that comparisons between corpora reveal differences in word distribution and patterning between users and contexts – between British and Jamaican English speakers, for example, or between situations where language is written and spoken. I compared the CorTxt frequency list with the British National Corpus (BNC), a 100 million-word collection of texts from a range of spoken and written discourse types including newspapers, letters, conversation, radio show call-ins and so on. Although collected in 1990s (over a decade before CorTxt), the BNC like CorTxt contains what can be called 'British English' and thus differences between the two may be put down to the specific nature of the text messages in CorTxt. Before reading on, can you guess which word tends to be most frequently used in this corpus of 'general' British English? Note that the order tends to be fairly stable across such corpora. Then, as you look at the BNC word list in Table 6.1 below, consider what, if anything, strikes you about the top ten words in the list. Did you guess the most frequent word correctly?

Two immediate observations spring to mind. *The* is the most frequent word, and what is particularly striking is how much more frequent it is than any other word – it is twice as frequent as the second word, *of* and nearly three times as frequent as *a*. The other thing that may strike you is that the most frequent words are all **grammar words** rather than **lexical items** – as

Table 6.1 BNC word frequency list

	Word	Frequency (per million words)	% of corpus as a whole
1	the	61847	6.18%
2	of	29391	2.94%
3	and	26817	2.68%
4	a	21626	2.16%
5	in	18214	1.82%
6	to	16284	1.63%
7	it	10875	1.09%
8	is	9982	1.00%
9	to	9343	0.93%
10	was	9236	0.92%
11	i	8875	0.89%
12	for	8412	0.84%
13	that	7308	0.73%
14	you	6954	0.70%
15	he	6810	0.68%
16	be	6644	0.66%
17	with	6575	0.66%
18	on	6475	0.65%
19	by	5096	0.51%
20	at	4790	0.48%

(from Leech et al. 2001)

well as the determiners *the* and *a*, there are the prepositions *of*, *in* and *to* and two forms of the verb *to be*, *is* and *was*. (Note that *to* occurs twice, as the infinitive – as in, *I want to go* – and as the preposition – *I want to go to the cinema.*)

In other corpora, it is to be expected that this distribution will change, and that somewhat different grammar words occur more frequently. If we isolate the spoken section of the BNC, for example, we find that the pronouns *I* and *you* are particularly frequent:

the	39605	–	104720.4	64420
I	29448	+	369238.5	6494
you	25957	+	385328.3	4755
and	25210	–	1134.5	27002
it	24508	+	151913.5	9298

(Leech et al., 2001)

Note, however, that *the* remains at the top of the list and that, regardless of the nature of any specialized corpus – computer science (James et al., 1994); psychiatric interviews (Dahl, 1979), romance fiction (Tribble, 2000) and short stories (Stubbs, 2001) – this is where it tends to stay.

CorTxt, however, departs in significant ways to general corpora. What differences strike you as you read the list in Table 6.2, on the next page?

Perhaps your most immediate observation was that the most frequently occurring word is not *the* but *you*. There are a number of other observations that could be made, but what I want to focus on is that the order of some frequently occurring words in CorTxt is a reversal of that in the BNC. That's to say, many words swap positions between the two frequency lists. Firstly, in CorTxt, *you* is more frequent than *I*. Secondly, *the* occurs less frequently than *a* in CorTxt, whereas in other corpora *the* can be three times as frequent as *a*. These are not the only examples – if we go further down the word list we can see that *have* and *is* are also reversed, as are *me* and *my* and *just* and *so*. However, the reversal of *a* and *the* seems particularly startling not only in their upset of the typical order but because of the generally low frequency of *the*, and the implications this may have for Txt.

The fact that *the* is far less frequent in texting than general language, while *a* retains a similar frequency, is to an extent unsurprising: Biber et al. (1999, p. 267) note that *the* varies more across registers than *a*, while Leech et al. (2009) document a gradual decline of *the* in British and American written language corpora between the 1960s and 90s. *The* is also generally less frequent in spoken corpora, and texting is widely thought to be 'like speech'. However, in no other corpora – even spoken ones – do the frequencies of *the* and *a* begin to compare with that in CorTxt. Another explanation may be abbreviation and the tendency for texters to omit words – perhaps *the* tends to be omitted while *a* is not. This may explain the reversed frequencies in part, but cannot fully account for the reversal. In a random sample of

Table 6.2 CorTxt word frequency list

	Word	Frequency (in 190, 516 words)	% of corpus as a whole
1	You*	7,884	4.12%
2	To**	4,976	2.61%
3	I***	4,257	2.23%
4	X	3,689	1.93%
5	A	3,580	1.88%
6	The	3,553	1.86%
7	And	3,171	1.66%
8	In	2,387	1.25%
9	For	2,057	1.08%
10	It	2,020	1.06%
11	Have	1,993	1.05%
12	Is	1,577	0.83%
13	Be†	1,567	0.82%
14	Me	1,555	0.82%
15	On	1,523	0.80%
16	Are	1,478	0.78%
17	Of	1,420	0.75%
18	At	1,393	0.73%
19	My	1,285	0.67%
20	Good	1,265	0.66%

*   *u* accounts for 3043 of the total occurrences of *you* (39 percent)
**   Unlike the BNC wordlist, *to* includes infinitive and preposition (i.e., it is treated more consistently as a wordform.
*** Unlike the BNC wordlist, *I* in Cortxt does not include its use in contractions such as *I'm*.
†   *b* accounts for 375 of the total occurrences of *be/b* (24 percent)

text messages, where *the* occurred 75 times and *a* 86, I gauged that *the* was omitted a further 34 times and *a* 16 times, in examples such as the following. Such an exercise is of course open to debate. Decide which articles you think are missing, and then check my decisions in the footnote.[1]

6.3   have good weekend.

6.4   You all ready for big day tomorrow?

6.5   have got few things to do. may be in pub later.

6.6   Cant think of anyone with spare room off top of my head

The figures suggest that *the* may indeed be omitted more often than *a*. However, if we include the omissions with the occurrences, then *the* would have occurred 109 times and *a* 102 times – *the* was still more frequent than *a*. It seemed worth looking for other factors. One remaining explanation appeared to lie in the commonly used phrases in which both *a* and *the* occur.

A brief note on *an*: *an* occurs less frequently in texting than it does in speech, at 1422 occurrences per million words, compared to 3430 in the BNC. Concordance lines show that it occurs frequently to the left of *hour*, and also with *email* and *amazing time*. Except for noting similarities with the phrases in which *a* will be seen to occur, there do not appear to be any implications of this for the frequencies of *a* and *the*, and *an* was not included in the analysis.

6.4 Phrases in CorTxt

Before going on to look at phrases including *a* or *the*, I looked more generally at the phrases that typify CorTxt. These are presented below in Tables 6.3 to 6.6 as three-, four-, five- and six-word phrases. With the exception of the six-word phrases (of which there were only 4), the ten most frequent of each have been selected. Note that, as I mentioned above, the shorter phrases often form part of the longer phrases; you saw above how *let you know* formed part of *just to let you know that*. As you read through each set below, consider how you would describe and categorize them.

The above phrases can be described as being highly interactive, in the sense that many refer directly to the interlocutor: *see you in a bit, look forward to seeing you, hope you have a good time*, and they often elicit responses or some form of further interaction: *did you have a good time, let me know when you . . ., what are you up to*. Others frame an utterance in a way that suggests concern for the interlocutor: *just to let you know that . . . .* Finally, some phrases are more 'formulaic' (and thus more semantically complete) than others: *see you soon, happy new year to you, i love u so much*. The phrases can be categorized into the functions listed in Table 6.7.

O'Keeffe et al. (2007) suggest that frequently occurring phrases or chunks act as a 'fingerprint' of the particular discourse type – that is, the phrases say something what a discourse is about. If this is so, we might posit that phrases in CorTxt reveal a highly interactive discourse, whose participants are concerned with consolidating intimate relationships, making future plans and organizing further interaction. It is interesting to compare this briefly with phrases seen to occur most frequently across written and spoken corpora.

Table 6.3 3-word phrases in CorTxt

3-word phrases in CorTxt		
1	Have a good	231
2	Let me know	163
3	See you soon	74
4	A good time	71
5	Do you want	68
6	How are you	65
7	Let you know	63
8	A good day	62
9	Happy new year	60
10	Give me a	53

Table 6.4 4-word phrases in CorTxt

4-word phrases in CorTxt		
1	Do you want to	40
2	Have a good day	35
3	Let me know when	34
4	Hope you had a	31
5	Let me know if	29
6	Have a good one	27
7	Had a good time	24
8	To let you know	23
9	Have a good week	23
10	What you up to	21

Table 6.5 5-word phrases in CorTxt

5-word phrases in CorTxt		
1	Hope you had a good	21
2	Just to let you know	17
3	See you in a bit	15
4	Let me know when you	15
5	Did you have a good	13
6	Let me know if you	11
7	Looking forward to seeing you	10
8	Happy new year to you	9
9	To let you know that	8
10	Hope you have a good	8

Table 6.6 6-word phrases in CorTxt

6-word phrases in CorTxt (all)		
1	did you have a good time	8
2	hope you had a good time	7
3	just to let you know that	6
4	do you want a lift tomorrow	5

The phrases that typify spoken English conversation relate to the management of the immediate interaction to a greater extent than in CorTxt, including the monitoring of the hearer's engagement – *you know what I mean* – and the parallel hedging of the speaker's position – I don't know if . . .; or something like that (O'Keeffe et al., 2007, pp. 71–5 and see Figure 6.8).

In contrast, the fingerprint of written data is 'a 'world-out-there' representation in that phrases relate referents to the real world – they are referential rather than interpersonal (O'Keeffe et al. 2007: 68). Note the impersonal constructions and prepositional relationships see Figure 6.9.

Thinking back to the word frequency list, the other observation that you could make from the frequently occurring phrases is how many include the word *you* (which you'll remember is the most frequently occurring word in CorTxt). My next step was to explore whether the frequencies of *a* and *the*

Table 6.7 Function of chunks in CorTxt

Function	Phrases used
Expressing wishes and sentiments	*hope you had a good* (*time*), *did you have a good* (*time*), *happy new year to you, happy birthday to you, hope you have a good, have a good* (*day, week, one, weekend*), *hope all is well, i love you so much*
Framing current interaction	*just to let you know* (*that*)
Referring to future (or other) shared interaction	*see you* (*soon, then, in a bit*), *looking forwardtoseeing you, do you want to meet, or do you want to, do you want to come, do you want me to, do you want a lift* (*tomorrow*), *good to see you, on my way*
Referring to future (texted) communication	*let me know when you, let me know if you*

Table 6.8 Functions of chunks in CANCODE (5-million word spoken corpus held at the University of Nottingham)

Function	Phrases used
Discourse marking	*you know* (the most frequent), *you know what I mean, at the end of the day*, and *if you see what I mean* (O'Keeffe et al. 2007: 71)
Facework and politeness	*do you think, I don't know if/whether, what do you think*, and *I was going to say* (O'Keeffe et al. 2007: 73)
Vague expressions	*a couple of, and things like that, or something like that, all the rest of it*, and (*and*) *all this/that sort of thing* (O'Keeffe et al. 2007: 70–5)

Table 6.9 Functions of written chunks in CIC, Cambridge International Corpus (Carter and McCarthy, 2006, pp. 832–7)

Function	Chunks used
Time and place	Prepositional phrases: *in the, on the, at the, out of the* Noun phrases + *of*: *the edge of the, the bottom of the, the side of the* Combinations: *in the middle of the, at the top of the*
Possession, agency, purpose, goal, and direction	*of a, of the, to the, with the, by the, for the*

in CorTxt could be explained in part in terms of the phrases in which they occur. I started with *a*.

6.5 Phrases with *a* in CorTxt

Two observations can be made about *a* in relation to phrases in CorTxt: firstly, many of the occurrences of *a* are 'phrasal'; and, secondly, the phrases in which *a* occurs include some of the most frequent. To take the first observation first, the fact that *a* is often used in recurring phrases can be seen by looking at a random set of concordances lines for *a*. Concordance lines (see Chapter 2), display occurrences of a **node word** (in this case, *a*) in context – that is, in the context of the words that occur immediately to the right and left of it. Phrases which recur to varying degrees in the corpus, and which are emboldened in Figure 6.1 below, account for 14 of these 20 lines.

This is of course only a very small sample, but it suggests that any attempt to explain the frequency of *a* in texting must make reference to the phrases in which it occurs.

Secondly, as the above concordance lines suggest, many of the phrases in which *a* appears occur very frequently. Of the above phrases, *have a good*

```
 1     t outside Hey buddy, us a bell when you finnish
 2 st arrived in and there's a couple of things we n
 3       oman and sounded like a pile of snot and tears.
 4  er Katie here and i have a new number. This is it
 5  at kav so there might be a bit of a selly oak poss
 6       me posted xx Depends a little whether nik joins
 7     mum company . . . Have a good time xx Mystery
 8     nd of person who needs a smile to brighten his
 9               in. We bought a couple a Xmas pressies. Wot u
10    da throw the night. have a good one x Cool cool.
11  ing.she's better now stil a bit dazed i think.i had
12      sumed we were getting a lift. . . Want me to boo
13  kered so better not. Hve a gud time tho Yipee i'v
14    ob than dave! Fab. Have a good week, don't work
15     ow tomorrow. Did u hav a successful shoppin tri
16   know I have just bought a fish and chip and mus
17     ow the address give me a txt. steve Hey hav se
18  nything about it.x Have a good day love to all Y
19    orean girl moving down a class tomo, poss new
20    u know wot i mean! Wot a slapper eh?! X Happy
```

Figure 6.1 Random sample of concordance lines for *a*

is the most frequent 3-word phrase in CorTxt (which you may remember from section 6.4), while the related phrase *a good time* is fourth, and *give me a* the tenth most frequent phrase. Finally, the 2-word chunk *a bit* evident in the concordance lines is also very frequent (202 occurrences). I looked at these in more depth. The phrase *have a good* occurs 236 times, followed by various references to time (see Figure 6.2).

As mentioned at the start of this chapter, the phrase can be adapted to different contexts, as we saw in *Have a good strike!* There is also variation in the adjective used:

- *nice* occurs 30 times to describe *lunch* and a *meal* as well as periods of time;

- *great* occurs 28 times, most frequently in *have a great time*;

- *lovely* occurs 15 times, most often alongside birthday or Christmas wishes, as in *have a lovely birthday*; or *Happy bday 2 u! Hope u have a lovely day.*

- *fab* occurs 14 times, predominantly in *Have a fab day.*

Other less frequent phrases include: *hope you have a spiffing good night, a smashing day, a wicked time* and *a wonderful afternoon.* There are also seven occurrences of *have a gud*, followed in six cases by *nite* – *Had a gud time at toni's wedding* and *Have a gud nite 2nite.* It is interesting to note the co-occurrence of eye dialect forms (see chapter 3).

Thus we can describe a function – that of wishing someone something – as being carried out through variations on a standard phrase which in most cases can be encapsulated by: *have a + positively-orientated adjective + time period.*

We can note further variations, by looking at *a good time* which occurred (in the initial phrase lists) 71 times, but only 30 times in the larger phrase, *have a good time.* It occurs elsewhere in structures such as *had a good time* (24) and *having a good time* (7) and *is a good time* (3).

Have a good	(236)	day	(35)
		one	(30)
		time	(30)
		week/wk	(24)
		night/nite	(22)
		weekend/wkend	(21)
		evening	(18)
		trip	(8)

Figure 6.2 *Have a good . . .* phrases in texting

6.7   Yeah will prob be around til end of the week. Had a good time but weather not been great. See you soon, k and l x

6.8   Good! Having a good time so far apart from the rain. Speak soon. Xxx

6.9   Hello! I'm back from gabon! I have lots i need 2 tell u- when is a good time 2 phone, i am on a train right now. NAME12 XXX

The other most frequent phrasing is *give me a* (53 occurrences) or *give you a* (21), which chiefly refer to future phone calls, text messages or other acts of interaction. So while have a good served a mainly phatic function, these phrases are pivotal to the organization of further interaction (see Figure 6.3).

Give me a missed call (which occurs once) is interesting as a phrasing which has surely come about with the use of mobile phones, to refer to the act of ringing a phone without it being answered in order to pass on your number.

6.10   What's happening?! Give me a missed call

Before moving on to *the*, I'd like to look at one more set of phrases which we mentioned briefly above in relation to O'Keeffe et al.'s (2007) analysis of spoken interaction, namely, *a bit*, *a bit of* and *a bit of a*.

The hedge *a bit* (which occurs 202 times in CorTxt) is generally thought to show consideration of an interlocutor. In spoken conversation, *a bit* does not simply serve to specify amount but instead, as Carter and McCarthy (2006, p. 64) state, it is 'deliberately vague and informal' and serves to soften assertions otherwise deemed by the speaker as direct or overly authoritative. Arguably, one example in Figure 6.4 amplifies rather than downplays assertions – can you spot it?

The exception is *quite a bit* in *But she talks quite a bit* (line 9) which serves to intensify rather than downplay. However, in this example as in the others, *a bit* can be described as playing an evaluative role, in that it marks statements as negative or critical. This is noted of spoken conversation by

give me a (53)	shout	(11)
	call	(10)
	text/txt	(8)
	ring	(6)
	bell	(5)
(I'll) give you a (21)	ring	(9)
	text	(4)
	call	(3)
	shout	(2)

Figure 6.3 *Give you/me a . . .* in texting

```
1    ing.she's better now stil a bit dazed i think.i had
2    hat she did, which was a bit lame, i thought tha
3    e fun! Am ok tho feeling a bit miserable in my bi
4    ws, am ok so will try for a bit of independence an
5    y local unfortunately it's a bit flat, infact it has n
6    ank you and see you in a bit. 10mins is your fri
7    ng anything. See you in a bit. How's it going? G
8    it? Well we are running a bit late... it turns out t
9    rial. But she talks quite a bit. So its ok. Any ad
10   i'll come up seaview for a bit. Xxx Just finished
11   rrow when I hope to feel a bit better Just got a te
12   eed2 ask u something, a bit bizarre just say se
13   en u would hear by? Im a bit use less 2 u really
14   te! Ok maybe 5.30 was a bit hopeful. . .we'v only j
15   ink Jeremy Clarkson is a bit sexy now! hope y
16   u guys later. See you in a bit. NAME298 Lol! Nah was
17   NAME46 for shopping in a bit. You lot? I reckon
18   o play with x Well thats a bit gay.. Make a tin fo
19   offered it to me already-all a bit mind boggling really...
20   avour ... Yep see you in a bit. Ex Might not have
21   an comes tomoz up for a bit of motown madness?
```

Figure 6.4 Selected concordance lines for *a bit*

```
1    Well done. Often a bit of a challenge to do it
2   rd. i know this is a bit of a cheek especially
3    eems to be. I had a bit of a cold but gettin bet
4   y touch! feel like a bit of a cow. But ta for th
5   . I know I've been a bit of a drip but I will start
6   dy wife are having a bit of a get together satur
7   at might have been a bit of a mean message to
8    thiing has proved a bit of a mistake i think- lo
9    il out tonight for a bit of a piss up, he's not
10  cancel lunch. Have a bit of a problem. Call you
```

Figure 6.5 Selected concordance lines for *a bit of a*

Carter and McCarthy (2006, p. 65), who give the examples: *It's a bit extravagant, isn't it?* and *He's a bit old to be driving.* The negatively oriented adjectives tend to be non-comparative (so that *He's a bit old* sounds negative, but *He's a bit older* does not).

In the concordance lines above, *a bit* occurs predominantly with such negatively oriented adjectives: *dazed, lame* (meaning *weak* or *pathetic*, as in *a lame excuse*), *miserable, flat, bizarre, useless, gay* (in its derisive sense, similar to *lame*) and *mind boggling.* Negative connotations can even be perceived in other, less obviously derogatory text messages such as line 14 above: *Ok so maybe 5.30 was a bit hopeful* (i.e. they did not make it on time), while the seemingly positive evaluation (line 15) that *Jeremy Clarkson is a bit sexy now!* can be seen as grudging or cautious with reference to the full text message: *Did you watch Top Gear? It was so funny, even I think Jeremy Clarkson is a bit sexy now!.*

Other exceptions may occur where *a bit* is followed by *of* (which occurs 34 times in CorTxt). As in lines 4 and 21 above, *a bit of* serves as a hedge but is less evaluative than *a bit.* It softens the strength of the texter's ambition in *so will try for a bit of independence*, and plays down the extravagance of the entertainment promised by *up for a bit of motown madness?* Similarly, *in a bit* (occurring 41 times) and *for a bit* (18 occurrences) modify the length of time involved and thus downplay the authority of the texter.

Interestingly, however, *a bit of a* (20 occurrences) reverts to the negative connotation also implied by *a bit*, as seen in Figure 6.5.

What this initial investigation suggests is that the frequent occurrence of *a* in frequently occurring phrases may help explain its overall frequency in CorTxt.

6.6 Phrases with *the* in CorTxt

Analysis of *the* in CorTxt reveals that a lower proportion of occurrences of *the* can be described as phrasal, as seen in the following randomly selected concordance lines (Figure 6.6). Seven of the 20 lines are labelled phrases (35%), compared to fourteen with *a* (70%).

```
1        t looks like you are ill in the morning ? X Neath
2     like cluedo but I'm sure the bishops won't mind.
3         imbo waiting to cross to the other side. Hence th
4     he lion says when I roar the whole jungle shakes
5     at list ..? Can you bring the suitcase to work. X
6         d little friends in town in the afternoon/evening.. J
7     little thing maybe? X Is the cd somewhere i can
8     u c d little thing i left in the lounge?it was free b
9         r lives together call u in the morning xxx am ho
10    ! And lo, it is printed, n the computer switched o
11        loads of exercise shit in the summer when are yo
12    ldlife expert. What job? The one in Belgium? Ok
13    ondon office for work for the next week.PHONENUMBER
14    london, and u shall hav the grand slam! X I am
15    r long, me! X Why dont the txts deliver? Maybe r
16    g. Would u be watching the rugby? Dunno if its
17    ow's the house without the chicks. quiet and tid
18    ook soonish and tell me the date i received my
19 will look out for NAME146. All the best! No definately-
20        after screaming child at the mo! u two gals run
```

Figure 6.6 Selected concordance lines for *the*

```
1    me up before u leave in the morning i need to get up
2  If not give me a call in the morning to make sure I wake
3  y, prob you'll see me in the morning. F x Yep will do
4  . How about meeting in the morning for s&m, i go
5  lives together call u in the morning xxx "its yours
6 a picture of it to you in the morning x OK seeya soon"
7    possibly pick me up in the morning. My car is not fi
8   u r re lesson! See u in the morning. F x "I'm saving my
9 mselves Yes ok will do in the morning "Only a couple of
10   They want you to ring in the morning if poss" "The bank is
```

Figure 6.7 Concordance lines for *in the morning*

As well as the prepositional phrases mentioned above, we also see the phatic formulaic phrase *All the best!* which occurred 20 times in the corpus.

So, the most frequent phrases in which *the* occurs are prepositional phrases associated with time and place (such as *in the morning* or *at the mo*) – rather than the interpersonal focus identified in phrases containing *a*. However, no one phrase seems to occur particularly frequently, and not as frequently as those with *a*, and it is this which may help explain the unusual relative frequencies of the two. For example, the most frequently occurring phrase, *in the morning*, occurs only 35 times, compared to 236 occurrences of *have a good* (the most frequent phrase with *a*) (see Figure 6.7).

Other references to time include *at the moment* (with 27 occurrences) and the slightly more frequent *at the mo* (33 occurrences) (see Figure 6.8).

```
1      Dying of pneumonia at the moment well got alittle cold
2        fine, on holiday at the moment just relaxing. I have
3      having a shit time at the moment but we will have it
4        able to do much at the moment as my CRB check has
5      get hold of anyone at the moment. I'll have to let
6    Doing my career plan at the mo. Thats an interesti
7    hard at college work at the mo. I've got so much to
8  in hospital. She is ok at the mo r u home alone
9  orague? I'm in ireland at the mo with the in laws! Go
10   is beta. I'm at home at the mo, that's why i wanted
```

Figure 6.8 Selected concordance lines for *at the moment/at the mo*

```
1 ng to gym and I'm in town at mo. So can we make it for
2 run here with my bro but at mo got stinking cold. Have
3  Can't return the camera at mo. Prob. Be able to make
4 chine! And sleeping badly at mo. Observation nxt wk –
5 Naughty gal! Yes, on bus at mo. Are you still in town?
```

Figure 6.9 Selected concordance lines for *at mo*

The number of times *the* is omitted from these phrases is interesting. While *at moment* occurs only three times, *at mo* occurs twenty-three times throughout CorTxt (see Figure 6.9): over two-thirds again the occurrences of *at the mo*. Of course, the same occurs with *a* which is, for example, omitted 52 times in the phrase *have good* (*time*, *day* and so on).

Other most frequent phrases are *the end of* (19 occurrences) and *the rest of* (17) which, as the concordances in Figure 6.10 show, refer predominantly to time. Again, the phrases are often involved either in coordinating shared activities (*it should be back by the end of week*) or as part of phrases similar to *have a good* (such as *enjoy the rest of your day*).

Looking first at *the end of*, those that do not refer to time often refer to physical locations – such as *near the end of Cornwall* – while exceptions involving *the rest of* include the presumably light-hearted *the rest of me* above. Again, as with *at the mo*, it is interesting to note the frequency with which *the* is omitted from these phrases. There are eighteen occurrences of *end of* in CorTxt, and ten of *rest of* (see Figure 6.11).

Other frequent phrases with *the* in texting include prepositional phrases referring to place or to travel: *on the way* (17), *on the bus* (6), *in the car* (10), *to the cinema* (13), *at the pub* (12), *in the pub* (18), and *on the train* (12), among others. As with time phrases, these highlight the role of texting in coordinating future social arrangements.

The 29 occurrences of *by the way*, a discourse marker involved in organizing text segments (see Chapter 5), are interesting because, while the time and place adverbs explicitly reflect the purpose of texting, *by the way* highlights interpersonal considerations in a similar way as with *a bit*. Specifically, *by the*

```
1 it should b back by the end of week - not happy
2  issue delivered by the end of the month. Deliver
3 nt to the run up to the end of term! Nothing els
4    near coming near the end of Cornwall now, so
```

```
1  looking forward to the rest of the month! See
2   to do? What about the rest of me?! What day
3 e thats cool, enjoy the rest of your day. Hey y
4  ice weekend, enjoy the rest of your night and
5    Should be in for the rest of the evening t
6  should be nice for the rest of the week.
```

Figure 6.10 Selected concordance lines for **the end of** and **the rest of**

```
1 nds good! Txt u towards end of day re exercise.
2 ·spuds r gud! Only until end of today. This is fro
3  ess. Won't find out til end of july - another co
```

```
1 'ham. Have a jolly good rest of week xx Hello! T
2  but Sat fine too. Enjoy rest of hols x We're her
3  orting tomo now. Enjoy rest of wk! E x Hope w
```

Figure 6.11 Concordance lines for **end of** and **rest of**

way indicates to interlocutors how the text segment which it introduces relates to previous sections of a text message, namely, a 'temporary digression from the previous segment or a shift in topic' (Carter and McCarthy, 2006, p. 262).

In CorTxt, *by the way* can either precede the 'text segment' it introduces (17 occurrences) or follow it (12).

6.11   Not yet. Just i'd like to keep in touch and it will be the easiest way to do that from barcelona. *By the way* how ru and how is the house?

6.12   Jolly good! *By the way*, NAME57 will give u tickets for sat eve 7.30. Speak before then x

6.13   At home *by the way*

Three text messages begin with *by the way*. (These should be seen in the context of the wider interaction, but unfortunately, previous text messages are missing from these exchanges.)

6.14   *By the way*, 'rencontre' is to meet again. Mountains dont. . ..

6.15   *By the way*, i've put a skip right outside the front of the house so you can see which house it is. Just pull up before it.

```
1   ian network! All fine here. Btw, am back friday morn
2    tty fab thanks 2 me! Hehe btw NAME87 where were
3  Tee hee. But ta for invite. BTW, running late and mi
4    elly, how r u? Hows work, btw how r they 4 staff
5   ws on what ur doin 2nite?! Btw do i nt get x x x's
6    monday, probably all day, btw did you know this we
7     wot the details Yeh yeh. btw NAME13s access have
```

Figure 6.12 Selected concordance lines for *btw* in texting

6.16   *By the way*, make sure u get train to worc foregate street not shrub hill. Have fun night x

Again, it is interesting to note that this frequent phrase also occurs in a form, the initialism *btw* (8), without *the*.

This brief analysis show how *the* occurs in prepositional phrases used for the purposes of discussing arrangements (*in the morning* and so on) and also in interpersonal phrases such as by the way. However, in explaining word frequency, we see a less strongly phrasal use of *the* than of *a*.

6.7 Chapter summary

In this chapter, I detailed an investigation of words and phrases in CorTxt, which used the corpus linguistics tool of frequency to drive the analysis. It is necessary to note that this approach was but one way in which an analysis could proceed, and other studies driven by different data sets or different purposes would be very different. I should add that my investigation was also driven by an attempt to work as much as possible with raw data – for example, with word frequency lists. Other studies may use 'keyness' (whereby the *significance* of a word's frequency is taken into account) and other statistical measures; it is now also possible to automatically generate variable phrases as well as fixed ones using Wordsmith Tools (see Notes on Methodology below).

This study illustrates how a particular way of approaching corpus data (through word forms and frequency) can reveal something different about the discourse; something which may not be evident through other analyses. The reversal of the frequencies of *the* and *a* is intriguing, and can be explained only in part by the speech-like nature of Txt and the tendency for texters to omit words. The other explanation is their occurrence in the phrases that recur throughout, and may be said to characterize, CorTxt. These phrases, as a 'fingerprint' of the discourse, reveal participants to be maintaining and extending relationships through the organization of future social arrangements through texting. Crucially, for the argument regarding the frequencies of *a* and *the*, *a* appears to occur more frequently in the phrases most frequently used to fulfil these functions.

As a final note, what then can we say about the function of phrases? For this, we must look to psycholinguistic studies. I noted earlier that phrases are seen to reduce users' processing loads, particularly in spoken conversation conducted in real time, because chunking reduces the items that speakers must retrieve from their 'information store'. Kuiper's (2004) studies of sports commentators and auctioneers, for example, suggest that speakers regularly performing under pressure rely on formulaic language to relieve the demands on their memory resources. Similarly, the easing of hearers' processing effort and their understanding of what speakers tell them is also achieved through formulaic language. According to Wray A. (2002, p. 95), formulaic phrases such as *I wonder if you'd mind . . .* draw hearers' attention to requests which may then be expressed in more novel ways. (Of course, speaker and hearer may not always share the same formulaic phrases, in which case the onus may be on the speaker to adapt to the hearers.)

Is this likely to be a function of phrases in texting? Probably. Although text message conversations are not conducted in 'real time', it appears that people often write quickly and may draw on ready-made phrases in order to convey a message as quickly as possible.

However, this role in cognition is not the only function that phrases are thought to fulfil. They are also seen to oil the wheels of interaction in other ways, by organizing speaker–listener relationships and constructing social identity, and it is these functions that I have focused on in the above investigation (in part because statements about the interactive role of functions are easier to defend in data-based analyses than assertions about cognition). As described previously, texters in CorTxt organize and monitor their relationship with their listeners though lengthy phrases such as *I just wanted to let you know that . . . .*

According to Wray A. (2002, p. 91), one reason for the fixedness of such formulae is to ensure hearers interpret utterances as polite, the effect of which is that such exchanges become rituals for which it is essential to learn the correct things to say in order to achieve communicative goals in smooth, non-face-threatening fashion (hence the apparent eagerness of parents to teach their children politeness formula: *don't forget to say X, did you say Y?* [Gleason, 1980, p. 252 in Wray A., 2002, p. 110]). Similarly, the use of phrases in CorTxt suggest a desire to be polite and to frame messages in ways that soften the potential abruptness of a statement.

Commonly used phrases may also express individual and group identity. Communities remember set phrases that distinguish them from others, from national anthems and pledges of allegiance to favoured quotations and rhymes (Wray A., 2002, p. 72). A language community is necessarily defined by the orientation of its members around shared language norms. Driven by 'desire to sound like others in the speech community' (Wray A., 2002, p. 75), individuals hear, store, use and thus contribute to stocks of politeness formulae, as well as shared turns of phrase and collocations. Inevitably, this use of formulaic language excludes those who do *not* belong to the group – see Kuiper's (1996) observation that formulaic sequences in auctions are restricted (despite the apparent need to reduce auctioneers' processing loads) by novice bidders present.

Text messaging practices have been described as 'codes' which outsiders (parents, teachers, journalists) find it difficult to decipher. These 'codes' (although arguably not usually as indecipherable as newspapers would have us believe) can be explained in part, like all language norms, by the phrases which emerge through interaction between a particular group of texters. What this also means of course is that different communities will use different phrases, and it is important – as I've argued throughout this book – not to see the phrases explored in CorTxt as necessarily reflecting those used by all texters.

6.8 Some notes on methods

My frequency word lists were generated using *WordSmith Tools*, available at a price online. One limitation to word frequency lists is that the significance of difference between frequencies cannot usually be assumed without statistical calculation of the probability that the observed differences are due not simply to chance (Leech et al., 2001, p. 16). This calculation can be done automatically using the keyword analysis tool provided by *WordSmith*, which compares a word frequency list to a reference corpus, such as the BNC (see Leech et al., 2001) to produce *keywords*. Keyword lists of course bring their own insights and limitations (Baker, 2004, pp. 349–57). And it should be remembered that both word frequency lists only ever serve as a way into the data and as an indication of what to explore (Sinclair, 1991, p. 31). Note that free software is also available, chiefly *AntConc* (http://www.antlab.sci.waseda.ac.jp/software.html). Software such as *WordSmith* and *AntConc* can also help in the identification and quantification of frequently occurring word strings or phrases.

NOTE

1. Have a good weekend; You all ready for *the* big day tomorrow?; have got a few things to do. May be in *the* pub later; Cant think of anyone with a spare room off *the* top of my head.

CHAPTER SEVEN

Everyday creativity in text messaging

7.1 Introduction

7.1   *[text message not included in corpus]*

    Chloe: Kind of. Just missed train cos of asthma attack, nxt one in half hr so driving in. not sure where to park.

           [text message not included in corpus]

    Chloe: Yes see ya <u>not on the dot</u>

           [text message not included in corpus]

    Chloe: Walking over.

           [text message not included in corpus]

    Chloe: From broad st. Can't walk fast, sets me off again. V nearly there.

Chloe, in her early thirties, and friend

Before looking at the kind of linguistic creativity illustrated by *not on the dot* in the above text message exchange, I'd like to think briefly about a wider connection between text messaging and creativity. Text messaging has inspired a range of creative responses in both poetry and art. Back in 2002, Emma Passmore won the second *The Guardian*'s SMS poetry competition (and £1500) with this entry.

I left my pictur on th ground wher u walk

so that somday if th sun was jst right

& th rain didnt wash me awa

u might c me out of th corner of yr i & pic me up

The judge, U.A. Fanthorpe, said: 'Clearly, the text poem has become an established form, and it has a head start because of its brevity. Many poems fail because they go on too long; some of these got by with hardly any words at all. I found that invigorating'. The idea that the constrained form of a text message is its artistic advantage is one I shall return to below.

To take another example, in October 2008, text messages sent by onlookers were projected (uncensored) onto a cloud of smoke over Trafalgar Square in London, thanks to art installation Memory Cloud, created by artists Stephen and Theodore Spyropoulos. Theodore Spyropoulos said, 'Smoke is the paper, and the light is the writing. It's a real conversation piece - people respond to what they see' (*The Guardian*, 17th September 2008).

Is there something about texting that inspires artists to use it in their work? On the one hand, the appeal of text messaging as an art form must lie in the fact that it serves as a powerful mode of personal expression and because of the intimate way in which people respond to it – so that a texting-inspired art installation becomes a 'conversation piece'. On the other, the need to be creative stems from the constraints within which a texter, or artist, must express themselves. As Fanthorpe went on to say, 'When words, or time, are limited, urgent sentiments come to the surface'; all that emotion and care packed into a hundred or so characters.

It is this same combination of self-expression and stringent constraint that nudges texters themselves towards linguistic creativity. In the third chapter of this book, I discussed how people respond to constraints such as the limited character allowance to put across complex social identities simply through the way in which they spell. Here are a couple of the messages I looked at.

7.2   Thankyou for ditchin me i had been invited out but said no coz u were cumin and u said we would do something on the sat now i have nothing to do all weekend i am a billy no mates i really hate being single

7.3   Ok that would b lovely, if u r sure. Think about wot u want to do, drinkin, dancin, eatin, cinema, in, out, about. . . Up to u! Wot about NAME408? X

Given the resources that texters have at their disposal with which to express themselves, variation in spelling can be seen as a creative and appropriate response to the technology and its communicative demands. In the media, 'textese' has been dismissed as 'dumbing down the English language' (Thurlow, 2006, p. 677) But what 'Txt' really illustrates is how the urge towards personal expression within such stringent constraints leads, as it were, to creative 'solutions'.

Now, if we look closely at the messages above, we can see that variation in spelling is not the only creative solution adopted by texters. For example, as I commented in Chapter 4, text message 6.2 above draws also on a speech-like clause combination. The focus of this chapter, however, are other creative strategies, of a kind associated with literary language but which are also frequent in spoken conversation: that is, repetition, metaphor, idiom and new word coinages. In the first message, the texter makes use of **repetition**. In particular, they use two three-part lists: *drinkin, dancing, eatin* and *in, out, about*. This is a rhetoric device, widely used in political speeches and advertising as well as everyday conversation. Think of the parallelism in Julius Caesar's *I came, I saw, I conquered* (or, in his words, *veni, vidi, vici*) and in a series of adverts for a French cheese: *Du vin, du pan, du Boursin* which accompanied images of idyllic picnics (itself exploited to good effect in the strapline of the more recent and playful Boursin adverts, *du vin, du pan, du tracteur*, as two lovers having a picnic are ploughed down by a tractor).

In the second of the two text messages above, the texter uses an idiom *Billy no mates* and this idiomatic language creates a more powerful evocative effect than would a more literal wording ('I don't have any friends', say). This brings us to the text message cited at the start of the chapter (6.1), where the effect lies not in the use of a familiar and evaluative expression, but the way in which it has been manipulated: *see ya <u>not</u> on the dot*. (Later in the chapter we shall see how another texter manipulates *billy no mates* for effect.) Again, the idea that texters may use idiomatic language goes against the general portrayal of texting as a curtailed and dry means of expression. What I want to show in this chapter is that language play of this kind occurs as a result of, rather than despite, the constraints, in allowing texters to express often intimate and personal emotions, and that in this way the constraints are best seen as affordances.

I shall start by looking at the work of researchers into everyday creativity in spoken language, before comparing this with examples of repetition, idiom manipulation and wordplay in CorTxt. Although there are similarities between the way in which language is manipulated in conversation and text messaging, we shall also see some forms of creativity uniquely encouraged by the affordances of the mobile phone.

7.2 Creativity in everyday interaction

What exactly do we mean by creative language use? The word is to an extent misleading because 'creativity' is associated with such things as originality, singularity and genius; the few among us with powers of creativity and invention tend to be lone individuals blessed with divine inspiration (or at least that of unknown origin). For that reason, some linguistic researchers prefer other terms – Guy Cook (2000) writes about language play; Joan Swann (2006) about artful language. But these terms do not quite hit the mark either. What we are interested in here is creativity as an ordinary, collaborative practice in which most people engage during normal interactions – sometimes but not always playfully, sometimes but not always artfully, sometimes but not always consciously.

A distinction suggested by Ronald Carter (2004) captures both the playful and the less conscious aspects of creative language. **Pattern re-forming creativity** is so-called because it stands out and disrupts the surrounding discourse, and includes overt, often amusing language play such as punning or playing with idioms. Carter's examples come from CANCODE, a corpus comprising 5 million words of spoken interaction. The following exchange, in which one participant manipulates an idiom and both participants laugh, illustrates the kind of creativity which Carter describes as pattern re-forming.

A: He won't forget this time.

B: Brian, can you see those pigs over my left shoulder moving slowly across the sky?

[A and B both burst into laughter]

(Carter, 2004, p. 23)

Although often amusing, pattern reforming creativity also serves various interpersonal functions. On the one hand, it can create or reinforce solidarity – as most immediately evident in the above spoken exchange, creativity can bind participants together, highlight shared backgrounds and show how and where viewpoints converge. However, it can also indicate divergence, as is potentially illustrated above with B's response, which shows where he diverges from A's expressed opinion. So, creativity can also be used to challenge people, put forward a contrasting view and highlight different ways of seeing the world.

In contrast, Carter's **pattern forming** or **reinforcing** creativity refers to a more covert echoing or repetition of sounds, words and structures, which both Carter and Tannen suggest structures everyday conversation. In the following example from Tannen (1989, p. 66), Deborah Tannen (herself a participant in her data) describes the mutilation of someone's finger in a 'contraption'. The grammatical structure in the last three turns acts as a kind of 'frame', which the speakers manipulate to indicate agreement with the others and to emphasize where their views differ. The point is that this example of language manipulation is not as conscious, nor as humorous, as the above and may not have been particularly noticed by the participants (except of course by the linguist, Deborah Tannen, hiding in their midst). There is, for example, no laughter accompanying these spoken turns.

David: What contraption?

Steve: I don't want to hear about it.

Deborah: You don't want to hear about it.

. . .

David: We want to hear about it.

(Tannen 1989: 66)

Tannen (1989) describes such repetition as a cohesive device and as an 'involvement strategy'. As an involvement strategy, suggests Tannen, repetition within an exchange can allow speakers to show 'listenership', as well as playing an evaluative role by providing emphasis, evaluating preceding utterances and indicating where views diverge. Utterances are, of course, rarely repeated verbatim but with variation in form – such as in the above example where only the 'frame' (*want to hear about it*) is repeated and the variation within it allows the speakers to compare their views with the initial speaker's (*You don't want to hear about it*) and contrast them (*We want to hear about it*).

The distinction between pattern forming and pattern re-forming creativity is not of course as straightforward as the above examples make it seem. It is not possible to distinguish the two without recourse to participants' intentions and reactions, and what people mean and what they think are generally not easily available to the researcher. Instances of repetition can in fact appear very noticeable and potentially humorous.

Deborah: Rover is being so good.

Steve: I know.

Peter: He's being hungry.

(Tannen, 1989, p. 63)

Most importantly, however, the distinction between covert echoing and language play also overlooks the argument that repetition may be a strategy or resource underlying *all* creative patterns, even overt and amusing language play. According to Tannen (1989, p. 97), repetition underlies creative strategies including punning and idiom manipulation and is 'a limitless resource for individual creativity and interpersonal involvement'.

To go back to our spoken examples, then, repetition underlies the creativity in *Brian, can you see those pigs over my left shoulder moving slowly across the sky?* just as it does in *Rover is being so good – He's being hungry*. The difference is that while the latter involves an immediate repetition across turns within a particular exchange, the latter is a kind of repetition across time – and across discourses. I pointed out above that the effect of the former comes from its departure from the canonical 'pigs may fly'. Paradoxically, however, its impact also comes from its 'sameness'; the fact that the speaker is drawing on a shared repertoire of cultural expressions. One has to be familiar with 'pigs may fly' to appreciate the irony of the reworded form. As Sarah North (2007, p. 539) puts it, creativity is novel in that it constitutes 'new combinations of existing elements rather than of creating something out of nothing'.

So, what we have with both pattern forming and reforming creativity is repetition, but in neither case is the repetition a matter of saying the same thing twice. Instead, the structures are 'crafted to be relevant' to the immediate context of the unfolding interaction. They have, in effect, been recontextualized rather than repeated. This is very evident in the case of *Brian, can you see those pigs over my left shoulder moving slowly across the sky*. However, the same can be said for repetition within and across turns. Even when someone repeats themselves, the utterance, even if repeated verbatim, will mean something different the second time around.

> Why is there repetition in conversation? Why do we waste our breath saying the same thing over and over? (Why, for example, did I write the preceding sentence, which paraphrases the one before?)
>
> (Tannen, 1989, pp. 47–8)

The repeated utterances are not the same; instead, they build on and exploit the original to make the overall meaning.

Where are we, in terms of defining creativity? The creativity we are interested in in this chapter is not the original work of a lone genius, but a collaborative practice in which people draw on and manipulate familiar expressions for various interpersonal effects in contextually relevant ways. The distinction between pattern forming and reforming is a useful one in encompassing both language play and the less obvious echoing or patterning of language forms, but it suggests a misleadingly clear-cut division between the two. In actual fact, in different ways, all creative language practices rely on repetition: that within an exchange or across discourses. We shall see this in the examples I shall show you presently from CorTxt.

Before I do so, let me say a word on the prevalence of creativity across various informal contexts. Creativity of the kind described above has been found to be a normal feature of spoken conversation by a number of linguistic researchers, including David Crystal (1998) as well as Swann, Cook, Tannen and Carter mentioned above. Research has also identified creativity in informal writing such as diaries and personal letters. In the study of death row prisoners in the United States and their British pen pals, for example, Janet Maybin (2010) found examples of metaphors introduced and then sustained across the correspondence, as well as a use of three-part lists such as we saw above.

Meanwhile, studies of computer-mediated communication reveal similarities with creativity in spoken language and also show how differences result from the distinct digital context. The similarities can be explained because, like spoken conversation, online interactions are often informal, relations are equal and participants, to use Carter's (2004, p. 110) phrase 'jointly co-construct playful discourse with the aim of aligning, harmonising and sharing ways of seeing, so re-forming and reinforcing the informality of the relationship'. At the same time, the visual aspect of computer-mediated exchange may increase participants' awareness of their language use – and hence the extent to which they play with language. For example, users may also return to and reflect on earlier messages in a way not possible in speech. In her study of an Internet discussion board, North (2007, p. 546) suggests online interaction 'is thus particularly favourable to punning, which can take place after a time lag which in face-to-face situations would scupper any humorous effect'. Goddard (2006) illustrates a similar observation with the following example of a pun from her chatroom data. Andrew's play on 'chat' can be linked back to the opening remarks between him and Ryan, and it appears that the pun is evident to both of them.

Ryan ≫ i like chat
Andrew ≫ its good isn't it
Ryan ≫ rather.
LucyN ≫ hi Andrew
Ryan ≫ we can all be friends
Andew ≫ Hi Lucy, I thought the chat had got your tongue, excuse the pun
Ryan ≫ nice

(Goddard, 2006, p. 257)

Text messaging similarly encourages a playful focus on language. As we shall see, repetition and wordplay serves to form both textual and social cohesion in texting, as it does in online chat – that is, linking together utterances and forming bonds between speakers. There are differences between online creativity and that in texting, due to the different constraints that users face. Unlike online chat, texting is relatively asynchronous and texters may read and reflect on their own messages more carefully before they are sent (encouraging what I shall call 'metacommentary', which I shall describe later). Texters may also tend to pick up on the language in the most immediate of their interlocutor's messages given that conversation threads are not easily accessible on mobile phones – at least before the popularity of smartphones (which is when this study took place). So, as we shall see, creativity in texting differs in some ways from both spoken and online practices.

In the following sections, I shall discuss examples of creative language use in CorTxt. I look first at repetition across and within turns, that is, how words or structures are echoed within the same exchange. We will see here that repetition plays a cohesive role, as well as an evaluative one. I then focus on two creative strategies: manipulation of idioms or fixed expressions and wordplay. You should see throughout how the particular affordances and the functions of text messaging shape the kind of creativity that occurs – so that it is sometimes but not always like that of spoken conversation. Please stop after each section to reflect on whether you recognize the creativity I describe in your own texting practices – either in the text messages you send or in those you receive.

7.3 Repetition across turns in CorTxt

Examples in which grammatical 'frames' are repeated across turns in CorTxt include the following. In each case, the repetition arises because the interlocutor is addressing a question posed in the preceding text message, or is echoing a sentiment expressed by their interlocutor, and so the function of the repetition is to provide cohesion. In other words, the repetition serves an **anaphoric** function – it refers back to earlier parts of the text, a function normally associated with pronouns or . However, the repetition also serves an evaluative function.

7.4   <u>Can you use foreign stamps</u> for whatever you send them off for? Xx

<u>Can not use foreign stamps</u> in this country. Good lecture x.

7.5   Hello! How r u? Im bored. Inever thought id get bored with the tv but I am. Tell me <u>something exciting has happened there</u>? Anything! = /

<u>Not a lot has happened here</u>. Feels very quiet. NAME6 is at her aunts and NAME15 is working lots. Just me and NAME43 in at the mo. How have you been? X

7.6   I am back. Bit long cos of accident on a30. Had to divert via wadebridge. <u>I had a brilliant weekend</u> thanks. Speak soon. Lots of love xxx

<u>I had a good time too</u>. Its nice to do something a bit different with my weekends for a change. See ya soon xxx

The repetition is cohesive in that it links the response back to the question (or back to the initial sentiment). It may be that this practice is considered necessary in ensuring clarity, given that there can be delays between an initial response and a response (i.e. because texting is **asynchronous**) and because a text message can contain a number of somewhat disjointed responses or queries. I once received *The latter!* as a response to a text message and, as my phone doesn't save my sent messages and my own memory is poor, I had no idea which of the options I had given my friend had been the last one. As well as this cohesive role, the echoing of interlocutors' words can be seen to show listenership (that the texters are listening and responding closely to their interlocutor's demands). At the same time, the ways in which each repeated part follows and departs from the original wording can be described as evaluative. In 7.5, for example, *Not a lot has happened here* emphasizes the extent to which the reality of the situation departs from A's need to hear that *something exciting has happened there*.

In each of the following examples, the second texter responds to the first by repeating a phrase, as above (shown by underlining). They then use the same syntactic frame to emphatically extend their sentiment (shown in italics). The repetition here is perhaps more playful than in the examples above.

7.7   Thanks honey but still haven't heard anything I will leave it a bit longer so not 2 crowd him and will try later - great advice thanks xxx hope <u>cardiff is still there</u>! Xxx

Sounds like a plan! <u>Cardiff is still here</u> *and still cold*! I'm sitting on the radiator!

7.8   Hi hope u r both ok, he said he would text and he hasn't, <u>have u seen him</u>, let medown gently please xxx

Hiya, sorry didn't hav signal. <u>I haven't seen</u> *or heard* from NAME79 and neither has NAME281, which is unusual in itself! I'll put NAME281 on the case and get him to sort it out! Hugs and snogs. Xxx

7.9   Did he say how fantastic I am by any chance, or anything need a bigger life lift as losing the will 2 live, do you think <u>I would be the first person 2 die from N V Q</u>? XXX

He said that he had a right giggle when he saw u again! <u>You would</u> *possibly* <u>be the first person2die from NVQ</u>, *but think how much you could sue for*! Xx[1]

As well as playing a cohesive role, the repetition in each case suggests a positive evaluation of the preceding utterance (in the sense of expressing agreement with it), and shows how the texter's response builds on the original utterance. These examples also illustrate repetition *within* a turn, as in 7.7, *Cardiff is <u>still</u> here and <u>still</u> cold*. As Tannen (1989, p.51) suggests, this device somewhat paradoxically adds emphasis both to the repeated part (*still*), and to the new information (*cold*) – and is explored with further examples later.

The need to connect ideas between text messages also means that, rather than pronouns being used as a cohesive device, nouns mentioned in a first text message are often repeated in the second. As in the examples below, these repeated nouns occur without the determiner or modifier.

7.10   Aah bless! How's <u>your arm?</u>

Arms fine, how's Cardiff and uni? Xx

7.11   Have you heard about <u>that job?</u> I'm going to that wildlife talk again tonight if uwant2come. Its that2worzels and a wizzle or whatever it is?! Xx

Hello. No news on <u>job,</u> they are making me wait a fifth week! Yeah im up for some woozles and weasels. . . In exeter still, but be home about 3. X

7.12   Hey there! Glad u r better now. I hear u treated urself to <u>a digi cam,</u> is it good? We r off at 9pm. Have a fab new year, c u in coupla wks! X

<u>Camera</u> quite good, 10.1 mega pixels, 3optical and 5digital dooms. Have a lovely holiday, be safe and i hope you hav a good journey! Happy new year to you both! See you in a couple of weeks! Xx

What is interesting about the above text messages is that the cohesive strategy is not particularly speech-like. In face-to-face interaction, it could be assumed that ellipsis, pronouns or other anaphoric references would be used – so that *Camera* in 7.12 would be replaced by *It's*. The use of this kind of repetition in texting to connect utterances in a second text message with relevant parts of the preceding text message again appears to be encouraged not only by the asynchronicity of texting but by the fact that, unlike online discussions, previous text messages are not available for reflecting on while the next are written (except in smartphones). However, in each case, repetition serves not only a cohesive but an evaluative function, which appears to be that of heightening familiarity towards the object in question. *Arms fine* and *no news on job* assumes in a casual fashion that the texter does not need to specify which arm or job they are referring to.

A final practice to be mentioned in this chapter is how the immediate repetition of phrases can recontextualize a phrase or word as a concept or 'thing' which can then be evaluated. This can be seen in the following exchange.

7.13   . . . Are you in the pub?

sorry, no, have got few things to do. may <u>be in pub later.</u>

I like to think there's always the possibility of <u>being in a pub later.</u>

Discussion of whether the first texter is in the pub becomes a discussion of the concept of *being in a pub later*, and this allows evaluation. In this case, an apparently positive view of *being in a pub* is expressed: a wryly humorous statement that also tells us much about the first texter's sense of identity. A similar process occurs in the following through repetition of the adjective *cheap* and its transformation into a 'thing'.

7.14   Well, I was about to give up cos they all said no they didn't do one nighters.I persevered and found one but it is very <u>cheap</u> so i apologise in advance.It is just somewhere to sleep isnt it?

I like <u>cheap</u>! But i'm happy to splash out on the wine if it makes you feel better.

In summary so far, much lexical and grammatical repetition across turns in CorTxt plays a cohesive role, as indeed it does in spoken conversation. However, cohesion in the text messages differs from that of spoken language. One example is the repetition of (reduced) noun phrases rather than pronouns, encouraged by asynchronous features of the medium. Repetition in CorTxt also plays an evaluative function, with recontextualized phrases serving to add emphasis and to evaluate preceding utterances. These phrases can signal both where texters converge and where they disagree: an urgent *Tell me something exciting has happened there!* met uncooperatively by *Not a lot has happened here.*

7.4 Self-repetition in CorTxt

Self-repetition in texting also plays an evaluative role. In this first example of self-repetition in CorTxt, we see repetition of the phrase *with the stick*.

7.15   Am watching house – very entertaining – am getting the whole hugh laurie thing – *even* <u>with the stick</u> – indeed *especially* <u>with the stick</u>.

This is in reference to the American medical drama *House*, in which British actor Hugh Laurie plays a doctor with a limp and walking stick. As in *Cardiff is still here and still cold*, the repetition serves to emphasize both the repeated part and the new information, in this case *especially*. The intensifier *indeed* emphasizes the structural similarity of the two phrases and highlights the way in which the effect of the second part builds on or exploits the first.

So, this should not be interpreted as a case of self-correction. Instead, *especially with the stick* adds to *even with the stick* to create the overall intended meaning (i.e. that the texter finds particularly attractive something which should apparently detract from Hugh Laurie's charm). The syntactic parallelism in this example illustrates the apparent role for repetition in indicating stance in text messaging. Similar examples include the following:

7.16   I think I'm waiting for the same bus! Inform me *when* <u>you get there</u>, *if you ever* <u>get there</u>. NAME71 x

7.17   <u>They can</u> try! <u>They can</u> get lost, *in fact*. Tee hee

7.18   I jus hope its true that NAME281's <u>missin</u> me cos i'm *really* <u>missin</u> him!
        You haven't done anything to feel guilty about, yet. Xx

The practices described above, whereby the repetition of a structure adds
to the overall meaning, are extended in a practice described below as
metacommentary. Metacommentary is facilitated by the affordances of the
texted medium that allow texters to refer to an earlier part of the same text
message and explicitly comment on it. In contrast to spoken utterances,
texting as a written medium leaves a record of an unfolding 'turn'; in
contrast to synchronous online discussion, texters may have more time or
inclination to reflect on text messages before sending them. The fact that the
medium also allows for 'mistakes' to be deleted suggests that the 'mistake'
and its 'correction' in fact combine to make meaning. In other words, the
metacomment refers back to and alters interpretation of the preceding part
to create meaning.

7.19   I'll have a look at the frying pan in case it's cheap or a book perhaps. <u>No
        that's silly a frying pan isn't likely to be a book</u>

7.20   Ok. Not much to do here though. H&M Friday, cant wait. Dunno wot
        the hell im gonna do for another 3 weeks! Become a slob- <u>oh wait, already
        done that</u>! X

7.21   Shall I bring us a bottle of wine to keep us amused? <u>Only joking</u>! <u>I'll bring
        one anyway</u>

The metacomment in 7.19, part of a discussion about buying Christmas
presents and designed to amuse, may have emerged as a consequence of the
texter re-reading the text message and noticing the grammatical ambiguity.
For this analyst and possibly the textee, the metacomment serves to
reinterpret what may otherwise be read as a straightforward suggestion. In
example 7.20, *Become a slob- oh wait, already done that!*, the metacomment
is integral to the meaning and alters interpretation of the suggestion that
the texter will *become a slob*, while reinforcing the texter's frustration with
the situation. Finally, *I'll bring one anyway* (7.21) rephrases the original
offer to bring a bottle to jolly along a holiday photo viewing session. The
utterance works as a whole to draw a careful balance between amusing and
not offending.

Other instances of repetition explicitly indicate texters' awareness of the
medium. Text messages drawing on references to predictive texting failures
include these.

7.22   If you text on your way to cup stop that should work. <u>And that should be
        BUS</u>

7.23   Urgh, coach hot, smells of chip fat! Thanks again, especially for the duvet (<u>not a predictive text word</u>). Xxx

7.24   Thanks NAME270 and NAME56! <u>Or bomb and date as my phone wanted to say</u>! X

In 7.22, *cup stop* becomes *BUS*; *duvet* becomes *not a predictive text word* and *NAME270 and NAME56* become *bomb and date*. It seems possible that the texters wished to share either their amusement at the technology's failure – examples 7.22 and 7.24 seem to me particularly likely to amuse; or their frustration, which may be more likely to account for example 7.23. As in examples 7.19 to 7.21, the effect of these metacomments relies on the apparent choice by the texters to comment on what they perceive as a mistake rather than deleting or correcting it (a choice not available in speech). In doing so, they draw attention to and recontextualize the original utterance – just as we saw in the other examples of repetition above.

7.5 Idiom manipulation in CorTxt

In this section, I suggest that the manipulation of idiom and fixed expression in CorTxt is, as in all discourses, a balance between repetition and divergence. That is, the idioms depend for effect firstly on participants' familiarity with a recognized and repeated expression, thus creating convergence in the sense that a shared repertoire is drawn on. The impact is heightened by the varying extents to which each idiom is altered within the particular context. This is illustrated in the example from CorTxt which I cited at the start of this chapter in its full context.

7.25   Yes see ya <u>not on the dot</u>

As the longer conversation showed, this text message was sent as part of an exchange held as Chloe made her long and painful way to a rendezvous with a friend. The utterance *see ya not on the dot* depends for its impact firstly on participants' familiarity with the expression *on the dot* ('exactly') before they can appreciate any intended evaluative impact within the context of this particular exchange. In this case, we could speculate that the choice of expression emphasizes the late arrival, and perhaps the breaking of an earlier promise to be on time. Its effect comes from a balance, in this particular context, between the familiar and the new. Other examples of fixed expressions are as follows.

7.26   Did you show him and what did he say or could u not <u>c him 4 dust</u>?

7.27   <u>I've got some salt, you can rub it in my open wounds if you like</u>!

7.28   Good good, <u>billy mates</u> all gone. Just been jogging, again! Did NAME42 enjoy concert? X

In 7.26, use of the idiom *c him 4 dust* illustrates the role that idioms play in increasing intimacy, heightening intensity and facilitating evaluation. As I suggested above, idiomatic language can have greater impact than literal phrasing. In this case, *c him 4 dust* appears to conjure up a vivid image of someone quickly and recklessly departing, without regard for those left behind. It does this very succinctly. We could conjecture that the use of this idiom is thus encouraged by the affordances of the medium, in particular the shortness of messages. This suggests a particular role for repetition (in the form of idiomatic language) in texting. At the same time, this use of the idiom is embedded in the particular context – as is reflected in the characteristically text-like orthographic variation.

In 7.27, the texter exploits the idiom 'rubbing salt in an open wound' presumably to point out some insensitive comment made by an interlocutor. In this case, its rewording further heightens the intimacy, intensity and evaluation. Its non-canonical form gives it fresh impact by indicating irony, while suggesting that the texter is also complicit in the harm being done: *I've got some salt*. Its rephrasing also makes it more personal, not only because it has been crafted for the occasion but because it directly address the interlocutor: *you can rub it in my open wounds if you like!*. Its impact relies on a shared understanding of the idiom which is being reworded and this increases the intimacy.

'Billy no mates', as we saw earlier in this chapter, refers to someone with no friends. In 7.28, the expression seems to have been interpreted as comprising analyzable components that allow *billy mates*, in reference to the friends Billy once had. The implication, presumably, is that the texter now feels friendless or alone. The sameness to and departure from 'billy no mates' lends it its impact, which relies on shared knowledge and some inference from the reader.

Having suggested earlier that such creative practices are 'overt' and noticeable, I'd like to address the question as to whether it is possible to gauge texters' awareness of their language play. Of course, to an extent it is not possible and can merely be conjecture. Linguistic awareness may, however, be apparent in the following through the texter's metalanguage – that is, the language they use to talk about their own language use. Even if the texter is simply revealing that they do not know how to finish or add to the idiom, *and all that!* seems to indicate awareness that they are drawing on (or repeating) the prefabricated expressions of others.

7.29   Don't give a flying monkeys wot they think and I certainly don't mind. Any friend of mine <u>and all that</u>!

The addition of *and all that!* also gives the impression that the texter is drawing on a much wider and presumably shared repertoire of supportive expressions (even if the truth may be that *Any friend of mine* is all that they can recall). A similar sense of awareness is suggested in the following.

7.30   Guess which pub im in? Im as happy as a pig in clover <u>or whatever the saying is!</u> X

7.31   here is my new address POSTALADDRESS-apples&pairs<u>&all that</u> malarky

Co-construction of idiom manipulation also suggests awareness, in that texters are picking up on and extending each other's creative language use. In the following, two texters discuss plans to meet the following week. We see the combination of two idioms in the first turn and how the interlocutor picks up on them in subsequent turns.

7.32   Sorry, left phone upstairs. OK, might be hectic but would be <u>all my birds with one fell swoop</u>. It's a date.

Can help u <u>swoop</u> by picking u up from wherever <u>u n other birds</u> r meeting if u want. X

That would be great. We'll be at the Guild. Could meet on Bristol road or somewhere - will get in touch over weekend. Our plans <u>take flight</u>! Have a good week x

Deliberately or otherwise, the two idioms which the first texter draws on, 'in one fell swoop' and 'two birds with one stone', are semantically quite closely linked: firstly, in that both refer to an arc – the throw of the stone and the trajectory of the swoop; and secondly, in that a bird is said to swoop down for prey. What is interesting, however, is the way in which the second texter picks up on the idioms and incorporates them into an offer to give A and friends a lift, *Can help u <u>swoop</u> by picking u up from wherever u n other <u>birds</u> r meeting if u like*. The close attention paid to the other's words heightens intimacy and level of involvement, and this is reciprocated in the final text message in which the metaphor is extended with *Our plans take flight!*

To sum up, recontextualized idioms in texting not only indicate intimacy and heighten intensity but also capture evaluative attitudes and emotions otherwise difficult to express in this constrained medium.

7.6 Wordplay

In this section, I shall look at two kinds of wordplay: word coinage, and then punning. Word coinage of the kind I am interested in tends to involve some degree of morphological inventiveness: that is, where people play with the morphemes that make up a word. Common examples in spoken conversation are the morphemes –*y* ('my eyes are bluey') and –*ly* ('it's greenly challenged', to take an example from Carter's corpus where friends are describing the night's meal in terms of the lack of vegetables). In effect, morphological inventiveness involves the combination of familiar elements into new forms. This can be seen in the following examples from CorTxt.

7.33   Hi - can you do me a favour, pleasey? Have a look soonish and tell me the date i received my ma certificate? Thanks <u>lotsly</u>! Xx

7.34   <u>Beerage</u> tonight?

In example 7.33, *lots* is given an ending typical of adverbs, –*ly*, which intensifies the sentiment and makes it sound more intimate. It does so, I think, partly because of the unexpected pairing of *lots* and *ly*, and partly because of the sound (*lotsly* is alliterative, while –*ly* resembles the diminutive –*y* seen above in *pleasey*). *Lotsly* seems to be part of a wider strategy to hedge a request through the use of morphology: as well as *pleasey*, there is also *soonish*.

In 7.34, *beer* is given a common noun suffix, -*age*, which may refer to an event larger than the drink itself. It can do this because of the suffix's association with nouns, and in particular mass nouns such as *coverage* or *baggage*. As with *lotsly*, the word is striking to the reader, in the way that it combines existing elements into a new form: again, it is the balance between sameness and difference. It resembles the tendency in Britain for railway station announcers to talk of the *platformage*. I have also heard the term *lolage* used in online chat. A similar process in CorTxt produces *workage*.

7.35   No worries, hope photo shoot went well. have a spiffing fun at <u>workage</u>. X.

In the examples below, wordplay appears to be encouraged by earlier parts of the utterance.

7.36   Printer is cool. I mean groovy. Wine is <u>groovying</u>

7.37   Hello! All well hope you are ok too. Looking forward to seeing you. R u driving or <u>training</u>?

In example 7.6, the texter corrects *cool* to *groovy* to describe the printer (this in fact occurs because their interlocutor had previously expressed preference for *groovy* over *cool*). The texter then plays on the polysemous meaning of 'cool' to describe the wine not as 'cooling' but as *groovying*.

Similarly, in 7.7, the apparent act of changing a noun to a verb in *training* (meaning 'taking a train') may be encouraged by the preceding verb, *driving*. This can also be seen in this transformation of the drinking game *I Have Never* into a verb, which again follows another verb *flowing*.

7.38   The wine is flowing and <u>i'm i have nevering</u>.

How can this wordplay be explained? Texters engage in it despite the fact that the practice often involves more key presses and the coinages are not recognized by predictive text devices. As the above examples suggest, the purpose is interpersonal: to evaluate, intensify sentiment or heighten intimacy. These examples also suggest a playful medium, and one in which its users are not primarily concerned with abbreviation and saving time. Finally, texters' capacity to create 'new' words in meaningful ways from existing elements suggests morphological awareness, as it does in spoken interaction.

Puns, which also occur in CorTxt, are typically described as exploiting grammatical, phonological or semantic ambiguities. As a feature of spontaneous conversational humour, puns are recognized by linguists as fulfilling various interpersonal functions in talk. North (2007, p. 548) suggests that verbal play in online discussion contributes in a rich, complex way to textual and social cohesion and creates common viewpoints. Like asynchronous online interaction, which allows participants time to reflect on messages and spot ambiguities, texting may be particularly suited to punning.

For example, in 7.39 below, the idiom *have the stomach for it* appears to be encouraged by the initial mention of *belly dancing*. Both the figurative and the literal meaning of the idiom are foregrounded, with the suggestion perhaps being that B's midriff may have some bearing on her aversion to the dance.

7.39   A: Ooh, 4got, i'm gonna start <u>belly dancing</u> in moseley weds 6.30 if u want 2 join me, they have a cafe too. F

      B: Not sure I have the <u>stomach</u> for it . . .

      A: Yeah right! I'll bring my tape measure fri!

      B: Ho ho - big <u>belly</u> laugh! See ya tomo x

Other examples are as follows.

7.40   A: Goodo! Yes we must speak friday – egg-potato ratio for tortilla needed! Xx

      B: Okay but i thought you were the expert

      A: Yes obviously, but you are the <u>eggs-pert</u> and the <u>potato head</u> . . . Speak soon! Xx

7.41   Have you been practising your curtsey?

I've got it down to a <u>tea</u>. not sure which flavour

Eggs-pert in 7.40, a discussion around a recipe for tortilla, not only works as a pun but is itself a morphological creation. *Eggs-pert* does two things – it refers back to 'expert' in the previous message and to 'eggs' in the turn before that, playing on the phonological similarity between *ex* and *eggs* presumably to suggest that the first texter is in fact the expert when it comes to this particular recipe. In other words, it repeats and combines elements of the earlier message to create a new form which has its own meaning. *Potato head* does two different things – it draws on a common idiom (actually not very appropriately, as the idiom usually describes someone as stupid) while referring back to the tortilla's other ingredient. In this case, the pun draws on a prefabricated expression but how it is interpreted (humorously, as someone knowledgeable in making tortilla) is shaped by its immediate context.

The exchange in 7.41 occurred prior to the second texter attending a lunch with the Queen. The second texter is male and unlikely to curtsey, and the question can be interpreted, in this light, as a playful meronym regarding his general preparedness for the occasion. He responds to his interlocutor's humour with *I've got it down to a tea*. This is a version of *getting it down to a tee* which could be described as a manipulated idiom, but which also makes a pun (accidentally or otherwise) on the homophone *tea/tee*. This may draw on an association between two very British institutions: the Queen and tea-drinking. The texter then reflects back on, and extends, the pun with *not sure which flavour*. This draws attention to the pun, while casting doubt on the effectiveness or nature of his curtsey (interpreted as his level of preparation).

While the chief function of these puns may be amusement, the close attention paid to interlocutors' words and the effort made to manipulate them heighten intimacy and show listenership. As examples of recontextualized difference, puns work on both the levels described in this study, drawing on and evaluating previous utterances while recontextualizing idioms and fixed expressions.

7.7 Chapter summary

In this chapter, I started from the observation that the fairly stringent constraints of text messaging have inspired a range of creative responses, in poetry, art, film. These same constraints – better seen as affordances – also shape the creative practices engaged in by texters as they use the medium to fulfil communicative and often highly expressive purposes. What I seek to do in this chapter is to show that spelling variation is not the only creative 'solution' tried by texters. I do this by describing how at least one group of mature, well-educated, largely monolingual texters draw on the kinds of creative practices documented in spoken interaction. (Pause for a moment to reflect on how the creative practices described in this chapter reflect yours.) These practices have previously been neglected in sociological and linguistic studies into texting which tend to focus on creativity in abbreviation, ellipsis, phonetic spelling and omitted spacing.

My investigation of CorTxt shows, firstly, that the creative strategy of repetition plays a significant role in cohesion in texting. Cohesive devices in texting such as the repetition of (reduced) noun phrases (*a digi cam* to *Camera*) are not very speech-like, but encouraged by asynchronous features of the medium. Creativity in texting also plays an evaluative role. Local repetition such as *They can try! They can get lost, in fact*, morphological creativity as seen in *beerage*, or idiom manipulation such as: *see ya not on the dot* suggest that the desire to display identity, indicate stance and emotions and signal a sense of intimacy and belonging are focal concerns when texting. However, to reiterate, texters do not indulge in expansive language play *despite* constraints of the medium. Instead, repetition, idiom manipulation, wordplay and metacommentary are shaped by the particular functions and affordances of the medium. As in much spoken conversation, texters engage in playful, intimate interaction; while the visual nature of texting may particularly encourage and facilitate a focus on form. Furthermore, unlike online chat, texters have time to reflect and craft their messages.

What are the implications for the debates surrounding texting? My findings relate to text messages composed by educated adults and should not be generalized to different social groups – you may or may not recognize the same practices in the text messages you send and receive. Instead, the findings highlight the need for parallel corpus-based research involving other groups, such as children. What this study shows, however, is that the affordances of texting can be exploited in creative ways according to the capabilities of the individual, and it thus challenges the assumption that texting *per se* is damaging to literacy. Research carried out by Beverly Plester, Clare Wood and colleagues (e.g. Plester and Wood, 2009) is already suggesting that the respelling practices engaged in by children as young as 10–11 correlate with greater achievement at reading and spelling in school tests. This greater understanding of the creative possibilities of texting suggests new considerations for research into links between educational attainment and text messaging.

7.8 Some notes on methods

This particular study emerged as a result of my 'noticing' examples of creativity when reading concordance lines or exchanges, in much the same way as Ronald Carter reports with CANCODE, in his groundbreaking study of spoken creativity. Creativity cannot be identified through automated searching, which relies on reoccurring and predictable surface features, and so, as with CANCODE, examples in CorTxt were found through reading extracts taken from the corpus. I have not therefore quantified findings. Instead, like Carter, I offer examples which I consider representative of different kinds of creativity occurring throughout the corpus. Inevitably, their representativeness, as Carter points out, 'must be taken on trust'. It should be pointed out that most text messages in CorTxt are *not* creative, including informative and transactional functions such as: *I'm in sollihul, do you want anything?* However, analyzing extracts from CorTxt suggests that as many as 10% of messages show some element of creativity.

7.9 Further reading

There is a growing literature on everyday language creativity. As well as Carter (2004), Cook (2000), Crystal (1998), Maybin and Swann (2006), and Tannen (1989), you could consult Swann et al. (2011), as well as works on humour and 'joking' (e.g. Norrick, 1993; 2003). For further discussion of language play in online contexts, see Danet et al. (1997), Danet (2001), Fung and Carter (2007a), Tagg and Seargeant (2012).

Note

1 National Vocational Qualifications (NVQs), are work-related qualifications set up in the UK in 1980s.

CHAPTER EIGHT

Performing identity through text messaging

8.1 Introduction

\<Thunder\>	sssssssssss *passes joint to kang* . . .
\<Kang\>	thanx dude *puff* *hold* \>:-)
\<Thunder\>	kang exhale. . . you will die:-)
\<Kang\>	*exhale*
\<Kang\>	;)
\<Kang\>	:|
\<Kang\>	:|
\<Kang\>	:\
\<Thunder\>	heheheh
\<Thunder\>	heheheheh
\<Thunder\>	that was great
\<Thunder\>	:-Q:| :| :\sssss:)

(Internet Relay Chat data, from Danet et al., 1997)

It was only really in the 1990s – after many people had been using the internet for several years – that researchers moved from a description of online communication as an impoverished, transactional means of exchanging information to reconceptualize it as a liberating, playful place in which you could discard offline identities and become 'quite literally, whoever you wish' (Reid, 1991, p. 16). The interaction at the start of this chapter is taken from one of the first studies to explore how identities are performed online. The participants in the Internet Relay Chat (IRC) chatroom are simulating a party and the smoking of a joint. Their performance is constructed through a variety of creatively deployed graphic symbols. Thunder simulates the exhaling of smoke through repetition of the letter <s>, and then uses asterisks to frame the action of passing the joint to Kang, who inhales and holds his breath, as shown by the concentrated forehead in the smiley > :-). Later, Kang represents the actions of holding and exhaling through other smileys:

> <Kang> :|
> <Kang> :|
> <Kang> :\

Thunder responds with his own, more elaborate performance of someone with a cigarette in his mouth, who holds and exhales in a line of <ssss> and then smiles: :-Q :| :| :\sssss :). Through their performances, Kang and Thunder create the illusion of a relaxed, informal situation and they construct themselves as young, playful daring party-goers. The point is, of course, that they may in 'reality' not be any of these things. 'Kang' and 'Thunder' are both nicknames, and it is impossible for other participants to know how old they are, where they are from, or whether they are male or female. Many studies of chatrooms in the 1990s picked up on this theme of online anonymity (e.g. Donath, 1999) and, in particular, the fact that anonymity allows people to deconstruct offline identities, and then reconstruct them (Reid, 1991). This is possible partly because chat users tend to interact with people they do not otherwise know; and partly because, in a virtual interaction, users cannot access much social information about their interlocutors, other than details which interlocutors choose to 'give' through what they write, or signals that they unconsciously or accidentally 'give off' (to use Goffman's [1959] terms). Thus, 'Babydoll', an IRC user in Reid's (1991) study, confesses:

> Well, I gotta admit, I shave a few lbs off of my wieght when I tell the guys on irc what i look like..

It is therefore tempting to see online and offline worlds in a binary, polarized relationship, with people in anonymous chatrooms (the online world) able to free themselves from identities which in the offline world are fixed, unitary and as much a part of people as their bodies. As Donath (1999) put it in her study of early online forums, 'in the disembodied world of electronic communication, identity floats free of the stable anchor that the body provides in the real world'.

But does such a dichotomy between online and offline identity exist? It is easy to think of situations in the offline world where people may perform identities that do not match who they appear to be in other contexts – a salesperson who puts on a welcoming smile and officious manner when a customer comes into view, someone trying to impress on a first date, teenagers with their parents as opposed to teenagers with their friends and most people when their boss comes into view. People generally focus on different aspects of their personality or call on distinct ways of behaving, with different people.

If we accept that people are able to perform various 'identities' in their interactions with different people, it becomes difficult to say which, if any, of these performances constitutes the individual's 'real' identity. Indeed, we can see that 'identity' is not fixed or stable; instead, it is something that we actively put together and present to others. What we call 'identity' is thus constructed through our interactions with other people – what we emphasize or foreground about ourselves, what we suppress, how we want to come across in a particular moment. That is not to say that we are free to be *anything* we want, because people are constrained to varying extents by their circumstances, the norms and expectations of the society around them, and by some sense of individual self (formed, in part, through previous interactions). We can see similar constraints online. For example, a man can choose an online nickname – or 'nick' – which suggests he is female, but he may not be able to give a convincing online performance as a woman. The point is that although the anonymity of the internet may provide opportunities for people to hide or foreground certain aspects of their identity, this extends – rather than contrasting with – offline practices.

One way in which the performance of identity via online communication does differ from offline, spoken practices is that people have different resources available to them. In face-to-face interactions, people can orient towards a particular identity through their clothes, manner, actions, general appearance and so on. In online communication, all social and personal information must be constructed through text, using graphic resources such as in the IRC chat at the start of this chapter. Throughout this book, you have read about the kind of linguistic resources available when texting – respellings that reflect spoken pronunciations or that index certain identities, the use of grammatical features and discourse markers associated with speech, the repeated use of certain phrases, parallelism, idiom manipulation and wordplay. Thus, although the nature of the identities that people convey through online interaction will be shaped by consideration of who they are addressing and interpersonal features of the particular online context, the way in which this identity is performed will necessarily be shaped by features of the technology.

In this chapter, I discuss how the contributors to CorTxt draw on these various linguistic resources to create or perform social identities. I start by discussing sociological and linguistic discussions of identity and interaction, and then look at some recent studies of identity performance online, before exploring how the linguistic resources described in this book contribute to the performance of identity in text messaging. The texters concerned – as with most texters – generally know each other well in offline contexts, and my argument is not that they seek to deceive their interlocutors or to construct identities that contradict their offline selves. Their identity performances draw on elements of their offline relationships, performances and personae, as well as their responses to the features and affordances of the technology, and the particular contingencies and demands of the immediate unfolding interaction.

8.2 Identity and interaction

The notion that **identity** is constructed in interaction owes much to the ideas of US sociologist Erving Goffman in the mid- to late twentieth century. Goffman (1959) described social interaction in dramaturgic terms. People in everyday interaction, he argues, work together to put on theatrical **performances** for audiences, while taking on the role of audience for the dramatic performances of others. He starts from the observation that even when people are engaged in a task, they are simultaneously acting a part. For example, like Preedy, an Englishman on holiday in Spain, when on their own, people may put as much effort into conveying a certain impression to those around them, as they do to *actually* reading their book or enjoying their inner thoughts.

> If by chance a ball was thrown his way, he [Preedy] looked surprised; then let a smile of amusement lighten his face (Kindly Preedy), looked round dazed to see that there *were* people on the beach, tossed it back with a smile to himself and not a smile *at* the people, and then resumed carelessly his nonchalant survey of space.
>
> Sansom, (1956) *A Contest of Ladies*, cited in Goffman
> (1959, p. 16)

When interacting, Goffman argues, people can normally be described as working in teams, whose members cooperate in maintaining a particular interpretation of the situation. Team members must therefore present a united front in the face of the audience, and not undermine their team mates. Teachers, for example, may avoid contradicting each other in front of their pupils: a teacher in a study cited by Goffman (1959, p. 95) said: 'Just let another teacher raise her eyebrow funny, just so they [the children] know, and they don't miss a thing, and their respect for you goes right away'. Unlike performers and audiences, team members also share a 'backstage' relationship that they perform when the stage curtains come down and they can relax into more informal roles. Consider how teachers act during a break in the staff room, in contrast to their behaviour on supervision in the playground or teaching in class; or how a married couple might relax once their guests have gone; or how differently waiters might interact in the dining room and in the kitchen. Goffman cites George Orwell as noting:

> It is an instructive sight to see a waiter going into a hotel dining-room. As he passes the door a sudden change comes over him. The set of his shoulders alters; all the dirt and hurry and irritation have dropped off in an instant. He glides over the carpet, with a solemn priest-like air.
>
> Orwell (1951, p. 68) cited in Goffman (1959, p. 123)

Often, of course, the backstage roles are as much performances as the ones at the 'front' – is a husband more 'himself' with his friends or with his wife? Goffman's argument is not that some interactions are more or less contrived or real than others, but rather that people's social lives comprise a complex show of constructed fronts as they collude in different teams – on stage or backstage – to present versions of themselves. As Goffman (1959, p. 245) puts it, a person's identity, or self

> is a product of a scene that comes off, and is not a cause of it. The self, then, as a performed character, is not an organic thing that has a specific location, whose fundamental fate is to be borm, to mature, and to die; it is a dramatic effect arising diffusely from a scene that is presented.

Goffman's social actors may appear unrealistically egotistic, goal-driven individuals, but the underlying analogy is useful in understanding the often unconscious ways in which people manage social interactions. His focus was not specifically on the linguistic resources that people use in identity performances. However, language is often a potent symbol of people's identities (e.g. in Wales, it may be said that language is the prominent emblem of Welsh identity) and can thus be a vital part of people's performances. Language can be significant in two senses: firstly, in that *what* people say constitutes part of their projected identity; secondly, in that *how* they say it – the level of formality, choice of vocabulary, accent, dialect features and so on – will be intricately linked, by the speaker and others, to their social identity.

The first point can be related to the notion of 'performativity'. Philosopher John L. Austin noted in *How to do things with words* (1962) that certain verbal utterances – such as 'I do' or 'I declare this library open' – do not describe a pre-existing state of affairs (as with 'oh, it's raining') but bring such a state into being. That is, through the act of uttering 'I do' or 'I declare this library open', one performs the respective acts of getting married or opening a library. In Butler's (1993) words, they constitute an 'aspect of discourse that has the capacity to produce what it names'. Austin called these utterances 'performatives' but very soon realized that other 'speech acts' could similarly be seen as bringing states into being. If you promise to do something, you perform the act of promising and you have tied yourself to a future course of social action; if you ask something of me, you have performed a request, and you are committing me to a future course of action. Thus, the acts of promising or requesting – or refusing, inviting, ordering, advising – themselves perform social actions and bring future actions and interactions into being.

Philosopher and feminist Judith Butler extended this notion of 'performativity' to address the construction of identity, specifically gender identity. She argued (in line with Goffman's work) that gender is constructed and reaffirmed through discourse, that is, the roles that we associate with men and women are the result of their repeatedly being performed in interaction with others. Thus, we can say that gender roles are discursively constructed. This insight highlights the fact that people are active producers of feminine and masculine roles, rather than having them passively assigned at birth, and it also explains variability in how gender is constructed. It is evident that people can, and do, perform gender differently depending on who they are with and other circumstances. Linguist Deborah Cameron (1997, p. 60) points out that '[e]ven the individual who is most unambiguously committed to traditional notions of gender has a range of possible gender identities to draw on' and suggests that

> [p]erforming masculinity or femininity 'appropriately' cannot mean giving exactly the same performance regardless of the circumstances. It may involve different strategies in mixed and single-sex company, in private and in public settings, in the various social positions (parent, lover, professional, friend) that someone might regularly occupy in the course of everyday life.

Being a woman, for example, can take a very different form when with a group of other women as opposed to being with a male partner. Goffman describes how American college girls would play down their intelligence and take on intellectually inferior roles to their boyfriends. For example, they 'allow their boy friends to explain things to them tediously that they already know; they conceal proficiency in mathematics from their less able consorts; they lose ping-pong games just before the ending' (Goffman, 1959, p. 48).

Cameron (1997) also illustrates this variability with her study of the conversations between a group of five heterosexual male college students in the USA while watching soccer on the television. Although they exhibit many of the features thought to be typical of male talk – competitiveness, jokes, insults, and conversation about sport – they also engage in a practice not normally associated with men, that of gossip or 'rapport talk'. In particular, the group engage in critically examining the appearance and behaviour of gay men they know. Cameron argues that this seemingly untypically male practice serves to establish their group identity as 'red-blooded heterosexual males' (1997, p. 62) which sets them apart from the homosexual group. In other words, their gossiping is not a subversion of masculine identity but a 'performance of masculinity' appropriate to the situation – the situation being a conversation between a group of heterosexual males anxious to define themselves as being *not* homosexual. In mixed-sex interactions, these men may avoid gossiping, in order to distance themselves linguistically from 'women' and define themselves as being not feminine. As Cameron (1997, p. 61) concludes, 'What counts as acceptable talk for men is a complex matter in which all kinds of contextual variables play a part'.

In relation to the second point, studies by sociolinguist Penelope Eckert elaborate on how, in their performances of identity, people draw on and adapt various linguistic resources, alongside other aspects of their manner or appearance. She focuses on the orientations of Californian high school students towards one of two social roles – jocks or burnouts. Jocks are 'squeaky clean' and school oriented, involved in either athletics or school politics, while burnouts reject school activities in favour of the downtown area where they eventually find jobs. Although jocks and burnouts in fact account for only half the high school students researched, the salience of their roles is such that others define themselves as 'in-betweeners', in relation to the two groups. And although the two social groups are strongly class related – few jocks are working class and vice versa – the exceptions suggest that allegiance to one or other of the social groups is more important in determining linguistic choices than social class.

> Like their clothing and activities, the jocks' linguistic style conforms with their institutional engagement and aspirations. Their grammar is overwhelmingly standard. The burnouts' anti-school stance, on the other hand, shows up clearly in their non-standard grammar. Thus, for example, it is not surprising that while the burnouts show a tendency to use patterns of nonstandard negation (e.g. I didn't do nothing), this pattern is rare in the speech of the jocks . . . . This little linguistic fact is not a reflection of what the jocks and burnouts 'know', since the burnouts do use a good deal of standard negation and there is no burnout who uses 100% non-standard negation. Thus while for some of the burnouts the use of non-standard negation might indeed come more easily, it is clear that in many cases it constitutes a stylistic choice.
>
> (Eckert, 2007, p. 127)

The use – or non-use – of non-standard grammar illustrates the fact that although, in Eckert's (2007, p. 125) words, 'the basic features of our dialect are set in place by the environment in which we grow up, the actual deployment of those dialect features – as well as of many linguistic features that are not part of regional dialects – is left to individual agency'. In other words, people can pick and choose from an existing array of available linguistic features in constructing their own style; a practice which Eckert calls 'bricolage'. In turn, people's stylistic practice serves to relate them to the social group, or social identity, which is associated with that style. And we can add that people's performances construct and then repeatedly affirm (or challenge) the connection between certain linguistic features, certain styles and certain identities.

In this section, I've explained how identity is constructed through performances that people put on in the course of their everyday interactions. Linguistic resources are used alongside other resources in the presentation of self, as people select from the linguistic features available to them – that is, ones that are socially meaningful in their communities and culturally acceptable – in order to foreground particular aspects of their identities. As discussed in the next section, online interaction is no different – although the linguistic resources and communities that people experience in an online situation may differ from in some ways from those which they are familiar with in offline contexts.

8.3 Performing identity online

What happens to someone's repertoire of potential linguistic markers of identity when they go online? We've already noted that, in much online communication, there is a reduced access to paralinguistic features – such as tone of voice and gesture – and to non-linguistic resources – clothes, appearance, posture – that form part of people's stylistic practices in offline, face-to-face interaction. The lack of these social features appears to focus attention on what is available: namely, textual and graphic resources (Androutsopoulos, 2012, p. 3), which are often constrained through limited character allowance, size of keyboard and screen, and so on. For example, people on Twitter can send only 140 characters per Tweet comprising words and emoticons (and, of course, URLs to other webpages); online chat users are constrained not only by space but also the speed with which turns are expected; and the mobile phone texters which I studied sent an average of around 17 words per message and they largely did so without the benefit of a QWERTY keyboard. Perhaps it is unintuitive for some that these constraints (or affordances) may in fact encourage creative performances. However, as you saw in chapter 7, brevity can encourage a creative manipulation of form, as people try to put as much expression as they can into the limited character allowance; this is of course also encouraged by the informality of the typical online or texted interaction.

One can also argue that the attempt to represent verbal and auditory cues in writing – as we've seen with respellings that reflect spoken pronunciations – relies on and in turn heightens users' awareness of these features (Danet et al., 1997). That is, in speech, someone can adopt certain pronunciations or dialect features without fully being conscious of what they are doing – but they will only recreate in writing those features of which they have some awareness and knowledge. Hence suggestions that people may represent a greater number of non-standard dialect features in online communication than in speech (Esther Asprey, pers comm., works with Black Country youth who draw particularly extensively on dialect forms online) or that people may draw creatively on the resources of a language they do not normally use in spoken conversation (Tagg and Seargeant, forthcoming, explain how the online mixed language practices of a group of Thai-English speakers contrast with their claims to speak only in Thai when speaking to each other).

Another factor is that communication online – say, on social network sites like Facebook – may be seen as more public than private spoken conversations, so that when somebody heavily uses dialect forms (or other features), they are carving out an identity for a group in the presence of (and perhaps in contrast to) various other groupings or outsiders. In contrast, online communities that are based around a shared interest rather than a geographical proximity may need to reach a shared sense of identity among individuals who are from varied backgrounds. Reid (1991) notes that

> [t]he emergent culture of IRC is essentially heterogeneous. Users access the system from all over the world, and – within the constraints of language compatibility – interact with people fromcultures that they might not have the chance to learn about through any other direct means.

So, what the above suggests is that features typical of much online interaction today – the resources available, the potential for a heightened sense of linguistic awareness, the formation of communities in new or public spaces – may encourage a particularly creative and concerted effort at the construction and performance of social and group identity.

A number of studies illustrate this in relation to particular online communities (Fung and Carter, 2007a; Jones, 2007; Tagg and Seargeant, forthcoming). For example, Jones (2007) shows how Welsh-English bilingual girls use the 'free' spaces of MSN – beyond the strictures of the family, the school and the wider political context – to construct identities by playing with and mixing English and Welsh in ways that they would not in spoken conversation. Jones (2007, p. 48) suggests that "MSN-ing' is fun for Ffion (one participant in her study) because she can play around with something that is taken so seriously by those around her, from her family to her teachers and political leaders'. What is taken so seriously in Wales is, as mentioned earlier, the Welsh language as a symbol (perhaps *the* symbol) of being Welsh. The identity that Ffion presents online, then, is one of deviance from the standard (language) norms around her.

Jones (2007, p. 45) concludes that 'the girls, through their choice of language alone, are positioning themselves as 'deviant' from the discourse of the Welsh language which dominates much of their lives'. In this case, the online context provides a liberating context in which the girls feel free to foreground certain elements of their (shared) identity, and to subvert the dominant discourses of the political and educational spheres. The point which I wish to draw out of this study is that Ffion's linguistic choices, and the identity she constructs on MSN, emerge from a particular constellation of contextual variables, both those that reflect and those that subvert her offline world.

In the next section, I look at examples of linguistic resources in CorTxt and speculate on the role they play in the performance of identity through texting. I suggest how the idea of identity as performance can serve not only to explain texters' linguistic choices, but can also explain variation in their practices, and is useful in assigning texters an active role in constructing 'Txt'.

8.4 Performing identity in CorTxt

One of the first things that struck me as I started analyzing the text messages I had collected was that although many texters appeared to adopt various strategies of abbreviation, it was far from evident that they were necessarily trying to keep their text messages short. In other words, brevity appeared not to be primarily or consistently their main concern. Abbreviated forms would occur in otherwise quite lengthy text messages, and factors other than the need for brevity were evidently involved in decisions as to which forms would be abbreviated, and how. Let me illustrate this with the following text message, which shows how texters' abbreviating practices can be both selective and partial.

> 8.1   Hey i know ur at work but i just wanted to let u know that i found my pen lid. . .it was in the bin:)x

There are two instances of compression in this text message, the homophones <ur> and <u> and the lack of spacing within *in the bin:)x*. However, it is notable that these occur in an otherwise unabbreviated sentence. We could suggest that there are further opportunities for abbreviating (in line with practices described in this book) – the texter could respell *know* both times as <no>, for example, and they could also compress the sentence grammatically, omitting the pronouns *i* and *it*. It is a somewhat dubious exercise to start rewriting a text message in ways that the texter *could* but *didn't* write it, but the point is that the homophones do not occur as part of a thorough attempt to abbreviate the text message. You have also seen this in relation to grammatical ellipsis in Chapter 4, in text messages such as the following where some elements are omitted and others are not.

> 8.2   R u sure they'll understand that! Wine good idea just had a slurp!

In this text message, the copular verb *is* and the article *a* are omitted before *good idea*, while the article is retained in *just had a slurp*. The need to abbreviate cannot provide a full explanation as to what is omitted and what is not, and this is the case across the corpus. Take, for example, the following text messages (also discussed in Chapter 4). In the first, the situational ellipsis and respellings stand out as marked choices in an otherwise lengthy and expressive text message. In the second, the occurrence of *Am* and *i'm* within the same text message illustrates the fact that there are choices available to texters which go beyond the simple need for brevity.

8.3   No <u>am</u> working on the ringing <u>u</u> thing but have whole houseful of screaming brats so <u>am</u> pulling my hair out! Loving u

8.4   <u>Am</u> on a train back from northampton so <u>i'm</u> afraid not!

If the point of respellings and situational ellipsis is not primarily or consistently to abbreviate, then what are people doing when they use shortened forms? You have seen throughout this book that people's text messages appear primarily to be concerned with interpersonal matters – that is, most or all of a text message tends to be given over to oiling the wheels of a relationship. One could argue that, if brevity were the overriding consideration, the texter who had just found their pen lid in the bin could simply have said 'I just found my pen lid in the bin'. The rest of the text message is 'padding', if you like, discourse markers and formulaic phrases which serve an interpersonal rather than a transactional role, and the use of which give little indication that the texter is overly concerned with message length. A similar point has been made about many text messages throughout this book. You may remember, for example, that the creative practices described in Chapter 7 involve the integration of apparently abbreviated forms (underlined below) into playful, interpersonally orientated and expressive text messages.

8.5   Ok that would <u>b</u> lovely, if <u>u</u> <u>r</u> sure. Think about <u>wot</u> u want to do, <u>drinkin,</u> <u>dancin,</u> <u>eatin,</u> cinema, in, out, about. . . Up to <u>u</u>! <u>Wot</u> about NAME408? X

8.6   Ok. Not much to do here though. H&M Friday, <u>cant</u> wait. <u>Dunno</u> <u>wot</u> the hell <u>im</u> <u>gonna</u> do for another 3 weeks! Become a slob- oh wait, already done that! X

8.7   Sorry, left phone upstairs. OK, might be hectic but would be all my birds with one fell swoop. It's a date.

Can help <u>u</u> swoop by picking <u>u</u> up from wherever <u>u</u> <u>n</u> other birds <u>r</u> meeting if <u>u</u> want. X

That would be great. We'll be at the Guild. Could meet on Bristol road or somewhere – will get in touch over weekend. Our plans take flight! Have a good week x

In 8.7, the second text message is an elaborate reworking of the previous utterance, in which the first texter's playful use of *all my birds with one fell swoop* is picked up on and incorporated into the response; in this context, it is hard to accept that the use of the homophones <u> and <r> are chiefly to do with reducing the number of characters. Instead, if we accept that text messages have a chiefly interpersonal orientation – towards, that is, maintaining or bolstering relations with the interlocutor – then it seems reasonable to argue that decisions regarding which forms to shorten, and how, are made with this in mind. So, it may be that respelt forms play a more significant role in the interpersonal construction of identity than in actually shortening a text message. Rather than describing texters as seeking to shorten text messages through the use of abbreviations, we can thus see them as putting on a performance; performing brevity, if you like, in the light of the interpersonal significance that certain forms take on as a result of past interactions (through texting and in online contexts) and the wider media discourses that circulate around Txt.

Of course, brevity is not the only impression that texters convey through their performances in texting. In Chapter 3, you saw how non-mainstream groups such as punk fans use eye-catching phonetic spelling to position themselves as differing from or opposing others; and how teenagers' use of respellings in text messages had a similar effect in positioning them in opposition to their parents. In more subtle ways, the respelt forms in CorTxt similarly position texters as being unconventional, playful and potentially subversive. Thus, Alison, a well-educated, literate young adult, adopts a highly deviant texting style involving alphanumeric sequences which in fact diverges even from the practices of her interlocutors.

8.8   Hi NAME219 hope unis ok&u'r feelin gud Hows it bin wiv NAME227 since u got bac? Gud news bout the playscheme Look in 4ward 2see in u soon hav missd u lotsa love NAME330

8.9   Sorry, there was no way i was gonna make the wildlife talk, Wich is a bugger cos i wanted2go2that1. I can't go out2night i'm afraid. I've got2do some stuff4mum and me and NAME281 r going2the brean rally2moro and I've gotta pick him up at 8.30am! Sorry4being lame! Xx

The impression that these features give is impossible to determine, but she may be creating a distinct and playful identity for herself as a texter. (Alternatively, she may be seen as overacting – perhaps responding too closely to the picture of Txt presented in the print media and thus betraying a lack of familiarity with the technology or the practices of people who use it. Interestingly, this is a performance which Alison has since informed me she no longer puts on.)

While other contributors to CorTxt do not engage in such extreme performances of Txt, in many of their text messages the occurrence of forms such as the letter homophone <u> – which is the most frequently used respelling in the corpus – stands out to mark the discourse as unregulated and non-standard. It is a form associated with internet discourse and graffiti, rather than with a regulated space like the classroom.

8.10   Good idea. I finish at 7 today. U̱ wanna do it at home? U̱ going out tonight?

8.11   U̱ still in meeting. I've brought some lunch for wen u̱ finished. How long u̱ gonna b? Xxx

8.12   god, don't be silly, not worried in the SLIGHTEST! i was just having NAME325 on – something u̱ missed earlier. really no big deal. a+

The shared use of such unconventional forms simultaneously serves to demarcate group identity and heighten intimacy between interlocutors. The homophone <u> in the above examples does not come across as critical or derogatory, but as affectionate and intimate – *u* is perhaps to *you* what *thou* once was, if that's not too fanciful a notion – signalling intimacy and equality. So, rather than seeing <u> as an abbreviation strategy, or even as part of an attempt to create a façade of brevity, we can see it as having taken on interpersonal significance, as a marker of non-standardness and of closeness.

So far, I have argued that the features that characterize Txt can best be described as emerging from the ways in which texters perform brevity and non-standardness. The other apparent motivation for linguistic choices in texting is the attempt to imitate spoken utterances. Throughout this book, I have drawn comparisons between texting and speech, and have frequently described practices in CorTxt as 'speech-like'. The following messages include many features associated with speech, or with the representation of speech in writing – long sentences in which elements are strung together by commas or no punctuation at all, spoken discourse markers (*yeah, hmm, oh*), colloquial contractions (*ditchin, kinda, wiv, ad*) and eye dialect (*coz, wot*).

8.13   Thankyou for ditchin me i had been invited out but said no coz u were cumin and u said we would do something on the sat now i have nothing to do all weekend i am a billy no mates i really hate being single

8.14   Well done, blimey, exercise, yeah, i kinda remember wot that is, hmm. Xx

8.15   Hey bird. i'm gonna email you my very almost completed diss in a min. do what you can and give me a shout when you're returning it. thanks. oh and how are you anyway

8.16   Hello beautiful r u ok? I've kinda ad a row wiv NAME99 and he walked out the pub?? I wanted a night wiv u Miss u xx

8.17   Thought *praps* you meant another one. Goodo! I'll look tomorrow xx

8.18   **Oh sorry** I forgot that you're not at school! Ok cool see u later x

Firstly, however, it could be pointed out that the imitation of spoken forms cannot, like abbreviation, be seen as a consistent motivation underlying linguistic choices. For example, you saw in Chapter 5 that texters used some discourse markers (such as *oh*) very frequently; and others far less frequently (*you know*), although both are typical of speech. Divergences from spoken discourse are also evident in the fact that while much ellipsis in texting follows speech-like patterns, others do not. The following text messages, for example, contrast speech-like (8.19) and note-like (8.20 and 8.21) ellipsis.

8.19   Easy mate, guess the quick drink was bit ambitious.

8.20   Evening v good if somewhat event laden. Will fill you in, don't you worry . . . Head ok but throat wrecked. See you at six then!

8.21   Don't worry, is easy once have ingredients!

Similarly, clauses can be combined in ways that reflect a spoken utterance – where they are strung together with commas – or into short somewhat disjointed-seeming sentences reminiscent of a written note or postcard.

8.22   Dude, if you see NAME10 then don't mention you've spoke to me, she wants me to go to the pub and I cant be bothered and my mom goes on holiday tomorrow.

8.23   God it's really getting me down just hanging around. I hate not knowing. What did NAME72 say? How would she know? They'd be crazy not to take u. I'm worried. X

So, what this means is that the imitation of speech cannot be invoked as a full explanation for linguistic choices. More importantly, however, it is worth considering why texters should sometimes choose to create an impression of orality. Look back at 8.13, 8.14 and 8.15 above. What do you think the linguistic choices achieve in each of the text messages above? In particular, what emotion or stance do you think each texter is trying to convey?

Susie, in the first text message (8.13), is clearly angry and wants her interlocutor to acknowledge the consequences of their actions – she also, unwittingly or otherwise, comes across as being filled with self-pity (*i really hate being single*). These emotions are conveyed not only through the content of Susie's text message but how it is constructed, namely because the lack of punctuation creates a hurried and intensifying effect which highlights her distracted state. In 8.14, the texter appears mildly embarrassed, and the string of discourse markers and vague language (*kinda*) suggests to a reader that they've been caught out and don't quite know what to say. And finally, you saw in Chapter 5 how the composer of the last example above (8.15) uses the typically spoken discourse marker (*oh and*) as a way of framing the final utterance as an afterthought and in so doing heightens the intimacy, informality and humour of the text message in a way that an initial greeting would not do.

In other words, in each case, the main concern is not to 'sound speech-like' but to fulfil interpersonal purposes – to express an evaluative stance, to heighten intimacy, to signal informality. The forms that are typically associated with spoken language can be seen as resources that texters draw on in creating an impression of informality and intimacy. Thus, if you like, they are performing a speech-like informality, just as they perform being brief and non-standard.

The foregrounding of one or other of these aspects – brevity, non-standardness, speech-like informality – is one way in which texters can vary the impression that they give to interlocutors. It has been evident throughout this chapter (and book) that variation occurs as a result of people's idiosyncratic texting preferences, as well as consideration of contextual variables such as who is being texted, when and why. The notion that people have a distinct texting **idiolect** – a linguistic style that is peculiar to one individual – underlies recent forensic linguistic analysis of text messages sent by people involved in criminal cases. As discussed in Chapter 2, Tim Grant of Aston University gave evidence in a case in which a girl's murderer sought to give himself an alibi by sending text messages from her phone – but in fact gave himself away through the features that distinguished the text messages he sent from those already in her inbox. On a less sinister note, it is possible to identity differences in individual style within CorTxt. One vivid example is provided by Alison who, as you saw above, consistently uses alphanumeric sequences in the text messages which she contributed to the corpus – such as *wanted2go2that1* and *Lookin4ward 2seein* – within lengthy, highly compressed text messages which diverge from her interlocutors' practices. Other examples include the following case studies.

Laura often uses eye dialect forms such as <wot> and <u>, and the forms appear to strike a relaxed, intimate and playful tone. Note that Laura also plays with 'fish and chips' in the first text message below by transposing the initial letters and producing *chish and fips*, and that she uses a series of three-part rhetorical structures in the last (as discussed in Chapter 7) – *drinkin, dancin, eatin, in, out, about*. The respellings combine with these instances of everyday creativity in creating a sense of play and fun that characterizes many of her text messages.

8.24   We had chish and fips, off to comedy nite at tremough in a min. Wot
        about u? X

8.25   Um, i dont think i really know wot ur on about. Is it hay bales? R u tryin
        to win a bet?x

8.26   Ok that would b lovely, if u r sure. Think about wot u want to do,
        drinkin, dancin, eatin, cinema, in, out, about... Up to u! Wot about
        NAME408? X

You saw an example of Susie's text messages earlier in this chapter (and
throughout the book), in which she fires a somewhat rambling, angry
riposte at her sister's decision not to see her that weekend.

8.27   Thankyou for ditchin me i had been invited out but said no coz u were
        cumin and u said we would do something on the sat now i have nothing to
        do all weekend i am a billy no mates i really hate being single

The resources used to construct this performance – strings of clauses linked
by *and*, *but* or nothing at all and a selective use of colloquial contractions
and eye dialect forms – in fact characterize many of the 33 text messages
in CorTxt (all of which were sent to her sister). Note how, in 8.28 below,
a number of 'mistakes' accompany the loosely structured sentences – *there
visas*, *cant*, *us* (rather than US), *thats all*. Even the juxtaposition of *4* (*for*)
next to the number (*3 years*) looks clumsy. All these features contribute to
the impression that she creates of being in an agitated rush. In the third
message, you can see the interesting juxtaposition of respellings (*Just to let u
no*) and the rhetorical flourish reminiscent of formal or dated speech – *and
lo and behold*.

8.28   NAME182s mum has just emailed and there visas have been denied and they
        cant reenter the us 4 3 years thats all she said what are they going to do!

8.29   Just to let u no i got home safe and lo and behold i got an even smellier
        man sat next to me on the way back lucky me!

Kate's text messages, in contrast to many of the above, do not generally
contain many respellings. Instead, they are characterized by the use of hyphens
which separate the short clauses that typify her style. Note how, in 8.30, she
draws on a creative parallelism (discussed in Chapter 7) which exploits these
hyphenated clauses. This is also the case in the third text message below,
where the final outcome – *but i might say no on our behalfs!* – is also given
more emphasis by the preceding hyphen. There is also some possible play on
the use of *behalfs* rather than the more conventional *on our behalf* which
may highlight Kate's evaluation of the invitation to Croydon.

8.30   Am watching house – very entertaining – am getting the whole hugh laurie thing – even with the stick – indeed especially with the stick.

8.31   Hello there – haven't heard from you in a while – hope all is ok – please text!

8.32   Hi- are you coming up this weekend? It is NAME28's husband's birthday on sat and we're invited for a meal in croydon – but i might say no on our behalfs!

Finally, you saw one of Darcy's text messages in Chapter 5, in which he used a spoken discourse marker in *oh and how are you anyway* as part of his construction of an email that was highly functional, yet informal and intimate. This performance is one he repeats throughout the corpus, particularly in situations where he is asking for favours or discussing sensitive subjects. For example, he uses *oh and* again, in 8.34 below. In general, the text messages below illustrate his use of intimate forms of address – *Hey bird, Hey dude, Hey you'r're a legend* – as well as phatic and mitigating phrases such as *Dunno if you got my message but if its possible*, and some idiosyncratic punctuation and capitalization practices. The lack of question marks can be attributed to his belief that they are not necessary in text messages, given the familiarity between participants and the fact that the word order makes it clear that a question is being asked. However, he does use full stops to separate lengthy phrases.

8.33   Hey dude. Dunno if you got my message but if its possible could you please try to find out if NAME571 has got a turkey outfit. Cheers dude. See ya soon

8.34   hey you're a legend no i won't be spending it on booze. from this day on i am be sensible with my money mode. my plan is to be out of overdrafts etc by the end of the year. thanks again. oh and i booked the thai place.

8.35   Have you still got some of my jom carrey dvd's. can i have them back please

Despite the distinct ways in which these texters 'perform' Txt, it is not the case that they are fully consistent in the way they present themselves through texting (and, indeed, forensic linguists will only give an indication of the likelihood that a text message could have been sent by a particular individual). It seems reasonable to suggest that texters are unlikely to give the same performance to everyone but will vary their texting style according to their relationship with their interlocutors (e.g. friend or parent), the communicative function of the text message (asking a favour or passing the time in a pub) and the circumstances in which they are texting (public or private setting, for example). In different contexts, texters are likely to emphasize and suppress certain elements of their identity and thus co-construct with an interlocutor in any one instance a shared understanding of the immediate situation that will differ in some respects to the performances given in other texted interactions.

I'd like to illustrate this briefly with some further examples from Laura, who contributed 806 text messages to my corpus. At the time of the exchanges cited below, Laura, female, was aged around 30 and living in England. The above text messages (8.24 to 8.26) showed Laura's tendency to use eye dialect respellings such as *wot* and *u* to index a speech-like informality. She also tends to sign off with *x* (rather than *xx* or *xxx*).

However, if we look at other instances of Laura's texting behaviour, we can see that certain factors encourage variations in the linguistic choices she makes. In the following message to a friend who was on her way to visit her and had texted to find out which junction to come off the motorway, we can suppose a connection between the communicative function of the text message (in particular, the need for clarity) and the lack of respellings.

8.36   Megan: Hellow do I come off 23 or 24 of m5?

Laura: 23

Laura: Left on roundabout. Right at bottom of hill at t-junction. First left just in Bridgwater. Left at very end of that road. Continue all the way to westonzoyland!

The following text message to Laura's father is similarly written without respellings, but perhaps for different reasons. Here, there are no respellings nor grammatical ellipsis as she begins the text message – *I am flying off* – while the rest of the sentence is abbreviated only in way that we could associate with birthday cards and other written letters – *so just wanted to say . . ..* In other words, here Laura downplays the informality and non-standardness of her other text messages. However, there are also other features that mark this as a text message – note, for example, the lack of capitals for *congo* or *monday*.

8.37   I am flying off for congo tonight so just wanted to say happy birthday for monday! See you soon. Love laura x

In other cases, Laura foregrounds the features which typically mark her style as being informal, intimate and non-standard. The following conversation took place while Laura and a friend, Beth, were both watching the same rugby match in different pubs and getting progressively drunker as the match progressed. In this interaction, we can see Laura and Beth co-constructing the role of tipsy rugby supporters getting carried away, as they show their support for rugby player Jonny Wilkinson and then discuss their drinking, through the use of short turns and exclamations, a lack of punctuation and colloquial contractions such as *fella*, *ya*, *yup* and *init*.

8.38	Beth:	Jonny jonny jonny
	Laura:	Just watch that fella run!
	Beth:	Im battered
	Laura:	Good on ya. Where are you now? I took a break and ate some ice cream, back to drinkin now!
	Beth:	Oh no im on second bottle of wine and 5 bottles of breezer!
	Laura:	Bloody hell you go girl
	(later)	
	Beth:	Laura im still drinking
	Laura:	Yup me too – great init?!

Finally, in other cases, it may be her interlocutor's practices which determine which features Laura foregrounds and thus shape her own performance. In writing to Alison – who uses alphanumeric sequences (such as *wanted2go2that1*) – Laura uses *2do*, a feature she does not usually adopt but which she may do in this text message in an attempt to align herself with Alison, who she is trying (unsuccessfully, as Alison's response shows) to tempt out.

8.39	Laura:	Did u want 2do anything tonight? That talk in ilminster, out in town, dinner even? – mum is going out! Or r u doing something wiv NAME281? X
	Alison:	Sorry, there was no way i was gonna make the wildlife talk, Wich is a bugger cos i wanted2go2that1. I can't go out2night i'm afraid. I've got2do some stuff4mum and me and NAME281 r going2the brean rally2moro and I've gotta pick him up at 8.30am! Sorry4being lame! Xx

Although I started by highlighting Laura's typical choices (<wot>, <u> and so on) my argument is not that we should see Laura as diverging from the norm in certain exchanges, or that some usages are more contrived than others. It would, in a sense, be odd if Laura wrote to her father in the same way as she wrote to a tipsy friend when watching the rugby. The above text messages are all part of Laura's constructed identity, various elements of which she foregrounds in different performances, by drawing to differing extents on the linguistic resources at her disposal.

One of the outcomes of describing Txt in terms of the shifting and flexible performances of the people who produce it is that it grants them an active role in shaping the discourse. This is because the features associated with Txt cannot be seen as inherently or inevitably 'features of Txt', but rather as emerging from people's interactions through texting. In Shortis's (2007b, p. 2) words,

[r]espellings of Txt are 'natural', functional and uncodified and are interpreted and replicated by immersion rather than by formal instruction ... it is an orthography remade by users in their practices rather than one which depends on being received, learned and directly replicated in the manner of the acquisition of standard language spelling accuracy.

Although the respellings used in Txt are not completely 'uncodified', given that style guides and lists of 'SMS acronyms' abound (see the internet), they tend to be codified in a post-hoc fashion and it is fair to say that most people do not learn how to respell by consulting them. Specifically, it is difficult to imagine a practice whereby respellings are 'received, learned and directly replicated' in text messages – except perhaps by parents trying to understand what their children are doing – in the same way that spellings at school must be memorized and then unvaryingly and repeatedly reproduced.

Instead, respellings emerge during interaction (or 'immersion') in response to various interactive factors: accommodation to the practices of interlocutors, the value that people place on certain linguistic features and the meanings they bestow on them, the fulfilment of particular communicative functions (e.g. how informal people wish to appear), individual or group reactions to the constraints or affordances of the technology, as well as adherence or subversion the dominant discourses which circulate with respect to Txt (as you saw in the discussion of media reports on textese in Chapter 1). In other words, texters do not *learn* the respellings which they use in Txt, but they acquire or develop them as they interact with their interlocutors and, through repeated use, affirm and reaffirm them as being what 'Txt' is. Shortis's analogy of the 'orthographic palette' (introduced in Chapter 3) is thus rather apt. As Shortis (2007b, p. 21) explains,

> the less defined, determinate spaces of what counts as literacy in new text forms have created a context in which there has been an extension of the orthographic palette of meaning-making potential beyond the standard forms listed in dictionaries.

As Shortis argues, the 'normal' orthographic palette available to writers usually presents a binary choice of right or wrong. In unregulated online contexts, an 'extended orthographic palette' presents texters with a range of respelling options. Texters, this suggests, are free to use this palette not simply to select options but to create and to mix new colours as interaction proceeds – to extend, for example, existing orthographic principles to produce what to them may be new forms.

What is true of spelling is also the case for other practices noted in this book. It is these which are often overlooked in linguistic accounts of texting practices. In Chapter 4, for example, you saw that texters oriented towards two grammatical styles – one that seemed to reflect speech, and one in which ellipsis and clause construction diverged from practices noted in spoken interaction. These are not two pre-existing styles from which people select; instead, the styles emerge as the result of linguistic choices made and reiterated by individuals, so that the repetition of their performance creates the illusion of a fixed style (just as a dialect emerges from the repeated performance of certain features by a particular group of people). This is explicitly the case with the patterns described in Chapter 6, where I described how a 'fingerprint' of texting in fact emerges from people's repeated use of certain phrases. And in Chapter 7, you saw how instances of creativity are often co-constructed in contextually relevant ways across an unfolding interaction.

So, in the same way that gender is not what people *are* but what they say and do, Txt can be seen not simply as the language forms that people *use* when they text, but as the forms that are *created* (or co-created) through the interactive practices of texters. Informed by interlocutors' practices, driven by shared communicative purposes and social norms, and moved to converge around shared linguistic norms, texters tend to repeatedly enact similar actions through texting and to draw in similar ways on linguistic resources to do so. The language features of Txt result as an accumulation of these repeated performances of brevity, non-standardness and a speech-like informality. Thus, we move away from static descriptive terms that describe the language ('abbreviated', 'speech-like', 'non-standard') to look at how language patterns emerge from what texters are actually *doing* through texting. And what they are doing is co-constructing – with their interlocutors – understandings of their situations and the interactions in which they engage.

8.5 Chapter summary

In this chapter, I started from the observation, often made, regarding the freedom that people appear to have in constructing (or deconstructing) identity online. And this may be true, in virtual interactions between strangers. However, a binary distinction between online and offline worlds overlooks the fact that identity always emerges from performance, and that all interactions can be seen as performances of identity. In performing identity through texting, people have access to a different set of resources than those to which they are accustomed in spoken, face-to-face interaction. In the absence of social and paralinguistic cues – gesture, appearance, tone of voice, clothes – texters have recourse only to the text in presenting themselves and co-constructing a shared sense of identity. The textual resources to which texters have access include respellings, as well as the use of speech-like grammatical structures and discourse markers, and they draw on different configurations of these features in different contexts, with different interlocutors, and for varying purposes.

It is true to say, however, that much of CorTxt is characterized by a playful manipulation of linguistic resources. You saw this particularly in Chapter 7, but also in examples within this chapter and others. Many contributors seem to delight in playing with words and do so not only to amuse themselves and their interlocutors but as a display of affection and intimacy. It may be that other corpora of text messages will reveal similar practices; after all, it appears that texting is generally characterized by intimacy between texters. At the same time, different groups may tend – or be able – to access different resources and to suggest intimacy and informality through different means.

8.6 Further reading

There is a vast literature on identity and its discursive construction. Sources that relate particularly to online identity construction include Papacharissi (2010).

CHAPTER NINE

Text messaging in the World: the state of the art and its future

9.1 Introduction

> To: 050-5550555
> Salam! Here z the plan :) gather in
> al-3in mall. by 8 dubai. @ 10:30
> withdraw $ then get the dresses,
> invitation cards, c fatheya saloon,
> henna @ 2, hair 4, all @ 4:30 +
> makeup :)- take some pics @ go to
> the wedd. @ 19:30. c yal lolo.
> Latefa, AAN

Although this book has so far focused on the practices of a network of British texters, text messaging is undeniably a global phenomenon. The above is an entry by an Emirati woman in the Extremely Short Story Competition (ESSC) on the Arabian Peninsula (2008). It draws on familiar respelling practices (such as <c>, <pics>), truncated sentences and graphic resources (the emoticons, &, @) and other features associated with texting – length, topic, format) to create what people from most places could recognize as a text message. In other words, the story depends for its effect on a shared idea as to what Txt is like and on people making instant connections between certain features and texting. At the same time, it is clearly embedded in a local context, and many features may not be familiar to people outside the United Arab Emirates, or at least the Arabic-speaking world – the greeting *Salam!* and the numbers used in *8 dubai* and *al-3in*, for example. The entry thus illustrates two points that I wish to make in this chapter – firstly, there are certain features widely, if not globally, associated with texting; secondly, texting as a global phenomenon nonetheless emerges from the diverse practices of different local communities. As I suggested in Chapter 1, texting can therefore be called a **glocalized** practice, a global phenomenon that comes into being through an accumulation of localized practices. What this means is that any study of a group of texters (such as that described in this book) must be set in the context of the diverse local practices that are collectively known as 'Txt'. The practices described in this book will reflect and differ from those adopted by texters elsewhere, and must be understood in relation to this wider picture. It is this wider picture – the similarities and differences between the ways in which Txt emerges in different English-speaking communities across the world – that I shall go on to explore in this chapter. Also evident is that people's linguistic repertoires will not only or always include English resources. I also touch in this chapter on the extent to which practices observed in English text messages also take place in other languages, on how people select and combine resources from more than one language and how they choose between languages.

At the same time, any study must be considered as one historical instance in an unfolding story of technological and social change. What is happening *now* differs from what was happening ten years ago and will presumably have changed again in ten years' time. Already, as I write, I am aware of changes that have already occurred since 2007, when I stopped collecting text messages. For example, the increasing popularity of the smartphone (with various features that differ from earlier models and through which the internet is accessible) must be having an impact on the decisions made by people deciding when to communicate by text message, when by email, when on a social network site and so on. One question I wish to address is the extent to which these rapid technological changes render futile any attempt to make general statements about technology-mediated communication, and this is the question I address towards the end of this chapter. I will reiterate the point (implicit throughout this book) that technology is in fact not necessarily central to understanding what is going on when people text. It is not the technology that shapes communication, but how people perceive and value the technology and, ultimately, what they *do* with it. Generalizations are thus limited not so much by the nature of the particular technology being exploited but by the practices and values of the particular communities of individuals exploiting it.

By exploring these two themes – the diverse local contexts in which texting takes place in the world today and its position along a line of rapidly changing digital technologies – I seek in this chapter to contextualize the local study outlined in the rest of this book.

9.2 Text messaging around the World

In Chapter One of this book, I alluded to the way in which texting so unexpectedly and explosively took off at the end of the last century. However, some countries were quicker than others to develop what has been called a 'mobile culture', and Britain (where my study took place) was by no means the quickest, even in Europe. By the turn of the millennium, Scandinavians – particularly in Finland and Norway – owned the most phones per capita and used them the most frequently. For example, in 2000, the population of Finland (5 million) sent 1 billion text messages (Kasesniemi and Rautianen, 2002, p. 170).

Outside of Europe, however, mobile phone use was by this time yet more entrenched in parts of Asia. With respect to texting, the Philippines has been termed the texting capital of the world, with South Korea, Singapore, Taiwan, Japan and Hong Kong not far behind. In these largely economically developed countries, choices between whether to text or to call have depended in part on cost as well as on social expectations. Lin and Tong (2007), for example, attribute the preference for calls over text messages in Hong Kong to the fact that talking loudly in public places receives less social opprobrium there than in other countries in the region where texting has been more popular. In general, however, mobile phone use by the early 2000s tended to correlate with a country's wealth, so that they had penetrated deeper into South East Asia, Western Europe, Australasia and North America, and had had least impact in the rest of Asia and in Africa.

However, this correlation between wealth and mobile technology has become more complex than the above suggests. This is largely because in many places mobile technology has proved less costly and more accessible than either landlines or computers. Thus, while the developed world came to mobile phones via landlines and its citizens are often likely to have used a computer before using a mobile, for many people in the 'global south' – south Asia, Africa, South America – the mobile phone has been their first experience of communications technology. Take-up in these regions can be explained not only by the realization on the part of NGOs and governments of the role that mobile technology can play in development but also by people seeking to access and exploit the technology that best fits their needs (Sey, 2011). As Ling and Horst (2011, p. 364) point out, at the end of the first decade of the twenty-first century, there are more mobile phones in the developing than the developed world – perhaps in part because of the relative population sizes – with four countries in particular, China, India, Brazil and Indonesia, accounting for a third of mobile phone subscriptions worldwide.

The people in developing countries who use mobile phones to send text messages (rather than to call) may largely comprise the wealthier and better educated groups, and studies of texting in such regions as sub-Saharan Africa tend to focus on university students (Deumert and Masinyana, 2008; Vold Lexander, 2011). This is due, on the one hand, to reduced levels of literacy among other groups and, on the other, to alternative, cost-driven social practices that have sprung up around the mobile phone. One such example is that of 'beeping', whereby leaving a missed call takes on a range of communicative meanings (Donner, 2007; Geirbo et al., 2007) which range from indicating that the call is to be returned, to announcing that someone has arrived or is waiting to be picked up, or simply to let the receiver know that the caller is thinking of them. The point of this practice is that it is free. Another practice which I noticed when in Cameroon on holiday was the setting up of mobile phone booths (a table and sunshade), each labelled 'Callbox', where people could pay to make calls on the stall holder's mobile, presumably to avoid either the cost of the handset or the temptation to use up too much credit.

This is not to say that texting is never used by some groups for the aforementioned reasons, nor that it *will* never be. There is evidence that texting can be used despite low levels of literacy – provided by, for example, Nagasaka's (2007) study of mobile phone use in the rural Philippines, or Kibora's (2009) in Burkina Faso. An Urdu-speaking Pakistani friend of mine, who spoke excellent English but struggled with writing it, once pointed out to me that texting offered a safe environment where 'misspellings' were tolerated, or even encouraged.

As discussed in Chapter 2, text messages are notoriously hard to collect, but small corpora from contexts across the world allow initial comparisons to be made, in terms of language use. In the UK, Thurlow and Brown's (2003) investigation of 544 text messages sent by British university students is often used as a benchmark by which subsequent studies evaluate texting practices and strategies. One such study, in Africa, was carried out by Deumert and Masinyana (2008), who analyzed 312 text messages collected from a total of 22 first-language isiXhosa speakers in South Africa aged between 18 and 27 and proficient to varying degrees in English; while Ekanjume (2009) looked at a selected number of text messages written by staff at the National University of Lesotho, and Chiluwa (2008) explored 61 text messages collected around Lagos and Ota in Nigeria. In the Arab-speaking world, Al-Khatib and Sabbah (2008) analyzed 181 text messages written by 46 Arabic-English bilingual students studying at universities across Jordan; and Haggan (2007) analyzed text messages submitted by Kuwaiti university students.

Other projects, in Europe and South East Asia, have been larger. Kasesniemi and Rautianen (2002) drew on an 8000-word corpus of Finnish text messages sent by children and teenagers. Fairon and Paumier (2006) collected 30,000 French-language text messages sent in Belgium as part of their worldwide project, *sms4science*, which has to date involved the collection of a similarly sized, multilingual corpus in Switzerland (Dürscheid and Stark, 2011), while the corpus held at the National University of Singapore (NUS corpus) contains 10,000 text messages. As with my corpus, in most of these cases, text messages are contributed by fairly young, internet-savvy, educated groups; unlike CorTxt, the majority of the corpora are multilingual and often characterized by switches between English and other languages.

In the next section, I look at what, if anything, texting practices across these contexts have in common.

9.3 A global SMS code?

In relation to their study of British texters, Thurlow and Brown suggest that three features lend text messages their distinctive air – message length, interpersonal focus and concentration of non-standard orthographic items – and the fact that studies of texting in other contexts tend to focus on these same characteristics suggests that they may have global validity. The characteristic length of a text message emerges chiefly from technological and cost-related reasons, although texters' purposes, their gender, and the circumstances in which they text, may also be a factor. Despite some variation, text messages are unlikely to exceed, say, 50 words and the average is likely to be 14 (Thurlow and Brown, 2003) to 26 (Deumert and Masinyana, 2008).

A related feature is message structure, given that texters do not always start a text message by using their interlocutors' name as a vocative (i.e. to address them with) nor sign off with their own name. Again, this may be partly because of the technology – people generally know who is texting them – and partly because of message length, as well as the nature of the communication (short, quick messages sent between people who know each other well and who often text preceding or following face-to-face interaction). Most of the following start with a term of endearment (although note that the Egyptian text message starts with a name) – *Hello bird*, *Aunty*, *Brur* – and are signed off with items such as *I'll give you a shout tomo at some point*; *Thnks*; *I'll c then. Sharp*; and *I really hope to see you all Soooooooooooooon*. Note that most allude to future communication.

9.1   Hello bird. Sorry i didn't ring. I'll give you a shout tomo at some point x

(from CorTxt)

9.2   Aunty, whnvr u drop by or whn we meet, pls bring the dvd. Thnks

Text message sent in Malaysia (Hassan and Hashim, 2009, p. 43)

9.3   Brur its 2bed one matras my darling is going 2 put me in shid in church. My money i have save have been decrease due 2 *da* Aunt Mayoly's funeral, & miner problst. So *da* case is coming very soon 3months preg. I'll c then. Sharp.

Matsuka, male English-isiXhosa speaker in South Africa
(Deumert and Masinyana, 2008, p. 126)

9.4   Hello Dalia, 7amdellah 3ala el-salama ya Gameel, we alf mabrouk 3alal el-shahada el-kebeera. Keep in touch. . . . I really hope to see you all Soooooooooooooooon

[Hello Dalia, Thanks God for the safe return, my sweet. Congratulations for the big certificate. Keep in touch ... I really hope to see you all Soooooooooooooooon]

Text message sent in Egypt (Warschauer et al., 2007, p. 312)

These text messages also illustrate the interpersonal and phatic nature of texting, which tends to be used for everyday purposes such as making requests (*whnvr u drop by or whn we meet, pls bring the dvd*), discussing personal issues (*My money i have save have been decrease due 2 da Aunt Mayloy's funeral*) and maintaining relations, good or bad (*Sorry i didn't ring, Keep in touch*).

Most studies of text messages written (at least in part) in English claim some similarity with the findings of research in other contexts in terms of the way that texters respell. These respellings can be seen as emerging from similar orthographic principles and constraints (see Chapter 3). The letter homophone <u>, for example, is used globally by texters, as the following text messages suggest.

9.5   Wow. . . U did it all nite ah. . . Hmmm. . . I got somethin on until 3 lk tt. . . Thk i'll msg *u* when i'm abt done k. . .

(NUS corpus, Singapore)

9.6   hw s d fmly?my lv 2 them n c *u* l8ta

(Lesotho, Ekanjume, 2009, p. 18)

9.7   *U* crossed my mind jst now, so I whisperd a prayr 2 ask God 2 take gud care of *u*, protct *u*, provide 4 *u*, abv all grant *u* ur heart desire

(Nigeria, Chiluwa, 2008, p. 53)

9.8   Plz try 2 giv urself a bit of a presure, stand up dont wait 4 2 long, its not fair even 4 *u* Thabo, but *u* must know 1 thing i care about *u* and i'l alwayz luv *u*.

(South Africa, Deumert and Masinyana, 2008, p. 125)

9.9   hi W how r *u?* hope *u* done well in the comprehensive exam ya rab. Listen
(X) needs some information 4m u, can I give him ur number or nt?

(Jordan, Al-Khatib and Sabbah, 2008, p. 37)

As these text messages also show, many of the respellings echo those noted
in CorTxt. I previously described consonant writing in the Malaysian text
message, and this also occurs in the Singaporean (<Thk>, <msg>, <abt>),
the Lesothan (<hw>, <lv>), the Nigerian (<jst>, <prayr>, <abv>) and
the Jordanian (<nt>). Other respellings include eye dialect forms (<nite>),
other homophones (<r>) and number homophones (<l8tr>, <2>, <4>).
The respelling <ur>, in the Jordanian and Nigerian text messages (9.7 and
9.9), is particularly interesting, given the fact that it is not strictly speaking a
phonetic respelling of *your*. You may remember that it occurred in CorTxt,
and it also occurs in other corpora.

9.10   hello how was ur wkend mine was gd r we stil havin d seminar

(Ekanjume, 2009, p. 19)

9.11   hmmm why don wan to check? Where u trip anyway? In ur hse or outside?
Oh okie gd gd

(NUS, Singapore)

Another almost-phonetic respelling, <4m> for *from*, similarly occurs in the
Jordanian text message. Such respellings are interesting in that we can posit
that they emerge in complex ways from people's interaction, rather than
simply following a phonetic spelling principle.

As the above examples may suggest, some studies report a greater use
of respellings than found, for example, in CorTxt or in Thurlow and
Brown's (2003) British texting study (e.g. Deumert and Masinayana, 2008).
However, it is important to remember that the number of respellings can
depend (as it does in CorTxt) on a number of factors (including research
purpose – Ekanjume, for example, claims to have eliminated text messages
without 'significant language features', which presumably refers to
respellings). In other of the corpora above, we see text messages with far
fewer respellings.

9.12   hey, i will be late for school, can u help me take notes.

(NUS, Singapore)

9.13   Dr. ndewo! Plse tell Chinanu dat I will lodge 5 thousand at past 3pm today.
She shld cope while I get ready to lodge more money.

(Chiluwa, 2008, p. 53)

9.14 LOVE IS A FEELING THAT'S SEEN IN ONE'S EYES. LOVE IS THE
      SIGHT OF SUNSET AND SUNRISE. LOVE IS THE JOY THAT MAKES
      PEOPLE SMILE, LIKE WHAT I WISH FOR YOU EVERYTIME

                                    (Deumert and Masinyana, 2008, p. 129)

Similar respellings appear to occur in other languages, at least those
written in a romanized script. The French respellings described by Fairon
and Paumier (2006), as well as by Anis (2007) in his study of 750 text
messages, reflect those described in this book, and similar strategies are
also noted for Swedish (Härd af Segersted, 2002), Finnish (Kasesniemi
and Rautianen, 2002), German (Doring, 2002) and romanized Arabic
(Haggan, 2007).

   However, it appears to be the case that some languages (or, in certain
cases, some scripts) are not generally abbreviated, or at least that texters
using these languages have been slower to adopt the strategies seen in other
languages. One such example emerges from Deumert and Masinyana's
(2008) study of text messages sent by bilingual isiXhosa and English
speakers in South Africa. While the South African texters abbreviated
English in a way that reflects practices elsewhere, they wrote out isiXhosa
text messages in a formal, conventional way. When asked, the participants
claimed that playing with spelling in isiXhosa was not only ridiculous but
impossible, and they rejected as either intelligible or authentic the example
text messages which the researchers wrote in abbreviated isiXhosa.
Deumert and Masinyana (2008) put this down to the different ways in
which English and isiXhosa are valued – while English is the modern,
playful language of the internet, isiXhosa is imbued with values of purity
and tradition and is closely tied up with a sense of local identity. Similar
distinctions may be made by Arabic, Greek and Chinese speakers, who
have been found not to play with the orthography of these languages, at
least when written in the (non-Roman) scripts traditionally associated with
each language (see Haggan, 2007; Tseliga, 2007; Su, 2007, respectively –
the last two focusing on computer-mediated communication rather than
texting).

   More recently, however, this distinction seems to be shifting, as practices
associated with English are apparently finding their way into other languages.
Deumert (forthcoming) reports that South African texters and internet
users appear now to be playing with spelling in isiXhosa, if not quite to the
extent that they do with English; and Tagg and Seargeant (forthcoming)
describe how a community of Thai online users lengthen words in both
English and Thai for various effects (similar to the Egyptian user's *see you
all Soooooooooooooooon* in 9.4 above).

   As well as these characteristic features (message length, purpose and
respellings), other texting practices may also extend across global contexts,

including the use of speech-like constructions and discourse markers, and playful language use. Although, as mentioned previously, most studies do not focus specifically on these characteristics, it is possible to pick out apparent similarities between text messages sent in various parts of the world. For example, text messages from the NUS corpus (in Singapore) reveal similar grammatical patterns as you saw in my British ones. The following show a speech-like situational ellipsis. Note also the familiar colloquial respelling <wanna> in 9.16 below.

9.15   Hello darling, had lunch? How's work? Another relaxing day at work? Jealous??

9.16   wanna meet up?

The Singaporean texters also use discourse markers associated with the spoken mode, such as *hmmm*, *Oh okie* and *rite* in the following text messages.

9.17   <u>hmmm</u> why don wan to check? Where u trip anyway? In ur hse or outside? *Oh okie* gd gd

9.18   <u>hmmm</u> sorrie I can't cfm juz as yet. . . it's free entry <u>rite</u>?

However, as in CorTxt, the Singaporean text messages are not always or consistently speech-like. In the following text messages, you can see other forms of ellipsis, which I called 'Dont worry, is easy' (as in 9.19 and 9.20 below) and 'Wine good idea' (9.21) when I discussed their occurrence in CorTxt in Chapter 4.

9.19   Hi dear, just finished my confirmation talk. * Was good, my boss is happy with my performance so far. . .? buy you dinner tonight if you are not working late. . . ?

9.20   Everyone, ate in the mtg room today. . . * Had dry macaroni. Soupy type is nicer.

9.21   Think weekend * better cos weekdays have to settle some stuffs

Studies of texting in other languages also suggest that grammatical ellipsis may take speech-like and 'note-like' forms. From her corpus of Swedish text messages, Härd af Segerstad (2002) contrasts speech-like ellipsis such as the omission of the first-person pronoun *jag* ('I'), with the omission of prepositions and possessive pronouns (such as *my* below) in ellipted structures that she likens to a 'telegram'.

9.22   kan inte ikväll. måste jobba. gillar dig i alla fall. KRAM x

[I] can't tonight. [Jag] have to work. [Jag] like you anyway. HUGS x

9.23   Stan Jönköping I sä fall. Lillasyster fyller 20, kalas. . .

[In] town [in] Jönköping in that case. [My] Baby sister turns 20, party. . .

(Härd af Segerstad, 2002, p. 224, p. 225)

Borochovsky-Bar-Alba and Kedmi (2010) similarly show with their collection of 3000 Hebrew text messages that texters often draw on spoken resources – they use a smaller lexicon typical of informal registers and often omit pronouns with present tense verbs. However, they also find that the Hebrew text messages share many features with written Hebrew, driven it seems (as in other corpora) by a greater need to abbreviate.

A final feature shared across many text messages is the playfulness that characterizes many of the text messages in CorTxt. Rather than revisit examples from Chapter 7 to illustrate this point, I'd like to extend discussion of a practice mentioned in Chapter 5, when Laura uses <wot> and the discourse marker *you know* to mark a teasing, ironic performance.

9.24   Jo: Do you have any ideas for NAME46?

      Laura: All he has said really is clothes. Why? Got some for me?

      Jo: Clothes?

      Laura: **You know,** wot people wear. T shirts, jumpers, hat, belt, is all we know. We r at Cribbs

As I discuss in Chapter 8, all interaction in texting can be described in terms of performance, but here Laura uses unconventional linguistic items to frame the momentary adoption of a voice that differs from her performance elsewhere in the texted exchange. This putting on of a different voice – one that is marked as being not her own – can be seen as being playful, intimate and evaluative. Here are three more examples.

9.25   Alan: happy birthday and welcome to the thirties club! i assume ur having a quiet, civilised time, sipping sherries and the like. . . . anyway, have big fun. c u sat. r

      Esther: Whash tha yer say? Er yesh shivilized very . . . Shavin ourshelves fer shaturday . . . Ta fer card (i think it looks more like NAME62 . . .) see you sat xx

In this first example, Esther represents through respelling and grammatical choices the speech of someone under the effect of alcohol, in response to

Alan's assumption that she is *having a quiet, civilised time, sipping sherries and the like. Whash tha yer say?* stands in contrast to the civilized sherry-sipping that Alan imagines. As well as the respellings (<Whash>, <yesh>, <shivilized> and so on), Esther lets trail off a somewhat confused sentence, *Er yesh shivilized very* and chooses the informal shortening *Ta*, which contributes to the performance. On the one hand, the response is undeniably playful; on the other, it serves to effectively contradict Alan's assumption, with whatever significance that has for the two.

In this example between the same two texters, Alan performs a formal, old-fashioned style through particular linguistic choices, towards which Esther also orients.

9.26 Alan: Good evening to you mrs esther! **here is me, alan!** i contact u with solemn news which may be difficult to bear! it appears, from my end, that birthday beverages will have to proceed in my absence. i truly regret this [. . .]

Esther: **Greetings me, alan!** Consider yourself excused.

Alan: [. . .] anyway, many good evenings to u! r

Esther: And several to you sir. Xx

The formality and dated style of Alan's text message can be seen in the address and the vocabulary choices: *contact, solemn, bear, beverages, proceed, absence* and *regret* as well as the sentence constructions. Esther picks up on these, responding with the old-fashioned greeting *Greetings* and the address *sir* and the formal *Consider yourself excused*. Evident in the performance is an element of irony, as seen in the odd phrases – *here is me, alan!* and *Greetings me alan!* – and the fact that elements associated with Txt creep in so that, despite the general formality, Alan chooses *u* over *you* and includes no capitals, and Esther ends the message with *Xx*. One interpretation may be that the dated style allows Alan to perform what must be a tricky social act – to excuse himself from attending his interlocutor's birthday party – by distancing himself from the act and expressing it in over-the-top statements. Esther's repetition of this style appears to signal her acceptance of his decision, and her attempt to uphold her interlocutor's face. Between them, the two texters perform a parody, which rests on the juxtaposition of the formal style and a style more associated with Txt.

This final example was included in chapter 5, as Kate uses the discourse marker *oh* as part of her playful performance.

9.27 Kate: Hi- text me if delayed – otherwise i'll be at station 2 collect at 12

Jo: Twelve twenty five. Okay, see ya then, national rail permitting. . . Looking forward already xx

Kate: As you well know i like to plan my day with military precision –
        therefore it amazes me that you gave your arrival time as 12.25 when
        it is clearly12.27 – for a busy professional like myself those 2 mins
        could make a lot of difference! I am now with – holding info about
        my disguise and will watch with delight as you struggle to find me!

Jo: suddenly appears we are ten minutes late. Sorry!

Kate: Oh- and it gets worse!

Kate is arranging to meet a visiting friend at the station and, on hearing
that her friend has not given her an exact time of arrival, effects the role of
an indignant and militant 'busy professional' (see the third text message in
the exchange). In actual fact, Kate would consider herself as being far less
precise in arranging her everyday activities – and presumably her friend
would agree – and the role she takes on here involves a reflection on her
own tendency to be late, as well as indirectly letting her friend know that
she has been sufficiently organized to look up the train times.

The South African texters in Deumert and Masinyana's study also
playfully put on voices that they mark as not being their own.

9.28 Zoleka: Wherefore out thou. . . Ahem. . . Where are u?

      Thami: Is this an sms from my oh-so-dear Julietta I see before me? I
               am here at last, my luv! What shalt thou cookest for thy sweet
               Romeo whenfore he visitest u?

      Zoleka: So, how's the univsty? There is a bottle of merlot and tofu
               waiting 4 u. How is ur schedulele? I have 2 c u my everlasting
               luv. . . hehaheha.

      Thami: Ur luv guzzling ale at expensive & pretensious but ugly place
               :-(. No castlehere :-)! My gold coins disapearring by the minute!
               With some friends now; they wana come.. They want *die wyn*
               [Afrikaans, 'the wine'] Can't get rid of them — out out damned
               spot! Hahehaha. Or do you wana cum ova rather? Let me knw.

      Zoleka: Oh Romeo wat u doin there! U r livin large! Wud luv 2 but my
               minister of transi ('transport') is absent. U guys can take a cab.
               when do i c u?

                                        (Deumert and Masinyana, 2008, p. 128)

As in the examples from CorTxt, the South African texters mix features
typical of Txt (such as the respellings <u> and <luv>) with an archaic
language (*thou, cookest*) that also draw on lines from Shakespeare
(*Wherefore out thou*). Their awareness of the incongruity between the two
styles is evident throughout, and indeed they foreground it, with Zoleka's
self-reflective *Ahem* marking her shift back to the more appropriate 'Txt':

Wherefore out thou. . . Ahem. . . Where are u?

Similarly, Thami's *Is this an sms from my-oh-so dear Julietta I see before me?* explicitly contrasts the Shakespearean references with texted communication in an apparently self-reflective way, while his laughter, *Hahehaha*, suggests a reflection on the texters' playfulness.

In their study of text messages in Hebrew, Borochovsky-Bar-Aba and Kedmi (2010) note that, despite a tendency towards using lexis typical of informal, spoken contexts, texters would incorporate what they call 'high-register' items in order to 'express cynicism, sophistication, or playfulness' (p. 22). The examples they give recall the *Greetings me, alan!* example from CorTxt.

9.29 le-xol man deva'ei (šuki ze ya'anu le-xol ha-me'unyan) *ze ha-telefon ha-xadaš šeli*

[*For whom it may concern (Shuki, that means to anyone who is interested) this is my new phone number*]

9.30 hey yafit! le-'or mezeg ha-'avir ha-nora ve-ha-maxsor be-rexev 'ani le-ca'ari lo 'uxal le-hagi'a ha-yom 'ani me'od roce lir'ot 'etxem21 ve-'et ha-bonbon. Todi'i li matai ze 'efšari. hamon mazal tov.

[*Hi Yafit! In light of the terrible weather and the lack of a car I will sadly not be able to come today. I really want to see you and the bonbon. Let me know when it will be possible. many best wishes*]

How can we explain the similarities that emerge in such far-flung groups? Researchers have posited the existence of a global SMS standard (Deumert and Masinyana, 2008; Deumert, forthcoming) or code (Blommaert, 2011), at least in relation to the respellings that are felt to be typical of texting. The latter label is in many ways an apt one, not least because Txt has popularly been likened to an undecipherable 'code' – 'hieroglyphs', according to a teacher quoted in *The Telegraph* in 2003 (Cramb, 2003) – and because of the similarities that span communities, geographical regions and even languages.

However, it is instructive to look beyond the label to consider how it helps us to understand what lies behind the construction of Txt. The problem with the term 'code' is that codes tend to be predetermined and somewhat fixed in form and function, and this contrasts with the active way in which Txt is 'remade by users in their practices rather than one which depends on being received, learned and directly replicated' (Shortis, 2007a, p. 2). To elaborate on the point, you saw (in Chapter 1) that the respellings used in texting are not new – they are not a secret code that texters have somehow stumbled upon – but instead they find their precedents in song lyrics, word puzzles, postcards, shop fronts, novel dialogue and so on (Shortis, 2007a,b). Particular forms, such as <wot>, and wider strategies of respelling, such as the use of <a> to represent schwa (as in <gonna>), are available to texters as resources on which they draw in constructing meaning and fulfilling interpersonal demands. The fact that respelling practices are similar across communities is due in part to texters' awareness of the same or similar forms and patterns and in part because orthographic principles across English-speaking communities (and other languages) constrain choices and imbue only certain forms with social meaning (so that <skool> is meaningful and <sguul> is not). But to say that texters are selecting from a constrained set of options is not to say that they are reproducing a code but that they are engaging in a social practice (see Chapter 3).

If Txt were a code, it is not one that has been learnt or prescribed – as argued here and elsewhere – and nor can texters be said to be copying or replicating the practices of another group. Instead, Txt emerges through the course of interaction – through immersion, as Shortis (2007b) puts it – in the process of texting itself (see Chapter 8). People draw on existing linguistic awareness and resources as they navigate the technology and respond to interlocutors' practices, expectations and demands. Of course, no community of texters across the world is likely to recreate Txt afresh through their practices, but will also draw on the wider discourses that circulate about the notion of Txt (at least as expressed in the media) as well as what may be global beliefs about the meaning of certain respellings (in English as in other languages), and these too will shape the language that people use in texting.

The term code also tends to obscure the fact that Txt – the language or discourse of texting – emerges not only as a result of particular respelling practices (which may often look code like) but also through the orientation towards certain grammatical styles, the adoption of phrases, the manipulation of idiom and structural parallelism and other graphic or text-based resources available to texters. And so we can consider Txt as emerging from the use of a fairly open, globally circulating set of possibilities or 'resources' which can be used as texters construct local social meaning and address immediate interpersonal demands.

These resources will, as they travel around the world, shift in terms of what they mean to, or how they are valued by, the texters who access and use them. The notion of globally circulating resources thus helps to explain how different practices emerge within communities, as we can expect to see differences in how people in different world contexts select and exploit the resources available to them.

9.4 Localized practices

One local factor behind differences between English-using texting communities lies in the fact that linguistic choices are often made by texters in order to reflect spoken or colloquial forms. These forms – and the values or meanings that attach to them – will often differ between communities. In Britain, it is probably fair to say that the dropping of /h/ at the start of words and the clipping of /g/ at the end of them tend to signal to many people a casual speaking situation and, in some cases, a lower class or less educated speaker. Such forms can also be strongly associated with traits such as laziness or sloppiness. Both are used in CorTxt. Susie, if you remember, clips the final <g> from a number of participle verbs in the following, as part of her construction of an angry riposte to her sister, and the forms occur in other text messages throughout CorTxt.

9.31 Thankyou for <u>ditchin</u> me i had been invited out but said no coz u were <u>cumin</u> and u said we would do something on the sat now i have nothing to do all weekend i am a billy no mates i really hate being single

9.32 Hey there. I am away for the weekend and bought some shoes. Was thinking about <u>chuckin</u> ur red green n black trainners 2 save <u>carryin</u> them bac on train. Feel free 2object.

9.33 hmm,i dunno if i'll feel like <u>goin</u> out realy, specially after long journey.plus i cant even afford to get in – but then it is a gd way of <u>gettin</u> home.xx

The following examples illustrate the omission of <h> from *had* (<ad>) and *have* (<av>). These occur with other colloquial respellings, including <wiv> (*with*) and <n> (*and*). The result is, as discussed throughout this book, the construction of an informal, colloquial, speech-like discourse – and one that is in some ways highly local.

9.34 Hello beautiful r u ok? I've kinda <u>ad</u> a row wiv NAME99 and he walked out the pub?? I wanted a night wiv u Miss u xx

9.35 Merry xmas2u 2. Hope uve <u>ad</u> lovely day. I <u>av</u>-walks on beach n loads nice food. Am full n knakrd now! Take it easy. NAME309 x

9.36 I don't think I'll be able do it I'm afraid. I'm gonna need be in bed really early onsat n prob won't be sorted anyway! Really sorry, u'll <u>av</u> great time anyway

The effect of capturing regional pronunciations is nicely illustrated in CorTxt with the variable respellings of something, as <summat>, <sumfing>, <summort>, all of which can be said to reflect differing British pronunciations. Interesting, many of these respellings occur in the phrase *or something*, which may be a particularly casual and evaluative use of the word.

9.37 Glasses!! I dont remember lightening? Tell of your address in case i have <u>summat</u> to send

9.38 Hi NAME219 did u decide wot 2 get NAME85 4 his bday if not ill prob jus get him a voucher frm virgin or <u>sumfing</u> xxx

9.39 Hi, drivin in in 15 if you want a lift. NAME268's giving a lecture that we're meant to be at or <u>summort</u>

Respellings across African contexts reflect a different set of local pronunciations and their role as markers of local identity. Matsuka's text message, which I looked at briefly in Chapter 1, illustrates the use of <d> to capture an African pronunciation of /th/ – as well as the local pronunciation of shit as /shid/ – and this is echoed in other corpora.

9.40 Brur its 2bed one matras my darling is going 2 put me in shid in church. My money i have save have been decrease due 2 <u>da</u> Aunt Mayoly's funeral,& miner problst. So <u>da</u> case is coming very soon 3months preg. I'll c then. Sharp.

'Matsuka' (Deumert and Masinyana, 2008, p. 126)

9.41 hw's <u>d</u> strike goin?any clses.wil visit u <u>dis</u> evnin

(Ekunjame, 2009, p. 18)

9.42 <u>De</u> class was slated 4 2moro but *CUSAT* has interrupted <u>dat</u> schedule so what about tues day @2pm? Have a nice wknd.

(Chiluwa, 2008, p. 53)

In his text message, as well as using <d> to reflect an African pronunciation of <th>, Matsuka also reproduces a local expression, 'its 2bed one matras', which depends for its humour on a particular pronunciation of 'too bad' as 'too bed' (Deumert and Masinyana, 2008, p. 127). As the use of this local phrase illustrates, the text message is full of other local forms: *brur* is 'brother' and *sharp* is 'cheers' or 'see you'. These give a strong sense of local regional identity to the text message. Other local items are evident in other corpora, from the Malaysian address *Aunty* to the Arabic 'God willing' (*enshalla*).

9.43 <u>Aunty</u>, whnvr u drop by or whn we meet, pls bring the dvd. Thnks

()

9.44 do I know him?! F u trust him ok no problem. Thx god the exam was very good I'll pass <u>enshalla</u>. shukran la3awatfik [thanks for your kind wishing]. Wht about ur thesis?

(Al-Khatib and Sabbah, 2008, p. 51)

As this last example illustrates, another way in which identities are forged within localized texting communities is through **code-switching**: that is, when people switch between one language and another. As I mentioned above, many of the corpora are multilingual, including Dürscheid and Stark's (2010) Swiss text messages, written in French, German, Italian and English; Deumert and Masinyana's (2008) isiXhosa and English corpus and Haggan's (2007) Kuwaiti corpus in which texters mix Arabic with English. Texters who have access to more than one language, and who can switch between them, can be seen as accessing an extended set of the resources available to monolingual texters. Social meaning can be enhanced not only by the choice of one language over another, but in the mixed forms that occur.

One example in the Singaporean and Malaysian corpora is the use of Chinese discourse particles in otherwise English discourse. The particles carry pragmatic meaning, of the kind that may be conveyed in English through tag questions and discourse markers like *you know*. However, for Chinese-speaking texters, the English equivalents may not quite capture the intimacy and evaluative effect of the Chinese particles. More than this, however, the juxtaposition of Chinese particles and English Txt may heighten the effect that the particles have – as markers of localness within a global discourse – so that they carry deeper significance than they would in wholly Chinese discourse (Fung and Carter, 2007a, p. 358). In the Singaporean text messages below, you can see the use of the discourse particles *lor*, *ah* and *lah*.

9.45   Hey. . . Can u meet me at yio chu kang station. . . U dun have to come out lor, juz pass me e stuff. . . How abt tt?

9.46   Enjoy ur supper.. but dun smoke too muchy ah

9.47   No lah. jst stay hm & rest. later go pick my gf up

(NUS Corpus)

Studies show that multilingual texters may draw on different languages to fulfil different purposes. Often, local languages appear to be chosen for the expression of particularly evaluative and intimate purposes, as well as in local cultural phrases such as *enshalla* and *shukran la3awatfik* (translated by the authors as 'thanks for your kind wishing') in the Jordanian message above (9.44). Meanwhile. English can be used as a distancing technique and, in many societies, for the prestige it brings. In 9.48 below, the texter euphemistically switches to English in order, in the words of one participant in the Jordanian study 'to be inoffensive, especially when we talk about matters relevant to love, disease, body functions, etc' (Al-Khatib and Sabbah, 2008, p. 56). In 9.49, the texter appears to be using fairly simple, easily learnt expressions in English which have come to function as 'marks of prestige'.

9.48   Hi 3aloush kefek? Yesterday I couldn't come to the class la2inu kan 3ind
       stomachache! Bti3rafi, it's the period time.

*[Hi Aloush, how are you? Yesterday I could not come to the class because
I had a bad stomachache! You know, it's the menstrual period time.]*

9.49   *hi sorry just checked my mob.* Lsn ana ma b2dar aji 3'er bokra coz 3andi
       ejazeh, ya seti ana b7akeki bokra lama awsal eljam3a *nighty (good night)*

*[. . .I can only come tomorrow, because the day after tomorrow I have
holiday, anyway, I'll speak to you tomorrow when I reach the university
. . .]*

(Al-Khatib and Sabbah, 2008, p. 57, p. 55)

The motivations for language choice vary across contexts – Chiluwa
(2008), for example, found that what he categorized as personal, religious
text messages contained fewer local language items than other types – but
the point is that the availability of different languages can be seen as part of
the set of resources facing texters in multilingual situations, which they can
exploit in creating meaningful exchange.

The emergent, ad hoc and active way in which this often takes place can be
illustrated through a particular localized, multilingual practice in the Arabic-
speaking world, namely, the use of number homophones to represent sounds
that do not have a correspondence in English. In the following example
from Al-Khatib and Sabbah's (2008) study in Jordan, <2> represents
the English word 'to' in *I wont 4get 2 bring* as well as the syllable 'to' in
'tomorrow': <2mr>. However, the numeral is also used in a way that may
not be familiar to non-Arabic speakers, in 'AL2O5T ALFADILAH' where the
numerals 2 and 5 have been used in the romanized script to represent sounds
in the word الأختالفاضلة ('sister'). The second texter quotes (in romanized
script) the form of address used by its interlocutor in the Arabic script and,
in so doing, recontextualizes the traditional Arabic into Txt.

9.50   الأختالفاضلة...الرجاءإحضارآتاب صقر معك غدا

☺ this z the 1st time someone calls me "AL2O5T ALFADILAH". . .☺ lol.
Anyway, don't worry, I wont 4get 2 bring the book 2mr. Take care.

This is illustrative of a wider practice, whereby texters and internet users
capture Arabic sounds that cannot easily be romanized. The practice of
romanizing Arabic – and particularly colloquial rather than classic Arabic –
was very limited prior to the advent of the internet and, where it did take
place (in guides for foreign learners, for example), sounds would be omitted
rather than represented through numbers. As Warschauer et al. (2007)
explain, the practice of using numbers arose in an ad hoc manner as texters

and internet users responded to the constraints of writing romanized Arabic online, and it is now a feature of texting (and internet use) across Arabic-speaking contexts.

9.51   Ra7aroo7 ma3a e'7ty 7aneen el7 f.la

[*I'll go to the party with my sister Haneen.*]

(Kuwait, Haggan, 2007, p. 440)

9.52   Hello Dalia, 7amdellah 3ala el-salama ya Gameel, we alf mabrouk 3alal el-shahada el-kebeera. Keep in touch. . . . I really hope to see you all Soooooooooooooooon

(Egypt, Warschauer et al., 2007, p. 312)

The saliency and significance of this practice for Arabic speakers is reflected by its use in the Emirati entry reproduced at the start of this chapter. In the story, the author uses the number homophone '3' as part of the Arabic city, al-3in, to represent a guttural Arabic sound which does not have a correspondence in English.

In this section, I've provided only a brief idea of the different ways in which Txt can emerge in different communities, due to the influence of local factors such as accent and dialect features and other languages, and the different values and meanings that attach to different forms. Just as Txt in CorTxt varied according to who was texting, why and whom, so it varies across (and within) geographically dispersed communities. Txt, then, is not a fixed standard or code but emerges from people's varying responses to particular contextual features. Despite the similar constraints that texters face – both linguistic and technological – there is a sense throughout the corpora discussed in this chapter that texting provides an unregulated space in which texters enjoy a certain freedom to exploit language in creative and meaningful ways, for deeply interpersonal reasons.

9.5 Looking forward

Texting is often grouped together with other forms of electronic or **digital communication** – where 'digital' is simply a technical term describing the technique of data transfer used by computers and mobile phones – which include interactions via internet platforms such as online chat, email and social network sites like Facebook. There is a tendency – on the part of the public, the media and the academic community – to assume that digital technology has transformed the way we communicate. Before going on to consider trends in texting, both as a digital technology and as a set of communicative practices, I'd like to reflect on the extent to which this 'exoticism' of digital technology – the positioning of texting and the internet as something new and 'other' – is helpful or accurate in describing the discourse of text messaging.

One counterargument is that digital communication, including texting, can in fact be seen as part of a longer tradition of informal written communication, alongside postcards, telegrams and letters. This is a point that I made in Chapter 1, so I shall go over it only briefly here. My argument in Chapter 1 was that texting should not be seen as representing a break with past practices, but rather as another example of how technology can be used to mediate communication. All written language is mediated by technology of some sort (from the pen and the postal service to the computer and the internet), and the nature of the technology – pen or keyboard, slow mail or email – will have some impact on its users' communicative practices. So, any description of the impact that current technology has on communicative practices must take into account the fact that this has always been the case: for example, the speed of the postal service similarly shaped how people wrote letters and postcards and for what reasons.

The second counterargument concerns the way in which current day researchers and media commentators approach digital communication with the awareness – and, indeed, the experience – of a time *without* digital communication (Herring, 2008). That is, someone who was born in, say, 1960, will have grown up without the internet or a mobile phone and would first have experienced them as an adult in their 30s or later. A line is sometimes drawn in the early 1980s, between those who grew up without digital communications technology (including Generation X, born between 1962 and 1982) and those who cannot remember a time without the internet and mobile phones (the Net Generation) (Herring, 2008). On the one hand, this awareness confers an advantage. Studying language is often about stepping back from everyday practices and approaching them as an alien might encounter human life, or a nineteenth-century British anthropologist would document an isolated tribe's practices. Conversation analysis – the detailed study of turn-taking and other features of conversation – is a good example of this, with its descriptions of how people relinquish turns and others take the floor in everyday interactions.

On the other hand, there are potential problems in the fact that, from the perspective of those who remember a world without it, digital communication is evaluated and understood in relation to non-digital communication, and it is the latter – face-to-face conversation, letter writing – that is considered the 'norm'. In comparison, digital communication is framed as being different, exotic, unknown and transformative. This leads to what Thurlow and Brown (2009) call the 'technologisation of communication', as the technology is foregrounded in descriptions of interactive practices.

In contrast, to many younger people, digital communication may be commonplace, 'unremarkable' (Thurlow and Brown, 2003) and in the process of 'slouching towards the ordinary' (Herring, 2004). There is less reason to focus on the technology as a defining feature of a communicative interaction if the technology has always been a part of such interactions and if comparisons are not being made with equivalent, non-digital means. Rather than focusing on *how* a communication is being conveyed (or mediated), young users may be more concerned with *what* is being communicated, to whom and why. Herring's argument is that a time will come when digital communication (and mobile technology) becomes the norm, rather than being compared to a pre-digital society, and at this point we may see discussions of its use move away from the technology and towards the communication itself. That is, when the Net Generation grows up, their perspective on digital technology as ordinary will become the dominant discourse.

This last assertion rests on some fairly static and absolute views, not least the assumption that everyone born after a certain date will be *au fait* with digital technology – in contrast, it is likely that some will have more experience and expertise than others. Secondly, the prediction ignores the fact that 'digital technology', and the practices that cluster around it, will themselves change. One recent shift has been from what is known as **Web 1.0** (where, e.g. users could access information) to **Web 2.0** (where users interact, participate and co-create content). It is likely that adults in, say, 2050 will be as uncomfortable with what will then be Web 3.0 or 4.0 and will compare these practices with the earlier ones that they are familiar with. A similar shift has taken place in mobile technology as smartphones integrate mobile functions with internet access. The point is that rapidly developing technology may always be an exotic, unfamiliar distraction, and thus we may always need to make an argument for focusing on communicative practices and what people are *doing* with the technology, rather than being hung up on the technology (Thurlow and Bell, 2009).

So, bearing this in mind, what further changes in mobile technology can we expect? I don't with to make predictions, but there are signs of present trends which suggest future practices. **Convergence** is one such trend, firstly in the sense that multiple digital platforms can be accessed on one device – texting, email, social network sites, content sharing sites, etc. And, generally, current trends suggest that this device will be increasingly mobile. New media is also becoming increasingly convergent in the sense that one platform – such as a social network site – contains many 'communication modes'. On a social network site, you can post status updates, load photos, leave postings on people's wall and communicate through instant messaging. As this suggests, such platforms are becoming multimodal, as image, video, and sound are embedded alongside text in such platforms. Smartphones differ from earlier incarnations in that users have access to a QWERTY keyboard – rather than a keyboard organized by numbers – and it is likely that phones will increasingly facilitate different scripts, which may impact on the extent to which speakers of languages written in scripts such as Greek, Arabic or Chinese use English and romanized forms of their written language.

The above is a brief description of a handful of emerging trends, and there are people better placed to comment on the likely technological developments. My point, however, is that it is difficult or impossible to predict how these developments impact on practice. I began this book by quoting from Cor Stutterheim, the creator of the technology behind texting, who explained that

> It started as a message service, allowing operators to inform all their own customers about things such as problems with the network. When we created SMS (Short Messaging Service) it was not really meant to communicate from consumer to consumer and certainly not meant to become the main channel which the younger generation would use to communicate with each other.

Nobody predicted that the texting facility added to mobile phones would become a widely used, expressive and important mode of communication. Similarly, it is difficult to know whether the increased capacity to input Arabic and other scripts will bring an end to the practice of romanization – or whether the practice has acquired a social meaning that will ensure its continuation. A similar point can be made with regards to the QWERTY keyboard and whether the increased speed and ease of effort it affords will lengthen text messages and discourage respellings – or whether texters will continue to draw on this as a resource in self-expression. Nor can we tell if convergence – in the form, for example, of a smartphone used for a range of purposes – will lead people to text more or less, for a more limited number of purposes or for a wider range. This brings me back to the argument that runs throughout this book – that it is not the technology but people's values and perceptions, and how they choose to exploit the technology for changing and individual communicative ends, that really shape the discourse of text messaging.

REFERENCES

Aijmer, K. (2002) *English Discourse Particles: Evidence from a Corpus.* Amsterdam: John Benjamins.

Al-Khatib, M. and E. H. Sabbah (2008) 'Language choice in mobile text messages among Jordanian university students', *Sky Journal of Linguistics* 21: 37–65.

Androutsopoulos, J. K. (2000) 'Non-standard spellings in media texts: The case of German fanzines', *Journal of Sociolinguistics* 4/4: 514–33.

—. (2012) 'Code-switching in computer-mediated communication', in Herring, S. C., D. Stein, and T. Virtanen (eds), *Handbook of the Pragmatics of CMC.* Mouton de Gruyter.

Anis, J. (2007) 'Neography: Unconventional spelling in French SMS text messages', in Danet, B. and S. C. Herring (eds), *The Multilingual Internet: Language, Culture and Communication Online*, pp. 87–116.

Asprey, E. (forthcoming) 'Black Country dialect and identity', in Seargeant, P. and J. Swann (eds), *English in the World: History, Diversity and Change.* London: Routledge.

Austin, J. (1962) *How to Do Things with Words.* Cambridge, MA: Harvard University Press.

Baker, P. (2004) 'Querying keywords: questions of difference, frequency and sense in keywords analysis' *Journal of English Linguistics* 32/4: 346–59.

Baron, N. (2000) *Alphabet to Email: How Written English Evolved and Where It's Heading.* London: Routledge.

—. (2002) 'Who sets email style? Prescriptivism, coping strategies, and democratising communication access', *The Information Society.* Oxford: Oxford University Press 18: 403–13.

Barros, C. D. M. (1995) 'The missionary presence in literacy campaigns in the indigenous langauges of Latin America', *International Journal of Educational Development* 15(3): 277–87.

Bennett, J. and G. Smithers (eds) (1968) *Early Middle English Verse and Prose.* Oxford: Clarendon Press.

Biber, D., S. Johansson, G. Leech, S. Conrad and E. Finegan (1999) *Longman Grammar of Spoken and Written English.* Harlow: Longman.

Blommaert, J. (2011) 'Emergent normativity and the politics of authenticity'. Talk given at the Mosaic Centre, School of Education, University of Birmingham, May 18th 2011.

Bolinger, D. (1946) 'Visual morphemes', *Language* 22: 333–40.

Borochovsky-Bar-Aba, E. and Y. Kedmi (2010) The nature of SMS discourse: The case of Hebrew, *Folia Linguistica* 44/1: 1–30.

Bradley, H. (1919) *On the Relations Between Spoken and Written Language with Special Reference to English.* Oxford: Clarendon Press.

Butler, J. (1993) *Gender Trouble: Feminism and the Subversion of Identity*. New York/Abingdon: Routledge.

Cameron, D. (1997) 'Performing gender identity: Young men's talk and the construction of heterosexual masculinity', in Johnson, S. and U.H. Meinhof (eds), *Language and Masculinity*. Oxford: Blackwell, pp. 47–64.

Carney, E. (1994) *A Survey of English Spelling*. London: Routledge.

Carter, R. (2004) *Language and Creativity: The Art of Common Talk*. London: Routledge.

Carter, R. and M. McCarthy (2006) *Cambridge Grammar of English: A Comprehensive Guide*. Cambridge: Cambridge University Press.

Chafe, W. (1982) 'Integration and involvement in speaking, writing, and oral literature', in Tannen, pp. 35–53.

Cheng, W., N. Greaves and M. Warren (2006) 'From n-gram to skipgram to concgram' *International Journal of Corpus Linguistics* 11/4: 41–433.

Chiluwa, I. (2008) 'Assessing the Nigerianness of SMS text-messages in English', *English Today* 24(1): 51–6.

Cook, G. (2000) *Language Play, Language Learning*. Oxford: Oxford University Press.

Cramb, A. (2003) 'Girl writes English essay in phone text shorthand' in the *Daily Telegraph*, 3rd March.

Crystal, D. (1998) *Language Play*. Cambridge: Cambridge University Press.

—. (2003) *The Cambridge Encyclopedia of the English Language*. Cambridge: Cambridge University Press.

—. (2008) *Txtng: The Gr8 Db8*. Oxford: Oxford University Press.

Dahl, H. (1979) Word Frequencies of Spoken American English. Michigan: Verbatim.

Danet, B. (2001) *Cyberpl@y: Communicating Online*. Oxford/New York: Berg.

Danet, B., L. Ruedenberg-Wright and Y. Rosenbaum-Tamari (1997) '"Hmmm . . .where's that smoke coming from?" Writing, play and performance on Internet Relay Chat', *Journal of Computer-Mediated Communication* 2/4.

Deumert, A. (forthcoming) 'Txtpl@y. Creativity in South African digital writing', in Allington, D. and B. Mayor (eds), *Communicating in English: Talk, Text, and Technology*. London: Routledge.

Deumert, A. and S.O. Masinyana (2008) 'Mobile language choices – The use of English and isiXhosa in text messages (SMS) Evidence from a bilingual South African sample', *English World-Wide* 29(2): 117–47.

Donath, J. (1999) 'Identity and deception in the virtual community', in Kollock, P. and M. Smith (eds), *Communities in Cyberspace*. London: Routledge, pp. 29–59.

Donner, J. (2007) 'The rules of beeping: exchanging messages using missed calls on mobile phones in sub-Saharan Africa', *Journal of Computer-mediated Communication* 13: 1–22.

Doring, N. (2002) '"1 bread, sausage, 5 bags of apples I.L.Y" – communicative functions of text messages (SMS)' *Zeitschrift für Medienpsychologie* 3.

Doyle, R. (1998) *The Barrytown Trilogy: The Commitments, The Snapper, The Van*. London: Vintage.

Dürscheid, C. and E. Stark (2011) 'SMS4science: An international corpus-based texting project and the specific challenges for multilingual Switzerland', in Thurlow, C. and K. Mroczek (eds), *Digital Discourse. Language in the New Media*. Oxford: Oxford University Press (in press).

Eckert, P. (2007) 'Messing with style', in Maybin, J. and J. Swann (eds), *The Art of English: Everyday Creativity*. London: Routledge, pp. 124–30.

Ekanjume, B. (2009) 'A sociolinguistic survey of the use of sms-text messages among NUL staff', *NJLC* 3(2): 14–31.

Extremely Short Story Competition (ESSC) (2008) see http://50words.org/overview-of-essc.aspx.

Fairon, C. and S. Paumier (2006) 'A translated corpus of 30,000 French SMS', *LREC*. Geneva.

Faulkner, X. and F. Culwin (2005) 'When fingers do the talking: a study of text messaging', *Interacting with Computers* 17/2: 167–85.

Fung, L. and R. Carter (2007) Discourse markers and spoken English: native and learner use in pedagogic settings, *Applied Linguistics* 28/3: 410–39.

—. (2007) 'New varieties, new creativities: ICQ and English-Cantonese e-discourse.' *Language and Literature* 16: 345–67.

Geirbo, H. C., P. Helmersen and K. Engø-Monsen (2007) *Missed Call: Messaging for the Masses. A Study of Missed Call Signaling Behavior in Dhaka*, (Internal Telenor publication). Fornebu, Norway: Telenor R&I.

Gillen, J. and N. Hall (2010) Edwardian postcards: illuminating ordinary writing', in Barton, D. and U. Papen (eds), *The Anthropology of Writing: Understanding Textually-Mediated Worlds*. London: Continuum, pp. 169–89.

Goddard, A. (2006) 'Discourses R Us: intertextuality as a creative strategy in Interactive Written Discourse', in J. Maybin and J. Swann (eds), *The Art of English: Everyday Creativity*. London: Routledge, pp. 251–60.

Goffman, E. (1959) *The Presentation of Self in Everyday Life*. London: Penguin.

Grinter, R. E. and M. Eldridge (2003) 'Wan2talk? Everyday text messaging', *ACM Conference on Human Factors in Computing System (CHI)*.

—. (2003) 'Wan2tlk?: everyday text messaging', *Proceedings of the CHI'03 Conference on Human Factors in Computing Systems* (Ft Lauderdale).

Groom, N. (2006) 'Phraseology and epistemology in humanities writing: a corpus-driven study', Ph.D. thesis, English Department, University of Birmingham.

Haggan, M. (2007) 'Text messaging in Kuwait. Is the medium the message?' *Multilingua* 26: 427–49.

Halliday, M. A. K. (1989) *Spoken and Written Language*. Oxford: Oxford University Press.

Hård af Segerstad, Y. (2002) 'Use and adaptation of the written language to the conditions of computer-mediated communication' PhD Thesis, Dept of Linguistics, Goteborg University.

Harkin, J. (2002) *Mobilisation: The Growing Public Interest in Mobile Technology*. London: Demos.

Hassan, N. and A. Hashim (2009) 'Electronic English in Malaysia: features and language in use', *English Today* 25(4): 39–46.

Herring, S. C. (2008) 'Questioning the generational divide: technological exoticism and adult construction of online youth identity' in Buckingham, D. (ed.) Youth, identity and digital media. Cambridge, MA: The MIT Press, pp. 71–92.

Hunston, S. (2002) *Corpora in Applied Linguistics*. Cambridge: Cambridge University Press.

—. (2003) Lexis, wordform and complementation pattern: a corpus study. *Functions of Language* 10/1: 31–60.

Jacobson, S. (1966) *Unorthodox Spelling in American Trademarks*. Stockholm: Almqvist & Wiksell.

Jaffe, A. (2000) 'Introduction: non-standard orthography and non-standard speech', *Journal of Sociolinguistics* 4(4): 497–513.

Jaffe, A. and S. Walton (2000) 'The voices people read: orthography and the representation of non-standard speech', *Journal of Sociolinguistics* 4(4): 561–87.

James, G., R. Davison, A. Cheung and S. Deerwester (1994) *English in Computer Science: a corpus-based lexical analysis*. Hong Kong: Longman, for the Language Centre, Hong Kong University of Science and Technology.

Jellinek, D. (2003) 'How to make those mobiles count', *The Guardian*, 8 October.

Johnson, L. (1975) 'Dread Beat an Blood'. Accessible http://www.last.fm/music/Linton+Kwesi+Johnson/_/Dread+Beat+An%27+Blood, accessed 14 November 2008.

Jones, S. (2007) 'Land of "My 9": Welsh-English bilingual girls creating spaces to explore identity', *Changing English* 14(1): 39–50.

Kasesniemi, E.-L. and P. Rautiainen (2002) 'Mobile culture of children and teenagers in Finland', in Katz, J. and M. Aakhus (eds), *Perpetual Contact: Mobile Communication, Private Talk, Public Performance*. Cambridge: Cambridge University Press, pp. 170–92.

Katz, J. and M. Aakhus (2002) *Perpetual Contact: Mobile Communication, Private TalkP public Performance*. Cambridge: Cambridge University Press.

Kesseler, A. and A. Bergs (2003) 'Literacy and the new media: vita brevis, lingua brevis', in Aitchison, J. and D.M. Lewis (eds), *New Media Language*. London: Routledge, pp. 75–84.

Kibora, L. (2009) 'Téléphonie mobile: L'appropriation du SMS par une « société d'oralité »', in De Bruijn M., Nyamnjoh F. and Brinkman I. (eds), *Mobile Phones: The New Talking Drums of Everyday Africa*. Bamenda (Cameroun)/Leiden: LANGAA/Africa Studies Centre, pp. 110–24.

Kuiper, K. (2004) 'Formulaic performance in conventionalised varieties of speech' in Schmitt, N. (ed.) (2004) *Formulaic Sequences: Acquisition, Processing, and Use*. Amsterdam: John Benjamins, pp. 37–54.

Leech, G., P. Rayson and A. Wilson (2001) *Word Frequency in Written and Spoken English: Based on the British National Corpus*. London: Longman.

Lin, A. M. Y and A. H. M Tong (2007) 'Text messaging cultures of college girls in Hong Kong: SMS as resources for achieving intimacy and gift-exchange with multiple functions', *Journal of Media & Cultural Studies* 21(2): 303–15.

Ling, R. and H. A. Horst (2011) 'Mobile communication in the global south', *New Media & Society* 13(3): 363–74.

Ling, R. and B. Yttri (2002) 'Hyper-coordination via mobile phones in Norway', in Katz, J. and M. Aakhus (2002) *Perpetual Contact: Mobile Communication, Private Talk, Public Performance*. Cambridge: Cambridge University Press, pp. 139–69.

Maybin, J. (2010) 'Intimate Strangers: creativity at the level of practice, genre and textual poetics in penfriend correspondence', in Swann, J., R. Pope and R. Carter (eds), *Creativity, Language, Literature: The State of the Art*. Basingstoke, Hants: Palgrave Macmillan.

Maybin, J. and J. Swann (2006) *The Art of English: Everyday Creativity*. Basingstoke: Palgrave Macmillan.

—. (2007) 'Introduction: language creativity in everyday contexts', *Special Issue of Applied Linguistics* 28(4): 491–6.

McCarthy, M. (1993) 'Spoken discourse markers in written text', in Sinclair, J.M, M. Hoey and G. Fox (eds), *Techniques of Description*. London: Routledge, pp. 170–82.

McEnery, A. M. and A. Hardie (2011) *Corpus Linguistics: Method, Theory and Practice*. Cambridge: Cambridge University Press.

McEnery, A., R. Xiao and Y. Tono (2006) *Corpus-Based Language Studies: An Advanced Resource Book*. London: Routledge.

Merriam-Webster's Dictionary of English Usage (1994) Springfield, Massachusetts: Merriam-Webster Inc.

Moon, R. (1998) *Fixed Expressions and Idioms in English*. Oxford: Clarendon Press.

—. (2008) 'Lexicography and linguistic creativity', *Lexikos* 18: 1–23.

Nagasaka, I. (2007) 'Cellphones in the rural Philippines', in Pertierra, R. (ed.), *The Social Construction and Usage of Communication Technologies: Asian and European Experiences*. Quezon City: The University of Philippines Press, pp. 100–25.

Norrick, N. (1993) *Conversational Joking*. Bloomington: Indiana University Press.

—. (2003) 'Issues in conversational joking', *Journal of Pragmatics* 35: 1333–59.

North, S. (2007) ' "The voices, the voices": creativity in online conversation', *Applied Linguistics* 28(4): 209–60.

O'Keeffe, A., M. McCarthy and R. Carter (2007) *From Corpus to Classroom: Language Use and Language Teaching*. Cambridge: Cambridge University Press.

Orwell, G. (1951) *Down and Out in Paris and London*. London: Secker & Warburg.

Papacharissi, Z. (2010) *A Networked Self: Identity, Community, and Culture on Social Network Sites*. New York: Routledge.

Plester, B. and C. Wood (2009) 'Exploring relationships between traditional and New Media literacies: British preteen texters at school', *Journal of Computer-Mediated Communication* 14: 1108–29.

Pound, L. (1925) 'The Kraze for "K" ', *American Speech* 1(1): 43–4.

Praninskas, J. (1968) Trade-Name Creation: Processes and Patterns. The Hague: Mouton.

Read, J. and P. Nation (2004) 'Measurement of formulaic sequences' in Schmitt, N. (ed.) (2004) *Formulaic Sequences: Acquisition, Processing, and Use*. Amsterdam: John Benjamins, pp. 23–35.

Reid, E. M. (1991) Electropolis: communication and community on internet relay chat. Ph.D. Thesis, University of Melbourne.

Rock, F. (2001) 'Policy and practice in the anonymisation of linguistic data', *International Journal of Corpus Linguistics* 6(1): 1–26.

Sansom, W. (1956) *A Contest of Ladies*. London: Hogarth.

Schiffrin, D. (1987) *Discourse Markers*. Cambridge: Cambridge University Press.

Schmitt, N. (ed.) (2004) *Formulaic Sequences*. Amsterdam/Philadelphia: John Benjamins.

Scott, M. (1996) *Wordsmith Tools*. Oxford: Oxford University Press.

Scragg, D. (1974) *A History of English Spelling*. New York: Barnes and Noble Books.

Sebba, M. (2007) *Spelling and Society.* Cambridge: Cambridge University Press.

Sey, A. (2011) '"We use it different, different": making sense of trends in mobile phone use in Ghana', *New Media and Society* 13(3): 375–90.

Shortis, T. (2007a) 'Gr8 Txtpectations: the creativity of text spelling' *English Drama Media Journal* 8: 21–6.

—. (2007b) 'Revoicing Txt: Spelling, vernacular orthography and "unregimented writing"' in Posteguillo, S., M. J. Esteve and M. L. Gea (eds.) *The Texture of Internet: Netlinguistics*, Cambridge: Cambridge Scholar Press.

Sinclair, J. (1991) *Corpus Concordance Collocation.* Oxford: Oxford University Press.

Sinclair, J. and A. Renouf (1991) 'Collocational frameworks in English' in Aijmer, K. and B. Altenberg (eds) *English Corpus Linguistics.* New York: Longman, pp. 128–43.

Stubbs, M. (2001) *Words and Phrases: Corpus Studies of Lexical Semantics.* Oxford: Blackwell.

Su, H.-Y. (2007) 'The multilingual and multiorthographic Taiwan-based internet: creative uses of writing systms on college-affiliated BBSs' in Danet, B. and S.C. Herring (eds) *The Multilingual Internet: language, culture, and communication online*, 64-115. Oxford: Oxford University Press.

Swann, J. (2006) 'The art of the everyday', in Maybin, J. and J. Swann (eds), *The Art of English: Everyday Creativity.* Basingstoke: Palgrave Macmillan, pp. 3–53.

Swann, J., R. Pope and R. Carter (eds) (2011) *Creativity, Language, Literature: The State of the Art.* Basingstoke, Hants: Palgrave Macmillan.

Tagg, C. (forthcoming) 'Texting and corpora', in K. Hyland, M.H. Chau and M. Handford (eds), *Corpora in Applied Linguistics: Current Approaches and Future Directions.* London: Continuum.

Tagg, C. and P. Seargeant (2012) 'Writing systems at play in Thai-English online interactions', *Writing Systems Research.*

Tannen, D. (1989) *Talking Voices: Repetition, Dialogue, and Imagery in Conversational Discourse.* Cambridge: Cambridge University Press.

Taylor, A. S. and R. Harper (2003) '"The gift of the gab"?: a design-oriented sociology of young people's use of "mobilze"!', *Computer Supported Cooperative Work* 12(3): 267–96.

Thurlow, C. (2006) 'From statistical panic to moral panic: The metadiscursive construction and popular exaggeration of new media language in the print media', *Journal of Computer-Mediated Communication* 11: 667–701.

Thurlow, C. and A. Brown (2003) 'Generation Txt? Exposing the sociolinguistics of young people's text-messaging', *Discourse Analysis Online* 1/1.

Thurlow, C. and K. Bell (2009) Against technologization: young people's new media discourse as creative cultural practice, *Journal of Computer-Mediated Communication*, 14: 1038–49.

Thurlow, C. and M. Poff (2012) The language of text messaging in S. C. Herring, D. Stein & T. Virtanen (eds), *Handbook of the Pragmatics of CMC.* Berlin and New York: Mouton de Gruyter.

Tribble, C. (2000) 'Genres, keywords, teaching: towards a pedagogic account of the language of project proposals' in Burnard, L. and T. McEnery (eds) *Third International Conference on Teaching and Language Corpora*, Peter Lang, pp. 75–90.

Tseliga, T. (2007) '"It's all Greeklish to me!" Linguistic and sociocultural perspectives on Roman-alphabeted Greek in asynchronous computer-mediated communication' in Danet, B. and S.C. Herring (eds) *The Multilingual Internet: language, culture, and communication online*, 116–41. Oxford: Oxford University Press.

Uthus, E. (2007) 'Text messages destroying our language' *The Daily of the University of Washington*, 7 May.

Vold Lexander, K. (2011) 'Texting and African language literacy', *New Media and Society* 13(3): 427–43.

Warschauer, M., et al. (2007) 'Language choice online: globalisation and identity in Egypt', in Danet, B. and S.C. Herring (eds), *The Multilingual Internet: Language, Culture and Communication Online*. Oxford: Oxford University Press, pp. 303–18.

Weber, R. (1986) 'Variation in spelling and the special case of colloquial contractions', *Visible Language* 20(4): 413–26.

Webster, N. (1828) *An American Dictionary of the English Language*.

Welsh, I. (1993) *Trainspotting*. London: Secker & Warburg.

Willans, G. (1953) *Down with skool! A Guide to School Life for Tiny Pupils and Their Parents*. London: Pavilion.

Wray, A. (2002) *Formulaic Language and the Lexicon*. Cambridge: Cambridge University Press.

—. (2008) *Formulaic Language: Pushing the Boundaries*. Oxford: Oxford University Press.

Wray, R. (2002) 'First with the message', *The Guardian*, 16 March.

INDEX